RECENT PERSPECTIVES ON AMERICAN SIGN LANGUAGE

Edited by **HARLAN LANE**
FRANÇOIS GROSJEAN
Northeastern University

 LAWRENCE ERLBAUM ASSOCIATES, PUBLISHERS
1980   Hillsdale, New Jersey

Lawrence Erlbaum Associates, Inc., Publishers
365 Broadway
Hillsdale, New Jersey 07642

Library of Congress Cataloging in Publication Data

Main entry under title:

Recent perspectives on American sign language.

Includes bibliographies and indexes.
1. Sign Language—Addresses, essays, lectures.
I. Lane, Harlan   II. Grosjean, François.
HV247.R4   419   80-14759
ISBN 0-89859-053-1

Printed in the United States of America

Contents

Preface

As its title promises, this book presents several current perspectives on American Sign Language: linguistic, psycholinguistic, developmental, neurolinguistic, sociolinguistic, and historical. Each chapter reviews recent literature comprehensively, but of course not exhaustively, and the six chapters taken together provide an overview of a very rapidly expanding field. We hope this review will be helpful to a variety of social scientists and educators, and to students who, in rapidly growing numbers, are enrolling in courses concerning the deaf community and their language. We have included an introductory chapter by Harry Markowicz that calls into question some common presuppositions of those who—like ourselves but a few years ago—encounter sign language for the first time.

This book is also appearing in French, as an issue of the journal *Langages;* however, Wilbur and Hoffmeister's discussion of research on sign-language acquisition appears only in this edition.

The present work was inspired by discussion with French deaf people at the Seventh World Congress of the Deaf in Washington, D.C. in 1975. We would like to dedicate it to the numerous deaf people who, in the tradition established by Jean Massieu, Ferdinand Berthier, and Laurent Clerc, are contributing to the study of their language. As the editors' prerogative, we mention those with whom we have worked personally: Bonnie Gough, Ella Mae Lentz, Carol Padden, Marie Philip, Ted Suppala, and Harmut Teuber.

HARLAN LANE
FRANÇOIS GROSJEAN

1 Myths About American Sign Language[1]

Harry Markowicz
La Maison des Sciences de l'Homme, Paris

American Sign Language is often described in the following ways: It is a universal language whose grammar is poor compared to that of spoken language; its vocabulary is concrete and iconic; it consists of gestures accompanied by facial expressions. The intent of this chapter is to show that these descriptions do not correspond to the observations and linguistic analyses of languages in the visual/manual modality.

MYTH: SIGN LANGUAGE IS UNIVERSAL

It has often been said that sign language is a universal language—easy to learn and therefore available to anyone for worldwide communication. This suggestion was made also by early writers on sign language, such as the Abbé de l'Epée, the French priest who founded public education for the deaf late in the 18th century, and Remy Valade, who wrote the first grammar book on French Sign Language in 1854. These authors believed that sign language imitates objects and events and presents them as they occur in nature, just as an artist paints the scene in front of him. According to Epée and Valade, sign language is a natural language that unites deaf people everywhere in the world. They suggested that if hearing people learned to communicate in sign language, the world would have an excellent, ready-made universal language.

---

[1]A longer version of this text has been published under the title "American Sign Language: Fact and Fancy" by Public Service Programs, Gallaudet College, 1977 (reprinted 1978).

Even a brief look at the known sign languages of the world invalidates this contention. American Sign Language, British Sign Language, Japanese Sign Language, Danish Sign Language and other sign languages differ from each other as much as spoken languages differ. A deaf traveler is no more able to understand the sign language of the country he is visiting than is the hearing traveler able to understand the spoken language. Deaf people do, however, enjoy some advantages in their efforts at international communication.

First of all, because they lack a certain inhibition about using gestures and because they are masters at pantomime, deaf persons from different cultures are usually able to communicate their basic needs to each other better than hearing people who speak different languages. In situations where there is no shared language, deaf persons act out and even describe a person or a thing without resorting to either spoken or sign language. They communicate among themselves with remarkable ease, although with reduced efficiency and less speed than in their own languages. It is this gestural communication that gives the impression that the deaf have a common sign language.

In some essential ways, deaf people often share more life experiences with deaf people in other countries than they do with the hearing people in their own country. The similar world view and values that result from membership in a common minority group may play a greater role for mutual understanding than previously supposed, and a shared language may be less important.

In addition, certain sign languages, just like some spoken languages, are historically related. In this way, communication is facilitated across national boundaries. French Sign Language (FSL) was brought to the United States in the early 19th century, where it mixed with the sign language used by deaf Americans previously (Woodward, 1978). This mixture became the standard sign language in the United States and parts of Canada. Today, although they differ greatly from each other, ASL and FSL share some of the same signs and grammatical features.

MYTH: REALITY MUST BE WORD-BASED

American Sign Language is often criticized for being "conceptual" rather than "word-based." ASL is in this respect no different from spoken languages, because the principal function of language is to convey concepts. However, in a sign language, concepts are represented by signs rather than words. ASL is not a code for English. It is an independent language in which the signs directly represent the concepts.

Sign language is the primary language for the majority of deaf adults, the one used in their everyday lives, outside of work. It is the principal unifying force for the deaf community, the main symbol of identification among its members (Markowicz & Woodward, 1978). Because only a very small percentage of deaf children have deaf parents, sign language is transmitted from generation to generation in the schools for the deaf, in particular in residential schools. The socialization of deaf children takes place essentially in these institutes (Meadow, 1972). Sign language is the native language for the majority of deaf children who grow up in residential schools, whether or not they have deaf parents or can express themselves orally.

Just like members of other minority groups, the deaf have varying contacts with English, depending on their competence in that language. A deaf person chooses the appropriate language according to the situation. To communicate with hearing people who have some knowledge of sign language, a pidgin is used—signed English that combines the syntax of English with a sign vocabulary. Thus, we find the classical situation of diglossia, characterized by a continuum of varieties between ASL and signed English. However, in this situation the pidgin is considered to be the prestige variety (Stokoe, 1970). Because the pidgin is used in formal contexts (such as at a conference or on TV) and to converse with nonmembers of the deaf community, it is easy to understand how many hearing people mistakenly concluded that it is a manual/visual code for a spoken language.

MYTH: SIGNS ARE GLORIFIED GESTURES

To a person unfamiliar with ASL, signs may appear to consist of random hand and body movements accompanied by various facial expressions. However, to speak of signs as glorified gestures, as is sometimes done, indicates a serious misconception. The analogy would be to describe a spoken language one does not know, as "noises" made with the mouth.

Linguists find striking similarities between the structure of spoken and sign languages in spite of the difference in transmission.

Signs are made by combining simultaneously handshapes, orientation of the palms, movements of the hand(s), and their location on or near the body (Stokoe, 1960). There are formational rules that specify the possible combinations for signs in ASL. Combinations that violate the rules are considered to be impossible ASL signs, although they may occur in other sign languages. It is noteworthy that the users of sign language are as unconscious of the rules of their language as those who use a spoken language.

Using old sign language dictionaries and films made by the National Association of the Deaf in 1913, researchers have compared present-day ASL with earlier stages of the language. Regular patterns of change have been observed and described by linguists (Frishberg, 1975). Regional, social, racial, and sexual variation in ASL is distributed in regular patterns, similar to the patterns observed in English (Woodward & Erting, 1975).

MYTH: SIGN LANGUAGE IS ICONIC

Sign language is frequently described as iconic or picturelike. There are several points to keep in mind when considering the question of iconicity of signs.

First, signs for the same concepts are different in different sign languages. Second, if signs were really iconic, hearing people would be able to understand deaf people's signing with only limited instruction. As the experience of students of sign language shows, learning to communicate in ASL requires as much time, effort, and motivation as is necessary for becoming fluent in a spoken language.

Third, signs that appear iconic when they are made in isolation are often unrecognizable by a nonsigner when they occur in a sign conversation. This results not only from the fast rate of signing, but also from the modification of signs that takes place when signs are made in sign sentences.

Fourth, iconicity does not appear to play a role in the acquisition of ASL by children. At the time a young child learns the sign MILK, a milk carton or bottle is probably his or her only experience of its source. The child may not learn until years later that the milk is obtained from cows by milking them. Thus the iconic element of the sign MILK is completely lost on the child.

Fifth, signers often offer "explanations" for signs. If each sign had a single explanation, the argument for iconicity might appear somewhat more favorable. But, even a brief look will show that some signs have several "etymologies." Take for example, the sign AMERICA, which has four widely used explanations; they cannot all be true etymologies. Popular etymologies of this type are often totally unrelated to the real history of the sign.

Although iconicity in signs is often exploited in poetic expression and also for coining neologisms (Klima & Bellugi, 1979), it does not seem to play a major role in ASL communication among native signers.

MYTH: SIGN LANGUAGE IS CONCRETE

One of the most popular myths about sign language is that although ASL can express concrete concepts, it is restricted in its capacity to deal with abstract ideas. However, as in oral languages, sign language has the flexibility and the creative processes necessary to invent new vocabulary as it becomes needed.

Users of ASL have a lot of contact with written and spoken English. Thus, they are able to draw on the very large vocabulary of the English language. English words are borrowed into ASL by means of fingerspelling. Battison (1978) has shown that certain often-fingerspelled words become part of the ASL vocabulary through regular patterns, in much the same way that words are borrowed from one oral language to another.

Other procedures for creating new signs have also been described, such as compounding or giving a new meaning to an existing sign. In both cases, a systematic modification of the sign takes place. Another way is to invent a sign based on a mimed representation (Klima & Bellugi, 1979).

ASL includes many signs for abstract ideas such as LOVE, FAITH, BELIEF, and TRUST. Although some signs have an iconic element, they function as symbols just like spoken words. When we read in a newspaper article that "The U.S. Fleet is *sailing* in the Mediterranean," in our mind we conceive correctly a fleet of large steel ships powered by oil-burning engines. Given what we know about modern naval warfare, we do not imagine that the U.S. Navy has acquired an armada of *sailboats!* We can abstract away from the original meaning of the word "sail" and assign to it a new meaning that applies to ships without sails. In the same way, even a sign that shows some iconic element is not restricted to its original meaning. As the need arises, signs take on new meanings.

ASL has ways of expressing nuances just as spoken languages do. There are no limitations on what can be handled in ASL except those set by the choice of topics normally discussed in that language by the members of the deaf community. The assumption that ASL is limited to informal exchanges because of inherent deficiencies in its vocabulary or lack of structural complexity is without basis.

MYTH: ASL IS UNGRAMMATICAL

Word-for-word translations from one language to another often result in ungrammatical or meaningless sentences as illustrated by the following French sentences.

1. Il fait chaud.
   It makes warm.   (It is warm.)
2. Tu me manques.
   You me miss.   (I miss you.)

On the basis of these examples, it would be foolish to suggest that the French language is ungrammatical.

The opinion that ASL is ungrammatical, or lacks a grammar, usually results from a sign-for-word translation of ASL into English. It is based on the assumption that ASL must be structured exactly like English. However, ASL is an independent language with its own grammar and its own vocabulary, and both are unrelated to English.

It is certainly true that ASL does not have some of the features found in English. On the other hand, the latter language does not make use of such features as location and directionality, which indicate grammatical relations in ASL. Because ASL consists of movements made in space, signers refer to particular people or things whether they are physically present or not, by pointing, or by shifting their eyes to a specific point in space. Several *locations* can be established and may remain for the rest of the conversation. In the English sentence "Bob insulted John and then he hit him," it is unclear whether the "he" refers to Bob or to John, but there is no ambiguity in the equivalent sentence in ASL.

Directionality, the second feature identified previously, also makes use of space for grammatical purposes. For example, the notions of "subject" and "object" can be included in some verb signs by means of the direction of the movement. Consequently, the sentence HE SHOWS ME is executed with one sign—SHOW.

I SHOW HIM is made by reversing the direction. By modifying the movement of these productions of SHOW to indicate continuous aspect, we obtain "He shows me continuously" and "I show him continuously," respectively. Inflections based on the form, the direction, and the quality of the movement appear to have an important function in the grammar of ASL.

REFERENCES

Battison, R. *Lexical borrowing in American Sign Language.* Silver Spring, Md: Linstok Press, 1978.

Frishberg, N. Arbitrariness and iconicity: Historical change in American Sign Language. *Language,* 1975, *51,* 696–719.

Klima, E., & Bellugi, U. *The signs of language.* Cambridge, Mass: Harvard University Press, 1979.

Markowicz, H., & Woodward, J. Language and the maintenance of ethnic boundaries in the deaf community. *Communication and Cognition,* 1978, *11,* 29–37.

Meadow, K. Sociolinguistics, sign language, and the deaf subculture. In T. O'Rourke (Ed.), *Psycholinguistics and total communication: The state of the art.* Washington, D.C.: American Annals of the Deaf, 1972.

Stokoe, W. *Sign language structure.* Buffalo, N.Y.: University of Buffalo, 1960.

Stokoe, W. Sign language diglossia. *Studies in Linguistics,* 1970, *21,* 27–41.

Woodward, J. Historical bases of American sign language. In P. Siple (Ed.), *Understanding language through sign language research.* New York: Academic Press, 1978.

Woodward, J., & Erting, C. Synchronic variation and historical change in American Sign Language. *Language Sciences,* 1975, *37,* 9–12.

2 The Linguistic Description of American Sign Language

Ronnie Wilbur
Boston University

INTRODUCTION

Recent studies of American Sign Language (ASL) have argued convincingly that ASL is a language in the full linguistic sense of the word. Research into the structrue of ASL began in earnest with Stokoe (1960), and only recently have the details of ASL acquisition, memory, perception, history, sociology, and educational implications been approached. Recent research in linguistics illustrates the variety of topics that has been investigated: sociolinguistics (Woodward, 1973a, 1973b, 1973c), historical changes (Frishberg, 1976), phonology (Friedman, 1976a, 1976b), syntax (Liddell, 1977), borrowings from English through fingerspelling (Battison, 1978), the pronoun system (Lacy, personal communication; Kegl, 1976a, 1976b, 1977), and the complete range of systems built on the indexic pointing gesture and their acquisition (Hoffmeister, 1978a, 1978b). These and other studies have highlighted many linguistic features of ASL. Extensive research on other sign languages has not yet been conducted. Of necessity then, this chapter focuses entirely on ASL. It may be presumed that many of the processes, if not the actual details, will be found in other sign languages when they are investigated.

PHONOLOGY

Stokoe (1960) investigated sign formation, which he called "cherology," treating it as analogous to the phonological system of oral languages. He defined three parameters that were realized simultaneously in the formation of a particular sign—DEZ (designator, handshape), TAB (Tabulation, location), and SIG (signation, motion). A fourth parameter, ORIENTATION, which refers to the orientation of the palm, was added later by Battison (1973; Battison, Markowicz, & Woodward, 1975). In oral languages, distinctive features are simultaneously combined to produce consonantal and vocalic segments. Analogously, the four Stokoe parameters are produced simultaneously to form signs.

In oral languages, physical constraints make certain combinations of featues impossible. For example, a vowel cannot at the same time be both *high* and *low*. Other combinations are not possible on purely linguistic grounds (e.g., in English all [+ back, – low] vowels must be [+ round]). Similar redundancy conditions have been described for combinations of sign parameters. Adherence to these conditions defines a possible sign, whereas violations are considered impossible or improbable. Klima and Bellugi (1975) have observed that signs that violate these conditions form a pool from which humor and poetry may be created. Some of the conditions on allowable signs may be attributable to constraints placed on the visual mode by perceptual mechanisms (Siple, 1978) whereas others, such as the Symmetry Condition (Battison, 1974), may be productively motivated as well. Still other conditions, such as those identified for contact in two-touch signs by Battison, Markowicz, and Woodward (1975), may be linguistically arbitrary.

Battison et al. (1975) give several examples of linguistic constraints on sign formation. Some signs involve two sequential contacts with the body. If the body is divided into four major parts—head and neck, trunk, arm, and hand—then only the combinations summarized in Table 2.1 are permissible for the first and second contacts. In addition, the second contact is constrained to a centralized position in the major contact area, so that a sign may go from head to center chest, but not from head to either shoulder or to a corner or side of the trunk. A constraint such as this, not required by physical limitations, but possibly an aid to perception, distinguishes signs from pantomime.

TABLE 2.1[a]
Permissible Contacts with the Body for Double-Contact Signs[b]

First Contact	Second Contact			
	Head	Trunk	Arm	Hand
Head	+	+	+	+
Trunk	–	+	–	+
Arm	–	–	+	–
Hand	+	–	–	+

[a]Based on Battison, Markowicz, and Woodward, 1975.
[b]+ indicates an acceptable sequence, – indicates an unacceptable sequence.

Battison (1974) described two further constraints related specifically to signs formed with both hands. Basically, there are three types of two-handed signs: (1) both hands move independently; (2) only one hand moves but both handshapes are identical; and (3) only one hand moves (the dominant one) and the handshape of the nondominant, nonmoving hand is restricted to one of a limited set of the possible handshapes. For the signs where both hands move, a Symmetry Condition exists, specifying that the handshapes and movement for both hands must be identical and that the orientations and movements of both hands must be identical or polar opposites (mirror images). For two-handed signs in which the handshapes are not identical (3 previously mentioned), a Dominance Condition exists, specifying that the nondominant hand must remain static while the dominant hand produces the sign. (The dominant hand is most often considered to be the hand used by the signer to make one-handed signs, and the moving hand is considered dominant in two-handed signs where only one hand moves. Kegl and Wilbur (1976) diverge from this practice by considering *any* moving hand to be dominant; thus if both hands are moving, they are both dominant, and if a signer first makes a one-handed sign with his right hand and then a different one-handed sign with his left hand, he has switched dominance). Furthermore, the nondominant hand can assume only one of the six most unmarked handshapes, which include:

1. S-hand: a closed fist.
2. B-hand: the flat palm.
3. 5-hand: the B hand with fingers spread apart.
4. G-hand: fist with index finger extended.
5. C-hand: hand formed in a semicircle.
6. O-hand: fingertips meet with thumb, forming a circle.

Battison pointed out that these six handshapes are considered the least marked because they are found in all other sign languages studied to date, they are maximally distinct formationally and perceptually, and they are among the first acquired by children learning the language (Boyes, 1973). Lane, Boyes-Braem, and Bellugi (1976) also note that these six handshapes constitute "69% of all the entries in the Stokoe, Casterline, and Croneberg dictionary (1965) and 81% of all the entries in a 1-hr. corpus of the signing of a deaf two-and-a-half year old. [p. 276]."

The constraints identified to date seem to be sufficiently powerful that historical changes in ASL have tended to take signs that did not conform to these conditions and modify them into signs that do conform (Frishberg, 1976). Descriptions of signs are available from as early as 1797 for Old French Sign Language and 1850 for American Sign Language. Significant changes can be seen in signs in the relatively short time since Long prepared his manual (1918). Frishberg (1975, 1976) reports that changes in signs over time have tended to increase the symmetry of a sign, increase the fluidity between parts of a sign, move signs to a more centralized location, and modify the formation of some signs so that the hands are the main conveyor of the information rather than the facial expression, body or head movements.

While on the topic of historical change of signs, one other aspect needs to be mentioned: borrowing from English through fingerspelling. There are two kinds—initialization of signs and creation of new signs.

The substitution of a handshape from the manual alphabet into a sign for the express purpose of making that sign somehow "correspond" to an English word is called intialization.Typically, a sign is initialized in several ways, thus creating several distinctive signs from a single ASL sign. Although some deliberate initializations clearly violate rules of allowable sign formation, others are linguistically permissible and may even be accepted into the daily language. The acceptance of such signs, and other invented signs, varies from person to person. Some deaf people, who have been told most of their lives that signing is "inferior" or "not grammatical," may feel that these signs are "improving" the sign language, that they make the sign language "more precise." Others recognize the artificiality of these signs and stigmatize people who use them as "obviously hearing signers" (even though some deaf people may use them).

Battison (1978) reported that short fingerspelled English words may change into signs through a variety of modifications. Medial letters may be lost, leaving only the first and last letters. The remaining handshapes may assimilate according to the number of fingers involved. At the same time, the handshapes may dissimilate along the open/close dimension (i.e., if the first handshape is open, e.g. 5, then the second will be closed, e.g. S, or vice versa). Movements may be added (remember that fingerspelled letters in the American manual alphabet, except J and Z, do not move except as a transition into the next letter handshape). These may include linear movement (for example, the new sign for ALL from fingerspelled a-l may move down a list to indicate all the items in a list, or sweep across the horizontal plane to indicate all the people or things) or reduplication (repetition, usually of open/close change in handshape). The location may also change (fingerspelled words are made in a constrained box about shoulder height on the ipsilateral side of the hand that is doing the spelling) to other areas within the signing space. And finally, the sign may add a second hand. These combined changes remove the word from the realm of fingerspelling into the lexicon of signs. Battison suggests that the target of these processes is to produce a double handshape sign (but not necessarily made with both hands) that changes its handshapes during formation. This process is presumably productive and open-ended. Spoken languages in need of a vocabulary item may invent new words, compound already existing words, or borrow words from other languages. These processes which allow borrowing from English (or theoretically any spoken language), provide ASL with the same word innovation options as other languages.

Some of the constraints that exist on the formation of possible signs are linguistic and not physiological. Clearly it is possible for two hands to move along different paths simultaneously (although it is often difficult, e.g. rubbing your stomach while patting your head). The nonuse of all the possible formational combinations provides a reservoir from which puns, rhymes, and art-sign (poetry and song) may be made (Klima & Bellugi, 1975). Challenging Tervoort's (1961) claim that signs are rarely used ironically or metaphorically, Klima and Bellugi investigated manipulation of signs for creative purposes. In addition to identifying sign puns several types of sign-play were found (these are creative uses which do not depend on the structure of English). Three basic processes were reported: (1) the overlapping of two signs; (2) the blending of two signs; and (3) the substitution of one value of a regular formational parameter for another.

Recent work in ASL phonology has resulted in a proliferation of proposed distinctive feature systems (Kegl & Wilbur, 1976; Lane et al., 1976; Tjapkes, 1976; Woodward, 1973a) as well as an argument by Friedman (1976b) that such feature systems were not yet warranted for ASL phonology. This topic is the focus of ongoing research by different researchers, as is the topic of utilization of a generative phonological framework for ASL (Wilbur, 1978). The details of these arguments are sufficiently complex as to be impossible to present in the space available here without eliminating all of the remaining information in morphology and syntax. A complete review may be found in Wilbur (1979).

In addition to descriptions of the sign itself, some recent investigations have begun to focus on phonological modifications that may occur when signs occur in context. The processes described later are not yet well-documented in the literature as synchronic processes, and may at some later date be shown to be dialectal, stylistic, or even fast signing phenomena. Battison et al. (1975) and Battison (1974) refer to assimilations of movement, location, orientation, and handshape, but do not provide examples of the degree to which they occur. Kegl and Wilbur (1976) report assimilations of location (regressive, the first sign moves to the location of the second sign), handshape (also regressive), and facial expression (apparently progressive).

Assimilation in general is a process whereby two unlike elements become more similar because of their proximity in context. This increase in similarity may result from the first formed element becoming more similar to the second (regressive assimilation), or from the second element becoming more similar to the first (progressive assimilation), or from modifications in both elements (mutual assimilation). In spoken language, these elements are sounds; in manual language, they are signs. In spoken language, the sounds may change their place of articulation, or their manner of articulation. Similarly, signs may modify their location, handshape, or other characteristics.

Assimilation of location has been observed between two consecutive signs. In each case so far, it has been regressive assimilation, with the second sign conditioning adjustment in the formation of the first sign. For example, in a signed version of "Three Little Pigs" (Kegl & Chinchor, 1975), in a sequence from the wolf to the three little pigs, the wolf signs LET ME IN repeatedly. In some cases, the formation of LET is modified in that the right hand moves from waist level (where LET is normally signed) to chest height, in anticipation of the formation of the sign ME. In a few cases, both hands of LET were raised to chest height in anticipation of the following sign. In another example, WE REFUSE, regressive assimilation of location causes the sign WE to *metathesize* its two places of articulation (contact first at right chest, then at left chest, becomes contact first at left chest, then at right chest) in anticipation of the formation of REFUSE at the right shoulder. The existence of this kind of internal metathesis has been overlooked previously, and even thought impossible.

The example WE REFUSE also illustrates assimilation of handshape, again regressive assimilation. The sign for WE is usually made with an H hand (or for some people with a G hand), or in initialized versions with a W, but is made with an A hand as an assimilation to REFUSE which is made with an A. Other types of handshape modifications which are observed are not strictly phonological; They include blending of an object into its verb (modifying the handshape of the verb GIVE to the shape of its object BOOK, thereby executing GIVE and BOOK simultaneously, written hereafter as BOOK-GIVE), the blending of numbers into nouns (changing the handshape of WEEK, which is actually "one week," to reflect two, three, or four weeks), and the creative combinations of handshapes with certain motions, locations, and orientations to produce name signs.

Our discussion of facial expression has been extremely limited so far. The role of facial expression, head tilt, eyeblink, and eye gaze are so important in the syntax of ASL that their functions are described in their relevant places. However, certain facial expressions are distinct to particular signs, for example the distinction between LATE and NOT-YET is that the latter is made with an accompanying slightly extended tongue whereas the former is made manually the same, but without the tongue (Baker, 1976). Thus, at some level, it makes sense to talk about signs that are made with distinctive facial expressions, or lexical facial expression. What has been observed is the assimilation of signs with neutral facial expression (i.e., lacking lexical facial expression) to signs with lexical facial expression. In at least one example, the assimilation is not regressive, but progressive. The sign for BIG may be made with puffed cheeks. The sign TREE has no lexical facial expression of its own. The sequence BIG TREE may be signed in a variety of ways. The simplest

2. LINGUISTIC PERSPECTIVE 13

(but not necessarily the most acceptable) form would be BIG TREE, with neutral facial expression on both signs. The next possibility would be the unassimilated version, with BIG made with puffed cheeks and TREE made with neutral face (acceptability doubtful). The assimilated version would have puffed cheeks held across the formation of both BIG and TREE. Another possibility is to delete the manual formation of BIG and have a coalesced sign BIG-TREE, in which the hands form TREE but the facial expression is puffed cheeks from the sign BIG. One linguistically impossible version is BIG with neutral face followed by TREE with puffed cheeks. The fact that this is unacceptable argues for treating this process as assimilation with copying onto TREE, rather than claiming that puffed cheeks alone is an alternate version of the sign for BIG (Baker, 1976). Within the description suggested here, the coalesced form results from assimilation followed by deletion of BIG. Similarly, the fact that it is not possible to have BIG without puffed cheeks but TREE with puffed cheeks (i.e., BIG [neutral face] TREE [puffed cheeks]) is explained by the fact that puffed cheeks cannot occur on TREE unless it is copied from BIG, and there appears to be no rule that would delete the puffed cheeks from BIG after assimilation has occurred.

Fischer (1973) discusses reduplication as a phonological as well as a morphological process, indicating two speeds of reduplication and possible co-occurring horizontal sweeping and rocking motions. She notes that fast reduplication cannot co-occur with rocking, and that slow reduplication cannot co-occur with the horizontal sweeping movement. These rules are formalized as:

1. Verb   → [+Reduplication]
2. [+Redup] → [±Fast]
3. [−Fast]   → [±Rocking]
4. [+Fast]   → [±Horizontal Sweeping]

Rule 4, for example, says that a verb sign that is made with fast reduplication may or may not have horizontal sweeping motion, and also (by omission) implies that fast reduplication may not co-occur with a rocking motion.

Friedman (1974, 1976b) presents both qualitative and quantitative data showing that signs tend to be produced larger, tenser, and more rapidly in their stressed forms than in their citation forms. In measurements made comparing stressed and unstressed signs, Friedman (1976b) reports that the mean duration of a stressed sign is 833 msec. compared to 366 msec. for unstressed signs. However, the actual movement part of this duration is only 150 msec. for the stressed signs compared to 267 msec. for the unstressed signs. The remainder of the duration is composed of "holds," either before and after the movement, before the movement but not after, after the movement but not before, or for some signs, no hold at all. Holds before the movement averaged 367 msec. for the stressed signs compared to 150 msec. for the unstressed signs, whereas holds after the movement averaged 617 msec. for the stressed signs compared to 100 msec. for the unstressed signs.

Changes in motion vary according to the type of movement in the citation form. Motion along a straight line, twisting motion, and motion that involves bending of the wrist are modified to become larger, more rapid, and tenser, while other nonstraight movements, such as circular, bending of fingers, bending of knuckles, opening, and closing, become tenser and more rapid, but by their nature of formation cannot become larger. Signs which involved repetition in their citation forms tend to lose that repetition.

The type of contact an unstressed sign has may also affect how its motion is modified under stress, as well as affecting its stressed contact. Signs that have two points of contact develop an arching motion between the first and second contact under stress. Some signs with one contact, either beginning or end, may also develop this arc. Signs produced with continuous contact in unstressed form retain that contact and instead of being made quicker, are made more deliberately and slower. Friedman reports measurements of mean duration of movement for the stressed signs as 467 msec. compared to 267 msec. for the unstressed signs.

Signs which are noncontact in their unstressed forms, usually those that are also straight movement and directional signs, add a final contact point, becoming what Friedman calls "end contact." Similarly, signs made with an initial contact in their unstressed forms tend to add a final contact, becoming "double contact." Interestingly, signs that are initially "end contact" tend to become noncontact when stressed, with the exception of those whose final point of contact is on the nondominant hand. This leads Friedman to suggest that the loss of contact in these stressed signs serves in the interest of avoiding possible bodily injury to the signer that might result from a large, rapid possibly ballistic sign making its final contact with the head (DUMB) or chest (MYSELF). Those signs that are made with holding contact in their unstressed forms become noncontact in their stressed forms, while also becoming straight action, large, rapid, and possibly ballistic, thereby making maintenance of contact a physical strain.

Friedman's analysis of stress illustrates the types of phonological processes that may be found in sign language when one considers the effects of context on the formation of signs. Further investigations may reveal some other factors that have not yet been recognized.

Battison (1974) describes types of deletion that may occur in ASL: (1) deletion of a contact (which can also be viewed as deletion of a location), (2) deletion of one part of a compound, (3) deletion of movement (e.g., loss of repetition in stressed signs), and (4) deletion of one of the hands in a two-handed sign. Bellugi (1975; Klima & Bellugi, 1979) discusses deletion in the context of the process of compounding. In particular, a compound sign may take only as much time to produce as an average single sign, thus requiring deletion and/or temporal compression of parts of the compound constituents. Frishberg (1978) has observed that historically, if one part of a compound sign is deleted, a "compensatory lengthening" of the remaining movement may result.

A major phonological process that occurs in ASL, blending, has only been dealt with in scattered reports. Blending of two signs into one is discussed by Klima and Bellugi (1975) in the context of creative sign formation for artistic purposes (including humor). Blending of numerals into nouns has been described by Chinchor (1978). Blending of noun objects into verbs as the phonological manifestation of NP Incorporation has been discussed in Kegl and Wilbur (1976) as well as Kegl (1977, 1978a, 1978b, 1978c). Other phonological processes, and their conditioning environments, remain to be identified.

MORPHOLOGY

Fewer morphological processes have been identified, but the data supporting them are more extensive. Reduplication serves many morphological functions in ASL. Frishberg and Gough (1973a) identify reduplication as a means of forming the repetitive form of certain time adverbs ("week" vs. "weekly") with speed of reduplication as a variable affecting meaning. This type of reduplication may be repeated several times, whereas the augmentative reduplication ("bowl" vs. "big bowl") formulated by Kegl and Wilbur (1976) may only be repeated once. Fischer (1973) indicates that reduplication may be used to indicate verb aspect, such as iterative, continuitive, and with horizontal sweeping, plural subject or object. Verbs can be divided into Stative (*appear, seem, looks like,* etc.) and Non-Stative (Active), which can be further divided into Durative (*sleep, talk,* etc.) and Non-Durative (*kill, win, find,* etc.). These divisions are semantic in nature and therefore expected to be appropriately differentiated in every language. Stative verbs must be reduplicated quickly while Non-Stative verbs can be reduplicated slowly or quickly, when reduplication is being used for aspectual marking. Slow reduplication of a Non-Durative verb is interpreted to mean that the action was iterated ("kept on Xing and Xing and Xing," as in "winning and winning and winning"), whereas slow reduplication of a durative verb indicates that the action was continued ("Xed for a long time," as in "talked for a long time"). In addition, a slowly reduplicated verb can be "rocked," in which case the sign is interpreted as meaning "Too much X." Fast reduplicated forms usually indicate a type of plural. If the reduplication is accompanied by a horizontal sweeping motion, the sign is interpreted as having either a plural subject or a plural object, each of which does X. Fast reduplication without horizontal movement is interpreted as "Habitually does X." Thus, the speed of reduplication, the rocking motion or absence of it, and the presence or absence of horizontal sweeping of the hands can be used to indicate various semantic realtionships.

Supalla and Newport (1978) discuss the use of repetition in the formation of deverbal nominals (nouns derived from verbs) and associated forms. Their discussion includes another aspect of sign formation that has not been characterized extensively, namely manner of formation (see also Friedman, 1976b). Supalla and Newport begin by defining two basic types of sign movement—unidirectional and bidirectional. Within the category of unidirectional, they identify three types, *continuous, holding,* and *restrained,* and within the category of bidirectional, they identify only two of these, *continuous* and *restrained.* They illustrate *continuous* with the example of someone swatting frantically after a fly and missing, *holding* as the abrupt end of the motion as the fly is squashed with the fly swatter, and *restrained* as the tense, controlled motion one would use to avoid splattering the fly all over the table (the hand usually bounces back from the contact, reacting to the abrupt stop and the tenseness of the muscles). Supalla and Newport observe that in verb-noun pairs, such as SIT and CHAIR, FLY and AIRPLANE, DRIVE and CAR, the noun required at least one repetition of the basic movement, whereas the verb, although possibly reduplicated in the manner discussed by Fischer, did not require it. Repetition is insufficient, however, to derive nouns from verbs. There is also a concomitant change in the manner of formation. Whether the verb is continuous or holding, Supalla and Newport indicate that verbs tend not to be restrained, the corresponding noun is restrained. Thus, FLY is unidirectional continuous and AIRPLANE is unidirectional restrained. SIT is unidirectional holding, whereas CHAIR is unidirectional restrained. DRIVE is bidirectional continuous, and CAR is bidirectional restrained. As indicated, verbs may be reduplicated for various aspectual meanings. Cyclic reduplication of nouns carries the meaning "X after X after X" (e.g., "car after car after car") and is a reduplication of the already repeated movement (distinguishing it from the repetition of the verb).

Various types of plural formation exist. Jones and Mohr (1975) concentrate on noun plurals. Nearly all nouns can form the plural with the quantifier MANY. Modifications for noun plurals include changing the number of hands used to make the sign, use of reduplication, and continuing the movement while adding a horizontal sweeping motion. Fischer and Gough (1978) describe four types of verb modifications for plural subject or object; these include the definite (individual), indefinite, collective, and dual.

The definite (individual) plural can apply to all verbs. It has a meaning that implies that each of the people or things performing the action do so individually, not collectively (i.e., something like "John left and Mary left and Bill left"). In addition, the people or things involved must be definite (i.e., it cannot be used for "some people left"). In order to understand how this process, and the others discussed later, work, it will be convenient to establish three arbitrary points in space in front of the signer's body: Point 1 will be about 6 inches away from the signer's body in front and will be on the right about even with the right shoulder and will be at mid-chest height; point 2 will be somewhere to the left of point 1, same distance away from the body and same height, toward the center of the chest area but not directly in the center (this mid-line is used for reference to the addressee, second person reference); and point 3 will be similarly placed on the signer's left, same height same distance from the body (the distance from the body, the height, and the degree of leftness or rightness are subject to a number of individual signer variables, as well as the total number of references actually being made). For ease of translation, John will be referred to with point 1, Mary with point 2, and Bill with point 3. The definite (individual) plural which corresponds to "John left and (then) Mary left and (then) Bill left" or "They each left separately" is made by facing point 1 and making the verb sign, then facing point 2, repeating the sign, and then facing point 3 and repeating the sign. This process includes repetition of the verb, a horizontal movement that is not a horizontal sweep, and a reorientation of the body and/or head and face, which is referred to as "body shift" (Kegl, 1976a).

The indefinite plural has a meaning implying that "many, but not necessarily all" of the people or things involved performed the verb action. It can be collective "Many of them did it together." The indefinite plural is formed by fast reduplication of the verb sign (without pauses in between) moving around in a horizontal sweep (suppose it starts at point 1 and arcs around to point 3).

The collective plural, which means bascially that everyone or everything is involved in the performance of the verb, is made with a single production of the verb sign accompanied by a horizontal sweeping of the hands, body and/or eyes. Thus the formation of the sign might begin at point 1 and end somewhere near point 3, or the sign could be made closer to a single point, perhaps point 2, while the head and/or eyes turn from point 1 to 3. All verbs that can form a collective plural can also form the indefinite plural, but not vice versa. However, a generalization as to what factors allow or prohibit collective plurals remains to be determined.

Fischer and Gough (1972) indicate a couple of alternate pluralization processes that can be used for the collective and indefinite plurals. These include using two hands where in the singular only one hand is used (possibly along with reduplication and horizontal sweep as described earlier) and incorporating number into the verb sign. If the verb is made with a G hand (same handshape as the number 1), then its formation with the V hand (number 2) is the plural that Fischer and Gough have termed "dual." The set of verbs that can take this form is limited. If the verb has a V handshape (LOOK), then the following forms can be made:

1. "John looks at me." LOOK (hand moved to point 1 to indicate John, hand faces toward signer to indicate me)
2. "John and Bill look at me." LOOK (one hand made as at point 1, left hand made as at point 3) (This is also the dual.)
3. "Everybody looks at me." LOOK (made with both hands as at point 2, not necessarily at points 1 and 3, and with 4 fingers extended on each hand instead of 2 [V hand] to indicate "many")

Also morphological in nature are the time and tense systems for ASL. It has been noted by many sign language researchers that ASL does not provide tense marking on each verb in each sentence as e.g., English does, nor does it require a tense marking on each sentence as do Walbiri and Luiseño. Instead, ASL allows the time of the conversation to be marked at the initiation of that conversation and does not require further marking (although it *may* be) until the time reference is changed (as for example in Malay). Fischer and Gough (1972), Frishberg and Gough (1973b), Friedman (1975), and Cogen (1977) have all addressed aspects of the time marking system in ASL and modifications that may occur within that system.

Frishberg and Gough (1973b) describe the ASL "time line," a line passing alongside the body from behind the head to a distance no greater than the full extent of the arm in front of the body, passing just below the ear. The space right in front of the body indicates the present, slightly more forward indicates near future, and greater distances forward reflect very distant future. The near past, of course, cannot be signed behind the body, so the space above the shoulder just about in line with the ear is near past, and distances further back over the shoulder indicate distant past. If no time is marked at the beginning of a conversation, it is assumed to be the time of the speech act itself, the present. Time can be established by the time adverbials discussed previously (YESTERDAY, NEXT THURSDAY, etc.), perfective markers (FINISH, NOT-YET) or the signs FUTURE, PAST, PAST-CONTINUOUS. The use of one of the signs FUTURE, PAST, PAST-CONTINUOUS causes a shift in the interpretation of the time line. For example, using the sign PAST causes the part of the time line that was previously interpreted as present to become past. Thus, within a conversation established in the past, the use of the sign TOMORROW might be interpreted as "the next day"(i.e., the day after the event that was just mentioned) rather than "tomorrow"(i.e., the day after the speech act itself). Thus, the base of time reference can be adjusted to permit time before and after a specified time in the past to be discussed in the present conversation.

One of the few obvious suffixes in ASL, that of the bound negative, was identified by Woodward (1973a, 1973b, 1973c, 1974). Several signs (this is not a general process) may affix this suffix to form the negative instead of using the separate negative signs available (NOT, DON'T, etc.). The negative suffix is thought to derive from the French Sign Language NOT. The signs KNOW, LIKE, WANT, HAVE, and GOOD can form a type of contracted negative with this suffix called Negative Incorporation by Woodward, whereas other signs form their negative with the ASL sign NOT, usually preceding the verb, or the signs DON'T, STOP, or REFUSE/WON'T. The traditional description given to the contracted forms is a description first of how the sign is made, followed by a description of the negative form, apparently involving "a bound outward twisting movement of the moving hand(s) from the place where the sign is made" (Woodward & De Santis, 1977). P. Jones (1978) has offered two additional generalizations concerning the negative morpheme: (1) the orientation of the negative morpheme is opposite to the orientation of the sign it is negating (KNOW and LIKE have inward orientation, they are negated with an outward orientation, whereas WANT and HAVE have an upward orientation and they are followed by a downward oriented negative); and (2) regardless of the handshape of the unnegated sign, the negative morpheme is made with a 5 handshape.

SYNTAX

The key to understanding ASL syntax, particularly word order, is the recognition that locations in space are used for inflectional purposes. Within the "signing space" (the allowable area in which signs may be made), signs may be moved from one location to another to indicate differences in subject and object. The verb GIVE, for example, may start at the signer's body and move out toward the addressee to indicate "I give you...," whereas the reverse would indicate "you give me...." One can establish locations in space for John and Mary, and then move from John to Mary to indicate "John gives Mary..." (actually "He gives her...") or from John to the addressee to indicate "John gives you...." Kegl (1976a, 1976b, 1977) formalized this process into a general system of verb agreement. The concept of verb inflection as used by Kegl (and earlier formulations by Frishberg & Gough, 1973a, and Fischer & Gough, 1978) contrasts with Fant's (1972) statement that "signs are not inflected as words are" (a position also taken in Friedman, 1977). A consideration of all relevant arguments (in Wilbur, 1979) leads us to concur with Kegl. This formalization provides a useful solution to what Kegl (1976b, 1977) calls "the word order controversy."

Word order in ASL had been the subject of concern long before linguists began investigating it rigorously. Educators had noticed only that sign language word order used by deaf children and adults was not the same as the spoken language. They considered the word order simply to be "incorrect." Fischer (1975) argued that ASL has historically changed to become a Subject-Verb-Object (SVO) language like English, possibly through increasing influence of English itself. She argues that orders other than SVO are allowable if topicalization occurs, if the subject and object are nonreversible (i.e., only one possible semantic interpretation is possible), and/or the signer uses space to indicate grammatical relations (i.e., the verbs are inflected). When other orders occur, Fischer identifies "intonation breaks" that mark these orders.

Fischer's paper basically argues that ASL has become a Subject-Verb-Object (SVO) language like English, possibly through increasing influence from English itself. Fischer constructed sign sequences and presented them to native signers for interpretation. The presented sentences consisted of various permutations of two nouns and a verb: NVN, NNV, VNN. (When either of the two nouns can be interpreted as subject or object, the sentence is referred to as "reversible," e.g. "John kicked Bill," but if only one noun can logically or reasonably be considered the subject or object, the sentence is "nonreversible," e.g. "John kicked the chair.") Fischer reports that the interpretations provided by her informants were as follows:

1. NVN was interpreted as SVO.
2. NNV was interpreted as either   a) conjoined subject-verb (N and N V), or
                                                   b) OSV
3. VNN was interpreted as either   a) verb-conjoined object (V N and N), or
                                                   b) VOS

Fischer's (1975) conclusions from these interpretations was that ASL is an underlying SVO language. This does not mean that SVO is the only allowable surface word order: "Other orders are allowed under the circumstances that (a) something is topicalized, (b) the subject and object are non-reversible, and/or (c) the signer used space to indicate grammatical mechanisms [p. 21]." Variations from the basic SVO order can be signaled by "intonation breaks," which Fischer characterizes as consisting of pauses, head tilts, raised eyebrows, and/or possibly other nonmanual cues. Thus NVN is interpreted as SVO, contains no breaks, and is considered the underlying order. N,NV may be interpreted as O,SV with the object topicalized and a break between it and the remainder of the sentence (an example of a topicalized object in English would be "As for the rhubarb, John ate [it]"). The sequence VN,N may be interpreted as VO,S with a topicalized verb phrase, followed by the subject with a break after the verb phrase (symbolized by the comma). (An example of a topicalized verb phrase in English would be "As for doing the dishes, John will.") In discussing Fischer's data, Liddell (1977) notes that although these three orders include the subject in all three sentence positions, initial, medial, and final, this does not indicate random word order in ASL. Instead, he adds the observation that "if the subject or object accompanies the verb, the subject precedes the verb and the object follows the verb [p. 109]."

Friedman (1976a) argues with Fischer's analysis, claiming that word order is relatively free (she also inconsistently argues that SOV is the basic underlying word order). Friedman claims not to have found the "intonation breaks" that Fischer describes, and suggests that this is because she is using discourse data whereas Fischer is using elicited sentences. Friedman proposes several "avoidance strategies" for handling potential ambiguity that might arise in ASL, which include the use of the body and space for distinguishing referents (but she does not consider these inflections).

Friedman (1976a) summarizes the discourse situation in ASL as follows:

1. Nominal signs are articulated and established in space, either by indexic or marker reference or by body position.

2. Verb signs are then (a) manipulated between or among these previously established locations for nominal referents or (b) articulated on the body which is in the appropriate pre-established position for agent or experiencer.

3. The first verb is assumed to have first person subject unless an actual subject is indicated. Subsequent verbs that also appear without overt subjects are still interpreted as first person. Whenever a verb appears without a subject in connected discourse, the subject is "assumed to be the same as the last one given, until a new subject is mentioned."

4. As indicated earlier, word order appears relatively free, with a tendency for the verb to occur last.

5. The appearance or nonappearance of a noun sign after its initial establishment in the discourse seems to be in free variation, with its appearance functioning possibly as an indicator of emphasis, contrast, or clarification.

6. At most, four or five different referent locations may be used within a single discourse. These locations can then be used for later pronominal reference [pp. 141–142].

Friedman suggested that ASL has a series of avoidance strategies for processing and producing signed utterances that are necessary to compensate for constrained syntactic rules. Fundamental to her approach is the claim that the recognition of iconic representation in ASL requires abandonment of standard linguistic notation and concepts. Other researchers have retained standard descriptions (Kegl & Wilbur, 1976; Kegl, 1976a, 1976b, 1977, 1978a, 1978b, 1978c; Liddell, 1977; Lacy, 1974), requiring whatever iconicity is present in the language to be constrained by linguistic rules for sign structure and syntax.

Before continuing with this discussion of the word order controversy, some further elaboration of the role of the point in space and its effect on the linguist's description of ASL is needed. Only Liddell's (1977) discussion of ASL word order does not depend on an analysis of the role of the point, as his description relies primarily on nonmanual indicators of grammatical function. As for the others, the point in space makes an enormous difference in their perspective on word order.

In Lacy's (1974) presentation of pronominal reference in ASL, he considered the point in space to be an "index" in the sense of McCawley (1970). McCawley suggested that for semantic representations, a clause is appropriately separated into a "proposition" and a set of noun phrases. Each noun phrase is associated with an "index" which indicates its position (role) in the proposition. An example from McCawley of the sentence "the man killed the woman" is:

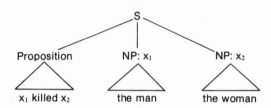

Lacy adopted this semantic representation for syntactic purposes in describing ASL by noting the parallel structure in ASL that associates each noun with a unique index. For Lacy, the pronoun itself was the pointing gesture to the point in space, and the pronoun could not be interpreted without its "index." He noted that personal pronoun "indexes" were placed in space according to several general rules. Neutral body position for the first verb of a discourse utterance is considered to be first person, as Friedman indicates previously. The center of the front of the signer is reserved for second person referent ("you"), and third person referents may be placed in space as we did earlier (all three points in a line) or alternating first third person referent on the right of the signer, 2nd third person referent on the left, etc.

Lacy (1973) reported that the point in space that locates each pronoun referent is sufficiently well-defined in three-dimensional space that once the signer establishes the location, other members of the conversation will direct their pointing so that a line extending from the end of the index finger (G hand) will (more or less) pass through the point location of the intended referent. This information adds to the claim that these pointing gestures are linguistically conventionalized in a way that pointing as used by nonsigners is not.

Friedman's (1975, 1976a) concept of the point in space is that it is the actual pronoun. Thus, pointing is simply a means of indicating which pronoun is meant, and starting a verb at a particular point may be viewed as a pronoun followed by a verb. This perspective contributes to her view that there are no inflections on the verb.

Kegl's (1976a, 1976b, 1977) concept of the point in space is an agreement point that, together with a deictic marker (not only the G hand, but also Å, Ψ, and B) may serve as an index for a noun phrase or pronoun, and which at the same time serves to mark the verb in the form of an inflection. Thus a verb made at some point, say point 1, is inflected in the sense that it has been moved to point 1 to agree with its subject. If a pronoun is present, it may be the body pronoun realized at point 1 to make the verb (e.g., body anchor verbs), or it may be a classifier (to be elaborated) handshape which will be made as part of the verb, or may be indicated by a preceding or following index made with a deictic marker; finally, it may be left null through a process of topic chaining (Kegl, 1976a).

These different linguistic descriptions of the role of the point in space obviously lead to different conceptions of how verbs behave in ASL, and subsequently how word order is to be viewed.

Kegl has identified a number of difficulties with Fischer's and Friedman's approaches. She notes, as did Friedman, the risk involved in presenting sentences to signers for interpretations or judgment as opposed to more naturalistic data, but at the same time, following Fischer's methodology, she presented similar sentences to signers, separating verbs according to whether or not they are inflected and used those which could be inflected.

When signers were presented with sentences in which the signs were in NVN order but the verb was not inflected, they interpreted the sentences as SVO. However, when asked when such a sentence would be used, they typically responded that an ASL signer would not sign the sentences that way, but that the sentences were understandable. They also suggested that hearing people might sign the sentences that way. One informant rejected all sentences which were presented without inflection on the verb.

When signers were presented with sentences in which the words were in the same order and the verb was inflected, the sentences were accepted as natural and were indicated as being preferred. If the verb was inflected and the words were in a non-SVO order, most signers accepted the sentences, but some indicated that they were stylistically awkward and that SVO order would be preferred.

The signers in Fischer's and Kegl's investigations were able to give consistent interpretations to sentences with uninflected verbs even though they are unacceptable in ASL. Kegl (1976b) attributes this to the bilingual nature of most signers. Although they may not be fluent readers and writers of English, they are nonetheless familiar with English in written and spoken form and in its signed equivalent, signed English. English has very little or no inflection on the verb (for person), no incorporation, no indexing (although there are pronouns and determiners which perform similar functions), and a fairly rigid fixed word order. Therefore, in cases where signers are presented with sentences which lack indexing and verb inflection, they may rely on English related strategies (namely word order) to determine grammatical relations. This bilingual phenomenon should be kept in mind.

Kegl's concept of the function of the point in space as part of an inflectional system in ASL also leads to an interpretation of the data different from

Friedman's. Friedman appears to be advocating avoidance strategies rather than syntactic structure for ASL (as exemplified by Edge & Herrmann, 1977). And although Friedman was concerned with separating verbs into their classes, she did so according to the number of arguments they could have and whether those arguments were semantically reversible. Kegl has separated verbs according to their inflection, and subsequently postulated the following solution to the word order controversy:

> Flexibility Condition: The more inflected
> the verb is, the freer the word order.

In ASL, order is free at the level of major constituents, that is, the ordering of noun phrases with respect to each other and to the verb, and ordering within the noun phrase may be somewhat free, but the NP itself cannot be broken up. The flexibility condition is consistent with the data reported by Fischer and Friedman, and accounts for the differing analyses presented by them. (Kegl also provides a formalization of the ASL phrase structures for NP and the verb complex, but the details are beyond the scope of this review.).

Liddell (1977) provides empirical verification of the "intonation breaks" reported by Fischer for orders other than SVO with uninflected verbs. Measurements of sign duration confirm that longer durations of signs contribute to the intonation breaks. His measurements indicate that a noun sign in initial position but not a topic (i.e., SVO) is roughly 11 fields (.18 sec) longer than the average duration of a noun sign in medial position (the shortest position). Signs in final position were approximately 17 fields (.28 sec) longer than medial position, whereas noun signs that were topics (i.e., S, VO or O, SV) were held about 22 fields (.37 sec) longer than medial position. Thus, his data indicate that part of the "intonation break" that Fischer referred to is a result of longer duration of the topicalized sign. Liddell also identifies a particular facial expression and head position that he calls *t,* which marks topics. The designation *t* refers to a combination of the head tilted backwards slightly and the eyebrows raised. It co-occurs with the topicalized sign, then disappears for the remainder of the sentence. Thus, the change of facial expression and head position after the topic, combined with the duration of the topicalized sign itself, provide the cues Fischer identified as intonation breaks.

Since Stokoe (1960), observers have noticed the important role of facial expression in the grammar of ASL. The use of the head nod for sentence negation and special expressions for yes/no and wh-questions were among the first identified. More recently, Baker (1976) and Baker and Padden (1978) have concentrated on lexical facial expression and on the role of eyeblinks in conditional sentences and questions. Liddell (1977), in addition to identifying the facial expression *t* that marks topicalization, also identified numerous other facial expressions which serve as an integral part of ASL syntax. These include adverbial facial expressions modifying the verb. For example, the facial expression Liddell calls "cs" (for "close shoulder") appears to have a meaning related to proximity of time or physical distance (e.g., "just yesterday," "brand new," "right in front," etc.). Other facial expressions (this includes head positions) have larger domains than the adverbials. The question and negation expressions may cover entire sentences, but may not also include topicalized (*t*) or asserted (*hn* for "head nod") elements. The establishment of domains for particular facial expressions allows Liddell to provide linguistic arguments for certain constituent structures. He is then able to argue for embedded clauses, in particular restrictive relative clauses. Relative clauses, as described by Liddell, may occur in initial, medial, or final position in ASL, and are accompanied by the facial expression *r* ("relative"), which includes raised eyebrows, backward tilt of the head, and raising of the cheek and upper lip muscles. Furthermore, ASL relative clauses appear to have internal heads; a sign that serves as the head of a relative clause is produced with increased duration (compared to the same sign when not the head of the relative clause).

Liddell also made some measurements similar to those he used to support Fischer's claim on an intonation break in non-SVO ordered sentences. In this case, he used the sign CAT in a variety of positions in a relative clause. He reports that in medial position, the shortest duration, CAT lasted about 14 fields (.23 sec), in final position, 24 fields (.4 sec), and in initial position, 20 fields (.33 sec). When CAT occurred in initial position in the relative clause, it was always as the object of an OSV sequence. Looking at DOG when it occurred in relative clauses as the subject, he found that in initial position and functioning as the head of the relative clause, DOG lasted 27 fields (.43 sec) but if not functioning as the head it lasted only 17 fields (.28 sec). In medial position, if DOG was the head, its duration was 22 fields (.37 sec) whereas if it was not the head, it lasted only 14 fields (.23 sec). Thus, the function of head of a relative clause contributes to an increase in sign duration, as does final position (as reported by Grosjean & Lane, 1977) and initial position (illustrated here by Liddell's findings).

Another aspect of sign language syntax is the pronominal reference system. Early descriptions of ASL reported that it had no pronouns, by which was meant that no overt separate sign was observed for the English equivalents of "he," "she," and "it" when they served as subject or object of a sentence. We have seen that these grammatical relations are indicated by spatial inflection on the verb (although the details of establishing NPs and agreement markers have been omitted). Friedman (1976a, 1976b) considered the point in space (where a verb is started or ended) to be a pronoun. Lacy (1974) considered only the pointing gesture to the point in space to be the pronoun. Edge and Herrmann (1977) considered both the pointing gesture and the point in space together to constitute a pronoun. Kegl (1976a; Kegl, Lentz, & Philip, 1976) considers the point in space to be an index for the noun and agreement marker for the verb. She identifies instead the process of pronominalization as the process of relating a particular characteristic (point in space, facial expression, rhythm of signing in story-telling, right or left hand when only two are needed, finger on nondominant hand) with a particular referent (Kegl, 1978a). Any use of that specific characteristic constitutes a reference to its unique referent. There are then several types of pronouns, among which are body pronouns, classifiers, and hand-indexing. Body pronouns, for example, include the use of the signer's body for marking first person singular, or when shifted to another agreement point, some other referent which is then considered to be the subject of the sentence. Body pronouns also include the use of real bodies in the environment (e.g., the use of a person present by pointing to him rather than establishing a different characteristic for him) and projected bodies, which function in space as third person reference. Another form of pronoun is the set of classifiers (Frishberg, 1975) that categorize objects by varying properties. Kegl and Wilbur (1976) reported that classifier substitution could occur for phonological purposes, such as avoiding the production of signs outside of the signing space or when blending of the noun into the verb (NP Incorporation) was phonologically impossible. Classifiers function syntactically as pronouns in place of nouns. Frishberg (1975) described them as "certain handshapes in particular orientations to stand for certain semantic features of noun arguments [p. 715]." Kegl (1976a) includes a tentative list of classifiers and their category definitions:

1. General person: the G handshape, usual orientation is fingertip up.
2. Ambulatory person: the V handshape, fingertips down.
3. Vehicle: the 3 handshape, orientation fingertips sideways (as opposed to the number 3, which has fingertips up), may be used for cars, motorcycles, boats, trains, etc.
4. Plane: the "plane" handshape, may be used for airplane.
5. Stationary object taller than wide: the "ten" handshape, used for objects such as bottle, lamp.
6. Flat objects that can be moved: B handshape, palm up, can be used for book, paper, mirror.
7. Stationary object taller than wide that cannot be moved: arm extended upwards from elbow to fingertips, B handshape, used for buildings, trees, flagpoles.
8. Flat object that cannot be moved: B handshape, palm down, can be used for floor, rooftop, ground.

9. Hollow curved object with rim: C handshape, can be used for glass, cup, jar, etc.

The exact specifications of these classifiers, and several others, are currently under investigation (Wilbur, Bernstein, & Kantor, 1978). As an example of how classifiers work, consider this example from an ASL version of "The Three Little Pigs." The signer describes the wolf climbing up the chimney of the third pig's house, falling down into a waiting pot of boiling water, in which he screams and squirms, and then escaping through the front door. In this description, the C handshape is used for the rim of the chimney as the wolf falls through it, and also for the rim of the pot of boiling water as the wolf first falls into it and then squirms around in it, and finally as the door frame through which the wolf escapes. The C handshape is *not* the sign for chimney, or pot, or door frame, but it substitutes for them in certain circumstances. In an acquisition study, Kantor (1977) demonstrated that classifiers were mastered much later than might otherwise be expected of one-handed signs. She found that children tended to make handshape substitutions—for example, substituting the motorically easier 5 handshape for the 3 classifier (vehicle) handshape or for the V classifier handshape, even though those same children could produce the 3 or V handshapes in nonclassifier signs like the number 3 or the sign SEE (made with V). Children as old as 7 were still displaying incomplete mastery of the classifier system, particularly in terms of knowing all of the objects for which a particular classifier could substitute. For example, they were able to use the 3 classifier for cars and motorcycles by age 4, expanded this to include trains by age 6, and finally added trucks and parked cars by age 7. This type of research supports the theoretical complexity claimed for the adult usage of classifiers, while at the same time demonstrating the developmental progression of ASL acquisition.

In their study of ASL conditionals, Baker and Padden (1978) reported that in conditional statements at least four changes could be observed between the first clause and the second clause: eyeblinks, release of nasolabial contraction, brow lowering, and initiation of head nodding. In conditional questions, at least two changes occurred. They report that in both conditional statements ("If it rains tomorrow, I will go to the library") and conditional questions ("If it rains tomorrow, will you go to the library?"), the "if" clause was marked with raising of the eyebrows. In the statements, but not the questions, the "if" clause was followed by an eyeblink. In the conditional statements, the second part would have the brows returned to their normal position, unless the statement was also negative, and changes in gaze direction and head orientation would occur as appropriate. In the conditional questions, the question part continued to have raised eyebrows, gaze at the addressee, and the head forward or cocked to one side. Finally, whereas ASL may have a lexical marker IF (Baker & Padden noted the fingerspelled i–f) in the first part, it does not have the equivalent of "then" as a sign in the second part.

As indicated, the yes/no question marker includes raised brow and wide eyes. For Wh-questions, the eyes are narrowed and the eyebrows are squished. ASL WH-questions have WH-words to signal them, but these words (WHO, WHEN, WHERE, WHAT, etc.) may occur in other than initial position (English Wh-words are restricted to initial position). Fant (1972) and Kegl (1977) observed that "bracing" may occur with Wh-question words, for example WHO PRO + GIVE + PRO$_{2p}$ BOOK WHO "Who gave you a/the book?" (literally, who gave you a/the book, who?"). Kegl considers this to be part of a more general bracing process in which a single word, entire phrase, or whole sentence can appear on both sides of sentence (initially and finally). Kegl also suggests that bracing may serve as a test for constituency, in that whatever may brace a sentence must be a constituent (this is parallel to Liddell's use of the scope of the nonmanual markers to determine if some element is part of a phrase or not).

Fischer (1974) reports several rules that appear to operate in ASL. She notes that Ross's (1967) Coordinate Structure Constraint is operative for ASL. She also notes that FOR is used to introduce purposive clauses (e.g., "for the purpose of") and that "unless" clauses are introduced by WITHOUT. She notes that auxiliaries in ASL include FINISH (perfective), BETTER (polite imperative), CAN, CAN'T, WILL, MUST, FROM–NOW–ON (future continuous marker), HAVE–BEEN (past continuous marker), NOT–YET (negative of FINISH), HAPPEN, SUCCEED, and possibly SEEM. These auxiliaries have the possibility of occurring at the beginning and/or end of a sentence without a change in meaning from its position in the middle of a sentence. In an embedded sentence Fischer (1974) states "the auxiliary can occur initially or preverbally, but not at the end [p. 17]." She postulates rules for Auxiliary Hopping (to move the auxiliary around), NP Fronting (for topicalization), Sentence Topicalization, and VP Topicalization. From the formalization of these last few rules, she concludes that Ross's (1967) Complex NP Constraint is also operative in ASL.

We have seen in this chapter that a variety of rules exist in ASL. None of these rules so far appears to be unique to ASL (except of course in how the output structure is constituted after application of morphological and phonological rules). We have seen how critical a linguist's perspective on the function of various aspects, such as the point in space, may be in affecting the linguistic description that is given and the conclusions that are drawn. The necessity of realizing constrained variability on word order, such as the Flexibility Condition, emphasizes the need for further grammatical description, and the subsequent utilization of this description in the teaching of sign language.

REFERENCES

Baker, C. What's not on the other hand in American Sign Language. In S. Mufwene, C. Walker, & S. Steever, (Eds.). *Papers from the Twelfth Regional Meeting, Chicago Linguistic Society*. Chicago: The University of Chicago Press, 1976.

Baker, C., & Padden, C. Focusing on the nonmanual components of American Sign Language. In P. Siple (Ed.), *Understanding language through sign language research*. New York: Academic Press, 1978.

Battison, R. *Phonology in American Sign Language: 3-D and digit-vision*. Paper presented at the California Linguistic Association Conference, Stanford, Calif., 1973.

Battison, R. Phonological deletion in American Sign Language. *Sign Language Studies*, 1974, *5*, 1–19.

Battison, R. *Lexical borrowing in American Sign Language*. Silver Spring, Md.: Linstok Press, 1978.

Battison, R., Markowicz, H., & Woodward, J. A good rule of thumb: Variable phonology in American Sign Language. In R. Shuy & R. Fasold (Eds.), *New ways of analyzing variation in English II*. Washington, D.C.: Georgetown University Press, 1975.

Bellugi, U. *The process of compounding in American Sign Language*. Unpublished manuscript, Salk Institute for Biological Studies, 1975.

Boyes, P. *Developmental phonology for ASL*. Working paper, Salk Institute for Biological Studies, 1973.

Chinchor, N. *The structure of the NP in ASL: Argument from research on numerals*. Unpublished manuscript, Brown University, 1978.

Cogen, C. On three aspects of time expression in American Sign Language. In L. Friedman (Ed.), *On the other hand*. New York: Academic Press, 1977.

Edge, V., & Herrmann, L. Verbs and the determination of subject in American Sign Language. In L. Friedman (Ed.), *On the other hand*. New York: 1977.

Fant, L. The American Sign Language. *California News*, 1972, *83*, 5.

Fischer, S. Two processes of reduplication in American Sign Language. *Foundations of Language*, 1973, *9*, 469–480.

Fischer, S. Sign language and linguistic universals. In *Proceedings of the Franco-German Conference on French Transformational Grammar*. Berlin: Athaenium, 1974.

Fischer, S. Influences on word order change in ASL. In C. Li (Ed.), *Word order and word order change*. Austin: University of Texas Press, 1975.

Fischer, S., & Gough, B. *Some unfinished thoughts on FINISH*. Working paper, Salk Institute for Biological Studies, 1972.

Fischer, S. & Gough, B. Verbs in American Sign Language. *Sign Language Studies*, 1978, *18*, 17–48.

Friedman, L. *On the physical manifestation of stress in the American Sign Language*. Unpublished manuscript, University of California, Berkeley, 1974.

Friedman, L. Space, time, and person reference in American Sign Language. *Language*, 1975, *51*, 940–961.

Friedman, L. The manifestation of subject, object, and topic in American Sign Language. In C. Li (Ed.), *Subject and topic*. New York: Academic Press, 1976. (a)

Friedman, L. *Phonology of a soundless language: Phonological structure of American Sign Language*. Unpublished doctoral dissertation. University of California, Berkeley, 1976. (b)

Friedman, L. (Ed.). *On the other hand: New perspectives on American Sign Language*. New York: Academic Press, 1977.

Frishberg, N. Arbitrariness and iconicity: Historical change in American Sign Language. *Language*, 1975, *51*, 676–710.

Frishberg, N. *Some aspects of the historical development of signs in American Sign Language*. Unpublished doctoral dissertation, University of California, San Diego, 1976.

Frishberg, N. The case of the missing length. In R. Wilbur (Ed.), Sign language research. *Communication and Cognition,* 1978, *11,* 57–67.

Frishberg, N., & Gough, B. *Morphology in American Sign Language.* Working paper, Salk Institute for Biological Studies, 1973. (a)

Frishberg, N., & Gough, B. *Time on our hands.* Paper presented at the Third Annual California Linguistics Conference, Stanford, Calif., 1973. (b)

Grosjean, F., & Lane, H. Pauses and syntax in American Sign Language. *Cognition,* 1977, *5,* 101–117.

Hoffmeister, R. *The acquisition of American Sign Language by deaf children of deaf parents: The development of the demonstrative pronouns, locatives, and personal pronouns.* Unpublished doctoral dissertation, University of Minnesota, 1978. (a)

Hoffmeister, R. *An analysis of possessive constructions in the ASL of a young deaf child of deaf parents.* Unpublished manuscript, Temple University, 1978. (b)

Jones, N., & Mohr, K. *A working paper on plurals in ASL.* Unpublished manuscript, University of California, Berkeley, 1975.

Jones, P. On the interface of sign phonology and morphology. In R. Wilbur (Ed.), Sign language research. *Communcation and Cognition,* 1978, *11,* 69–78.

Kantor, R. *The acquisition of classifiers in American Sign Language.* Unpublished master's thesis, Boston University, 1977.

Kegl, J. *Pronominalization in American Sign Language.* Unpublished manuscript, MIT, Cambridge, 1976. (a)

Kegl, J. *Relational grammar and American Sign Language.* Unpublished manuscript, MIT, Cambridge, 1976. (b)

Kegl, J. *ASL syntax: Research in progress and proposed research.* Unpublished manuscript, MIT, Cambridge, 1977.

Kegl, J. *ASL classifiers.* Unpublished manuscript, MIT, Cambridge, 1978. (a)

Kegl, J. *Indexing and pronominalization in ASL.* Unpublished manuscript, MIT, Cambridge, 1978. (b)

Kegl, J. *A possible argument for passive in ASL.* Unpublished manuscript, MIT, Cambridge, 1978. (c)

Kegl, J., & Chinchor, N. A frame analysis of American Sign Language. In T. Diller (Ed.), *Proceedings of the 13th Annual Meeting, Association for Computational Linguistics. American Journal of Computational Linguistics,* Microfiche 35. St. Paul, Sperry-Univac, 1975.

Kegl, J., Lentz, E., & Philip, M. *ASL pronouns and conditions on their use.* Paper presented at the Linguistic Society of American Summer Meeting, Oswego, N.Y., 1976.

Kegl, J., & Wilbur, R. When does structure stop and style begin? Syntax, morphology, and phonology vs. stylistic variation in American Sign Language. In S. Mufwene, C. Walker, & S. Steever (Eds.), *Papers from the Twelfth Regional Meeting, Chicago Linguistic Society.* Chicago: The University of Chicago Press, 1976.

Klima, E., & Bellugi, U. Wit and Poetry in American Sign Language. *Sign Language Studies,* 1975, *8,* 203–224.

Klima, E., & Bellugi, U. *The signs of language.* Cambridge: Harvard University Press, 1979.

Lacy, R. *Directional verb marking in the American Sign Language.* Paper presented at the Summer Linguistic Institute, Linguistic Society of America, University of California, Santa Cruz, 1973.

Lacy, R. *Putting some of the syntax back into semantics.* Paper presented at the Linguistic Society of America Annual Meeting, New York, 1974.

Lane, H., Boyes-Braem, P., & Bellugi, U. Preliminaries to a distinctive feature analysis of handshapes in American Sign Language. *Cognitive Psychology,* 1976, *8,* 263–289.

Liddell, S. *An investigation into the syntactic structure of American Sign Language.* Unpublished doctoral dissertation, University of California, San Diego, 1977.

Long, J. *The Sign Language: A manual of signs.* Iowa City: Athens Press, 1918.

McCawley, J. Where do noun phrases come from? In R. Jacobs & P. Rosenbaum (Eds.), *Readings in English transformational grammar.* Boston: Ginn, 1970.

Ross, J. *Constraints on variables in syntax.* Unpublished doctoral dissertation, MIT, Cambridge, 1967.

Siple, P. Constraints for sign language from visual perception data. *Sign Language Studies,* 1978, *19,* 97–112.

Stokoe, W. Sign language structure: An outline of the visual communication system of the American deaf. *Studies in Linguistics,* Occasional Papers No. 8, 1960.

Stokoe, W., Casterline, D., & Croneberg, C. *Dictionary of American Sign Language.* Washington, D.C.: Gallaudet College, 1965. (Revised Ed., Silver Spring: Linstok Press, 1976.)

Supalla, T., & Newport, E. How many seats in a chair? The derivation of nouns and verbs in American Sign Language. In P. Siple (Ed.), *Understanding language through sign language research.* New York: Academic Press, 1978.

Tervoort, B. Esoteric symbols in the communicative behavior of young deaf children. *American Annals of the Deaf,* 1961, *106,* 436–480.

Tjapkes, S. *Distinctive feature analysis of American Sign Language: A theoretical model.* Unpublished master's thesis, University of South Florida, Tampa, 1976.

Wilbur, R. Sign language research. *Communication and Cognition,* 1978, *11.*

Wilbur, R. *American Sign Language and sign systems: Research and applications.* Baltimore: University Park Press, 1979.

Wilbur, R., Bernstein, M., & Kantor, R. *The semantic domain of classifiers in ASL.* Paper presented at the MIT Sign Language Symposium and at the summer meeting, Linguistic Society of America, Urbana, Ill., 1978.

Woodward, J. *Implicational lects on the deaf diglossic continuum.* Unpublished doctoral dissertation, Georgetown University, Washington, D.C., 1973. (a)

Woodward, J. Interrule implication in American Sign Language. *Sign Language Studies,* 1973, *3,* 47–56. (b)

Woodward, J. Some observations on sociolinguistic variation and American Sign Language. *Kansas Journal of Sociology.* 1973, *9,* 191–200. (c)

Woodward, J. Implicational variation in American Sign Language: Negative incorporation. *Sign Language Studies,* 1974, *5,* 20–30.

Woodward, J., & DeSantis, S. Negative incorporation in French and American Sign Language. *Language and Society,* 1977, *6,* pp. 379–388.

3 Psycholinguistics of Sign Language[1]

François Grosjean
Northeastern University

In this chapter we review a number of studies pertaining to the psycholinguistics of sign language. We begin by summarizing those studies whose goal was to determine if sign language is as effective as spoken language for communication. Having responded in the affirmative to this question, we present an account of the studies that have demonstrated the psychological reality of certain aspects of the structural organization of sign language as it is described by linguistics. Next we study the production of sign language—what it has in common with spoken language and in what ways it is different—as well as the perception of sign: psychophysics of rate, iconic memory, and on–line processing of signs presented individually and in sentential context. We end the chapter with a résumé of studies bearing on the role of memory in sign language communication.

Because our space is limited and because of a lack of systematic research, this chapter will not treat the following aspects of psycholinguistics of sign language: communication between signers of different sign languages, the role of the figurative aspect of sign language and its perception and memorization, perception and production of contrived signing systems (such as Sign English), spoken—sign language bilingualism, and the acquisition of sign language as a native language. The latter topic is reviewed by Hoffmeister and Wilbur elsewhere in this book. Two further preliminaries: Although most of the studies that we cite are concerned with American Sign Language (ASL), we believe that the processes of production, perception, and memorization that will be examined are for the most part descriptive of other sign languages

---

[1]Translated from French by Harlan Lane.

as well. Moreover, these processes should be compared to those for oral language and consequently we will attempt to clarify as far as possible the relations between the activities of the signer/observer and those of the speaker/listener. Psycholinguistics is addressed, after all, to the perception, understanding, and production of all languages, whether spoken or sign. No model of linguistic performance can be complete unless it describes those aspects of encoding and decoding that are specific to the modality of communication, oral or visual, and those that are common to all languages whatever their modality of perception and production.

THE LANGUAGE OF SIGNS AS AN INSTRUMENT OF COMMUNICATION

Several studies have been concerned with the question of whether sign language is as effective as oral language in everyday communication. The results of these studies have exerted considerable influence on a number of linguists and psycholinguists, some having concluded from these that sign language is not a symbolic system of communication at the same level as oral language. The general scheme of these studies is as follows: a sender transmits to a receiver various items of information concerning a scene (evoking, for example, the relations subject–verb–direct object–indirect object), or concerning an object (car, flower, fish, geometric figure, etc.) or the face of a person. The task of the receiver is to use this information to select the item that has been described from among an array of similar items. The correct or erroneous choice by the receiver thus becomes an index of the effectiveness of communication.

In a study of this type, Schlesinger (1970) wanted to study how certain grammatical relations are expressed in Israeli Sign Language (ISL); namely, subject, verb, direct object and indirect object. In one of the stimulus arrays, there was a man, a bear, and a monkey. The six drawings in this array represented the six possible permutations in the format "X gives Y to Z" (the man gives the monkey to the bear: the monkey gives the bear to the man, etc.). The experiment using this particular array is the one that Schlesinger describes in detail and hence we consider it at some length here. Thirty deaf subjects, divided into 15 sender-receiver couples, participated in the study. Schlesinger undertook a detailed examination of the structures used by the subjects in their communication. He noted that many different syntactic structures were used, that the verb was never placed at the start of the sentence, and that the adjective was always placed after the noun that it modified. Furthermore, among the 20 subjects who produced "complete sentences" (sentences, according to Schlesinger, that included a subject, a verb, a direct object and an indirect object) the signs arranged themselves as follows: subject (S), direct object (DO), indirect object (IO), but also as follows: IO, DO, S, and also S, IO, DO. Schlesinger concludes that Israeli Sign Language apparently has no systematic rules allowing a distinction between the functions of subject, direct object, and indirect object.

This conclusion was the object of a critical analysis appearing in a report of the New England Sign Language Society (1976). We note here simply that the syntactic analysis by Schlesinger is highly disputable: He eliminated utterances containing several sentences, he was uninformed about certain visual indices that would assist in identifying sentences (body movement, facial expressions, rhythm of production, use of the space by the signer, among others) and his analysis was based to a large extent on the erroneous premise that grammatical relations in Israeli Sign Language are expressed exclusively in a linear fashion and cannot be realized in parallel.

As concerns the effectiveness of communication, Schlesinger reports a 74% successful communication for couples that used "complete sentences"; 54% when only one member of the pair used such sentences; and 44% for the pairs who never produced such sentences. These percentages are well below those that we might expect from a similar experiment in oral language (however it should be noted that Schlesinger did not run a control group made up of hearing subjects, which would have aided in determining whether the results obtained from the deaf subjects were due to the inherent difficulty of the task or to the absence of good communication between senders and receivers).

A very similar experiment is reported by Hoemann (1972). His goals were to gain a better understanding of the development of communication among deaf children who acquire ASL and to compare their linguistic ability with that of hearing children of the same age. Two groups of hearing subjects, averaging 8 and 11 years of age, and two groups of deaf subjects with the same average age participated in the experiment in sender–receiver pairs. Here three different tasks were employed: description of pictures, description of symbols presented from various perspectives, and explanation of the rules of a game. The results obtained were quite similar to those reported by Schlesinger; we will restrict ourselves here to those from the first task. For the group of 8-year-olds, the percent effective communication, that is, the percent of correct selections by the receiver, was 36 for the deaf, 53 for the hearing; for the 11-year-olds the corresponding percentages were 59 and 84. Hoemann concludes that deafness constitutes a handicap in peer-to-peer communicating even with manual methods. To explain these results he proposes a general experiential deficit, which affected both the acquisition of a conventional linguistic system by the deaf children and their development of formal communication skills.

Several years later, Oléron (1978) undertook a similar study with users of French Sign language (FSL). He used the same general format as Schlesinger and Hoemann, but employed six different experimental settings. The first involved six groups of five pictures representing living things. Each group contained the picture to be described, a scene representing the relations subject–verb–direct object, and four pictures evoking the same relations but with variations concerning one or the other of the three syntactic terms. The second setting, constructed along the same lines as the first, presented relations of the type subject–verb–direct object–indirect object. Pictures presenting different views of an object and of its relative position, of geometric forms, of fishes, of flowers and a "maquette" including various objects broken into diverse groups along its surface, constituted the stimuli in the other situations.

Oléron used two groups of subjects, one deaf and the other hearing. There were 10 boys and 10 girls in each group with practically identical ranges in age (15 years, four months to 19 years, eleven months for the deaf and 15 years, 0 months to 17 years, eight months for the hearing). Ten pairs of subjects of the same sex were constituted in each of the samples. The experimental procedure was practically identical to that of Schlesinger and Hoemann: Communication was conducted in one direction only and the experimenter provided no information at the time of picture selection. Furthermore, the messages from the sender were videotaped (which Schlesinger had failed to do).

The results obtained by Oléron are very similar to those reported by the first two authors. The rate of effectiveness of communication of the deaf was well below that of the hearing: 71.7% for the deaf receivers and 91.7% for hearing receivers as regards correct choices in the first situation; in the second setting, the scores were 58% and 82%, a difference that was reproduced approximately in the other settings. We do not discuss here the very detailed study of syntax and lexis that Oléron undertook on the utterances that were produced by the deaf subjects. Let us note however that this author, like Schlesinger, had difficulties in demarcating sentences and that his transcription of the utterances did not sufficiently take into account the information provided by sign inflection and by nonmanual channels of sign communication. We know, for example, that movements of the eyes, the head, and the body are often used to demarcate simple sentences and clauses in complex sentences such as relatives, subordinates, conditionals, etc. (see Baker, 1976, 1977; Baker & Padden, 1978). Oléron does not report using these cues in his syntactic analysis of the sign utterances. The conclusions put forth by Oléron concerning the effectiveness of the deaf in communication are rather revealing. He writes that the transmission of information is certainly less effective in the gestural language of the deaf than in spoken language. He hastens to add however that the finding depends nonetheless on the conditions in which research was accomplished. Oléron then invokes several factors that may partially explain the results he obtained: the level of language mastery of the subjects, the conditions under which they learned and used sign language, possible areas of lack of correspondence between the experimental conditions for the deaf and those for the hearing, the possible difficulty for the deaf sender to put himself in the place of the receiver, etc. He adds, however, that it is nonetheless difficult to account for the results solely by pointing to these factors and proposes that the detailed examination of gestural productions brings to light various characteristics which in all likelihood bear the major responsibility for these difficulties in communication.

On the basis of these three studies we might conclude that manual language does not allow as effective communication as oral language. Indeed, three different sign languages were used (Israeli, American, and French) in three different experiments and roughly the same result was obtained in each: a level of communication among the deaf of 74% or below and much higher scores for the hearing communicators.

Such a conclusion would be quite wrong, however. In what follows we report two experiments in which deaf and hearing subjects give very similar results and we undertake to show that Schlesinger, Hoemann, and Oléron did not sufficiently control the sign language proficiency of their subjects nor the particular system of manual communication that they used (all three investigators report this problem in their studies but none gives it the importance that it merits). Bode (1974) replicated as best she could the conditions of Schlesinger's experiment. She added a group of hearing subjects and very carefully controlled for the level of mastery of sign language of her deaf subjects (13 of her 16 subjects had learned ASL before the age of six). The percentage of descriptions correctly interpreted by the receivers was 95 for the hearing group and 86 for the deaf group, a difference of 9% that was not statistically significant. Bode concludes that ASL indeed contains mechanisms for communicating information concerning agent–object–indirect object relationships, which are comparable in effectiveness to those in oral language. She also casts doubt on the results obtained by Schlesinger concerning the effectiveness of communication in Israeli Sign Language and the purported absence of a system that allows the expression of the grammatical mechanisms cited earlier. According to Bode, a hearing control group, such as that used by Oléron, and a homogeneous set of deaf subjects chosen with respect to their dialect and their level of mastery of manual language should have been included in the design of Schlesinger's experiment.

Jordan (1975) asked a group of hearing subjects and a group of deaf subjects who used ASL to describe pictures of faces. The receiver was to select the picture described among 23 others. The results showed that the users of ASL communicated as well as the hearing subjects (4.83 errors in 24 presentations for the deaf, 3.96 for the hearing, a nonsignificant difference). Moreover, Jordan revealed that the deaf used fewer cues than the hearing to describe the pictures and that their productions were shorter than those of the hearing subjects; however the two groups used the same visual cues in their descriptions.

It seems, then, that when the homogeneity of dialect used by the subjects is controlled and when their perfect mastery of the dialect is assured, communication in sign language is as effective as that in oral language. Schlesinger himself was partly aware of this and Oléron commented that his 20 deaf subjects knew and used the gestural language of the deaf but that the experimenter did not test their proficiency in this respect. It would be interesting to know what type of manual communication was in fact used by the subjects in the experiments of Schlesinger, Hoemann, and Oléron and how proficient they were in that system. Certain subjects probably had a good knowledge of the oral language of their country and may well have utilized some form of sign language that was influenced by the oral language; others, perhaps less competent in oral language, may have used a form of the national sign language that was more authentic. (This situation is more complex in Israel where the population has a variety of linguistic backgrounds.) It is thus possible to advance the hypothesis that some of the sender–receiver pairs did not use exactly the same sign language or dialect, which would of course hinder effective communication. For example, many ASL signers can understand users of Sign English, but the inverse is seldom true. Not only were some of the pairs of subjects used by Schlesinger, Hoemann, and Oléron probably mismatched in this regard, but also the experimenters did not confirm that their subjects were truly fluent in the relevant manual languages. It seems probable that a certain number of subjects were not fluent signers, especially if they had learned to sign relatively late (deaf children of hearing parents often begin the acquisition of sign language when they attend a specialized school for the deaf and encounter children of deaf parents). Three additional questions ought to be asked: What dialect of sign language is learned in these schools? How long does it take to achieve mastery of a sign language? Do the deaf children of hearing parents ever succeed in achieving the same level of mastery as that attained by the deaf children of deaf parents, who learn the language quite early and in a familial environment? These questions were probably not asked by the experimenters when they selected their subjects. Moreover, and what is perhaps more serious, the results were used to form conclusions on the effectiveness of sign language in general whereas they merely reflected the varying competence in sign language of the samples of subjects employed. As Bode (1974) and Jordan (1975) have shown, when subjects are chosen for their knowledge of sign language and with proper consideration of the dialect they are using, then communication in sign language is as effective as in oral language.

LINGUISTIC DESCRIPTION AND
PSYCHOLOGICAL REALITY OF SIGN LANGUAGE

Although the linguistic analysis of sign language is still in its early stages, as is clear from Chapter 2 by Wilbur, some experimental studies have begun nonetheless to describe the psychological reality of certain aspects of the structural organization of sign language as it is characterized by linguists.

How do these studies differ from those undertaken with oral languages in the 1960s? The first difference concerns the mere number. They are not numerous, as the research in sign language is recent and many psycholinguists are more aware now of the problems associated with this type of research. But a second difference concerns the linguistic models themselves. These are often incomplete or even nonexistent when it comes to sign language. The traditional order of investigation—model first and psychological reality of the model second—has thus sometimes been inverted. Beginning with experimental findings, various investigators have proposed structural descriptions of some aspects of sign language; see, for example, the study of Lane, Boyes-Braem, and Bellugi (1976) concerning distinctive features for handshape, and the study by Grosjean and Lane (1977) on the surface structure of ASL sentences. In what follows we summarize briefly the main results obtained in this domain and then proceed to other aspects of psycholinguistics of sign language such as perception, production, and memory.

Stokoe (1960, 1966) proposes that a sign is made up of three parameters: handshape, location, and movement. To these Battison (1974) adds a fourth: the orientation of the hand(s). Thus, one question that has had a lively interest for investigators is the following: Are signs in fact decomposed into these parameters by signers and sign observers, or are they solely a product of linguistic analysis and thus without any psychological reality? As it turned out, the reality of these parameters was shown by several studies. In an experiment on the short-term memory for lists of signs (described in greater detail in the last section of this chapter), Bellugi, Klima, and Siple (1975) showed that errors of recall were not related to the meaning of the original sign but rather to the values of its formational parameters. The signs erroneously recalled differed from the stimulus sign in one or more formational parameters, thus indicating the psychological reality of the description provided by Stokoe.

An examination of errors made during the production of ASL—slips of the hand—likewise confirms the psychological reality of the formational parameters of signs. Comparable spoken language studies not only have confirmed the psychological reality of certain descriptive units such as words, phonemes, and distinctive features (see Fromkin, 1971, 1973; Garrett, 1975) but they have also given clear evidence for the formational rules that are used in the construction of syllables and words. Newkirk, Klima, Pedersen, and Bellugi (1979), in an analysis of 131 errors of production in ASL, wished to demonstrate the validity of the parametric analysis of sign and to evaluate certain rules for the formation of signs (for example, the symmetry constraint on handshape in two-handed signs). The authors noticed from the outset that very few errors (7%) were a result of entire sign substitutions; the greater part concerned rather the substitution of one parameter value for another, thus supporting the hypothesis that signs are organized in terms of these parameters. Among the parametric errors, 50% concerned handshape, 10% location, and 8% movement. These errors broke down into three categories: errors of substitution, where the values of parameter X in signs A and B are exchanged (when, for example, the handshape of SICK and that of BORING are switched); errors of anticipation, where the value of parameter X in sign B is used by anticipation in sign A (for example, in the phrase SIGN BASIS O–F POEM, SIGN was articulated with the K handshape of POEM instead of the index finger G shape required); perseveration errors, where the value of parameter X in sign A is maintained in Sign B. We should note that these types of errors were observed not only for the three major parameters, handshape, location, and movement, but also for the minor parameters, orientation of one or both hands, place of contact of the sign, and hand arrangement in two-handed signs.

The errors detected by Newkirk et al. (1979) not only provided evidence for the independence of formational parameters in the construction of signs but also for rules of sign formation. Although certain errors yielded signs that already exist in ASL, the majority were possible but nonexisting signs (only 4% of the errors proved to be impossible in ASL). These errors were constructed from precise combinatorial rules that the authors illustrated in their study. These rules apply, for example, to the constraints governing the use of contacting regions for particular handshapes in particular locations or again to the symmetry of two-handed signs. The latter rule stipulates that two-handed signs with both hands active require the same movement to be executed by each of the two hands (Battison, 1974, 1978). This rule was used in 21 of 22 errors, thus revealing its role in the production of sign language. Newkirk et al. (1979) conclude their study by stating that production errors provide striking evidence for the psychological reality and the independence of individual parameters of ASL and that they bring supplementary evidence that signs are organized sublexically according to a set of formational rules.

Research on the psychological reality of structures and rules in sign language took a further step in a study by Lane, Boyes-Braem, and Bellugi (1976), which was concerned with the organization of hand configuration at the level of distinctive features. Several studies on spoken language have shown that the phoneme is not the smallest unit of linguistic analysis; rather the distinctive feature seems to lay claim to this title (Chomsky & Halle, 1968; Miller & Nicely, 1955; Wickelgren, 1965, 1966). Lane et al. (1976) undertook to determine if handshapes are composed of distinctive features and if a model of these feature assignments would predict errors of perception in an experiment on the identification of signs in visual noise. If a description in terms of distinctive features is justified in sign language, we may conclude that the analysis of phonemes in terms of features is not unique to spoken language but rather that it is rooted more profoundly in the properties of language processing. These authors used a procedure similar to that of Miller and

Nicely (1955) but adapted to the visual modality. A series of 20 signs without meaning, representing the 20 hand configurations widely used in ASL, was videotaped and mixed with visual noise so as to induce subjects into error during the identification of the signs. The confusion matrices were analyzed by means of computer programs for hierarchical clustering (D'Andrade, 1978) and multidimensional scaling (Shepard, 1962, 1972). This analysis revealed a specific organization of handshapes with the degree of finger extension being the most important organizational factor. Lane et al. (1976) used their results to arrive at a model of hand configuration in terms of distinctive features. The model predicts identification errors at a level of r = .6 and is also compatible with findings on errors for sign memory and in sign production. Although the model was revised and extended by Stungis (1978), the earlier study was the first to show that the formational parameters of signs, and in particular, handshape, are decomposable into distinctive features, and the first to propose a linguistic model of these features based on experimental findings. In studies of spoken language, as we mentioned previously, linguistic models have almost always preceded the psychological investigations by several years.

At the level of the sentence, studies on the psychological reality of linguistic structure in sign language have also been undertaken with some success, but there are rather few to report. This is in part attributable to the lack of a partial, not to say complete, grammar of ASL on which these studies could base themselves. (See, however, Fischer, 1973, 1975; Kegl & Wilbur, 1976; McCall, 1965; Stokoe, 1960, 1966.) The few studies that have been undertaken all show that sign language syntax plays an important role in the processing of language by the signer/observer and that sign sentence constituents are functional units. In a molar demonstration of this fact, Hoemann and Florian (1976) showed that anomalous sentences in ASL are judged less meaningful than grammatical sentences and that immediate recall is better when the signs are in the expected grammatical order. In another study, Tweney and Heiman (1977) presented signs to deaf subjects in grammatical sentences and ungrammatical strings, each containing one nonsense sign. They found that the recall of the nonsense signs and indeed the recall of the meaningful signs were both better when they were positioned in sentences rather than sign strings, thus highlighting the importance of grammatical structure in decoding sign language. Tweney, Heiman, and Hoemann (1977) undertook a series of experiments using visual disruption as the paradigm: Signed messages were subjected to varying amounts of disruption using repetitive temporal interruption. Subjects were asked to look at the sign strings and then to repeat in ASL exactly what they had seen. The first experiment showed that nongrammatical lists of ASL signs proved to be quite resistant to disruption compared to equivalent lists of English words, and in the second experiment, ASL sentences proved more resistant to disruption than lists of semantically anomalous signs or unstructured lists. The authors concluded from this that ASL intersign structure has psychological reality. Other studies have examined more closely the functional units in sign language sentences. Baker and Padden (1978), for example, find that the eye blinks of the signer and of the sign observer respect the boundaries of constituents. Eye blinks have been found regularly between subject and predicate, between the verb and the direct object, and between a temporal indicator and the rest of the sentence. Twoney, Liddell, and Bellugi (1978) have demonstrated the psychological reality of relative clauses in ASL. They used seven types of sentences from simple sentences (subject, verb, direct object) to sentences with complements, and relative clauses. All the sentences were recorded on videotape with superimposed visual noise. The task of their subjects was to report each of the sentences as accurately as possible and a transitional error probability was calculated at each sign boundary. The results showed that in general there was a greater probability of making an identification error at the boundary between clauses than within clauses. The authors conclude that the structure of relative clauses as proposed by Liddell (1977) on linguistic grounds and more generally, embedding in sign, have psychological reality.

Other techniques have also been used to get a firmer grasp on the importance of syntax in sign language. Grosjean and Lane (1977), for example, wanted to determine if the duration of pauses in ASL (these are revealed in continuous signing by a hold in the movement of the hands between two signs) could serve to delimit sentences and immediate constituents within them, and if the durations of the pauses between signs could serve as a guide to the assignment of surface structures to the ASL sentences. We should note that this approach, like that of Lane et al. (1976), sought to use experimental results as an aid in suggesting a linguistic model. Five deaf subjects, all native users of ASL, signed a text containing 52 signs at five different rates. The analysis of their productions furnished, among other things, the locations and the durations of their pauses. Grosjean and Lane found, first of all, that the distribution of pauses in the text was not arbitrary, that longer pauses seemed to mark the ends of sentences whereas shorter pauses were to be found within those sentences. At the slower rates, the investigators obtained pause values between every pair of signs which allowed them then to construct a hierarchical structure for each sentence. These were very similar to the provisional surface structures assigned by linguists. The durations of the pauses indicated not only the breaks between simple sentences and coordinate sentences, but equally the boundaries of constituents inside these sentences. The average durations of the pauses, expressed as a percent of the total pause time between and within sentences, were as follows: between sentences, 47%; between conjoined sentences, 28%; between the noun phrase and the verb phrase, 22%; within the noun phrase, 1%; within the verb phrase 2%. Grosjean and Lane conclude that the average pause value between two signs corresponds to the order of the syntactic break between those signs.

This line of investigation has shown therefore that certain aspects of sign language grammar, which is still being elaborated, have psychological reality: units at the phonological level (distinctive features, and parameters of sign formation), and at the syntactic level (constituents, clauses, sentences) are truly functional in the encoding and decoding of sign language. In what follows we summarize studies that have analyzed the production, the perception, and the recall of utterances in sign language.

THE PRODUCTION OF SIGN LANGUAGE

In one of the very first studies from the Salk Institute for Biological Studies, Bellugi and Fischer (1972) compared the rate of production in English and in ASL. They asked three bilingual English/ASL speakers to tell a story in ASL, in English, and also in the two languages simultaneously. (The signing in this latter task probably resembled manual English more than ASL but this does not invalidate the conclusions.) The authors separated the articulation time from the pause time in English and ASL and calculated the rate of articulation in the two languages. The results showed that the rate of articulation in spoken language is almost double that in sign language (4.7 words per second and 2.37 signs per second). As regards the bilingual production, in which signing and speaking took place concurrently, they found an increase in pause time in both English and ASL as compared to the monolingual rendition, an increase that may be explained by the greater cognitive effort required for the simultaneous production in two languages. But again the rate of articulation was clearly less in sign language than spoken language. This difference can be explained by the fact that the articulation of a word requires less displacement of the articulators than that of a sign, where the arms and the hands move over a distance that can range from the top of the head to the waist of the signer.

Bellugi and Fischer (1972) next undertook the analysis of rate in terms of underlying propositions and discovered a fact of major importance: The two languages were characterized by comparable speeds—1.27 seconds per proposition in English and 1.47 seconds in sign in the monolingual productions (the range was from 1 to 2 seconds in both languages.) The communication of a message given in sign language and in oral language thus takes about the same time although the rates in terms of words and signs per second are different. The authors reconciled this result with that preceding by observing that sign language is heavily inflected and hence a sign sentence has fewer "words" than its English counterpart. Moreover, concurrent movements of the body and facial expressions provide additional channels of communication utilized by signers (see Baker, 1976, 1977; Baker & Padden, 1978). From these results we can conclude that sign language is not transmitted more slowly than oral language, as one might have thought from a superficial analysis of rate of utterance in the two languages, and we can further postulate that every language whether oral or visual, will probably have an information rate of approximately the same value.

Grosjean (1977, 1979) likewise compared the production of English and ASL. He summarizes these results in a 1978 article where he proposes that the two languages share, at least in part, a common production mechanism that is influenced by the rate of output, the semantic novelty of the message, the syntactic structure of the sentence, and the necessity of producing groups of words or signs of approximately equal length. Grosjean (1977) showed that speakers and signers produce a range of rates that is almost identical when they go from a slow to a fast production rate (a range of 2.6:1 for the signers and 2.7:1 for the speakers). This suggests that despite the different articulators that come into play in oral language and in sign language (tongue, lips, jaw in oral language, and hands and arms in sign language), there exists a common central system that determines the strategies used in increasing and decreasing rate.

Grosjean (1979) then studied the ways in which the signer and the speaker change their rate. He found that both modify their articulation time and their pause time but that the signer introduces greater changes in articulation time whereas the speaker prefers to modify pause time. Moreover, the slight change that pause time undergoes when the rate is modified in ASL is due to comparable changes in the number and length of the pauses and not, as in English, to a much greater change in the number of pauses than in the average length. The explanation put forward for these differences was connected to the differing respiratory behaviors in speech and sign; sign production takes place independently of breathing whereas speech output is highly dependent on the intake of air. A slower production rate in sign simply implies a slowing down of the articulators whereas in speech it means shorter runs of speech (the air reserve after intake is used up on fewer words) and hence more pauses.

Grosjean pursued his study by examining the factors that influence the durations of signs and of words and those that affect the frequency, duration, and location of pausing in the two languages. Klatt (1976) lists the following factors that influence the durational structure of syllables and words: the psychological and physical state of the speaker, the speaking rate, the position of the element within the paragraph, emphasis, semantic novelty, the length-ening at the end of the word and of the sentence, the inherent duration of segments, effect of linguistic stress, etc. Grosjean showed that four of these factors are also influential in determining the durations of signs. In the first place, each sign has its inherent duration. The distribution of the sign durations at normal speed turned out to be skewed to the right—the average duration of signs was .36 sec (median .33) and the range was from .18 sec to .68 sec. An analysis of sign duration in relation to hand configuration, place of articulation, and number of hands used in the execution of the sign, revealed that these factors do not play a major role in accounting for the inherent duration of signs. The movement involved in a sign, however, is a major contributor: Signs that are made with a movement involving the hands and the arms are twice as long (.6 sec) as those in which only the hands are involved (these signs last only an average of .3 sec). Further, signs in which the hands alternate and where the movement is repeated will have a duration that is longer than those in which there is more direct movement.

In the second place, rate of utterance affects the sign duration: The greater the rate the shorter the sign and vice versa. In the third place, the duration of a sign (like the duration of a word) is affected by semantic novelty. When a sign is presented for the second time in the course of signing a text, its duration is reduced by approximately 10%. And finally, we find that the signs at the end of sentences are about 12% longer than within the sentence.

These findings support the general hypothesis that oral and sign languages share, at least in part, a common underlying production mechanism. This view is strengthened when we examine the pause distribution in English and in ASL. As we noted in the preceding section, Grosjean and Lane (1977) found that the duration of pauses in ASL—as in French and English—signals the importance of the syntactic breaks. Some differences were found, however, between the performance structures of the sentences (that is to say the structures deduced from experimental findings, here pausing) and the formal linguistic structures. Grosjean, Grosjean, and Lane (1979) had previously shown this mismatch in spoken English, and they were led to recognize that performance structures respond to at least two major, but sometimes conflicting, constraints: the need to respect the linguistic structure of the sentence and the need to balance the length of constituents during speech production. They proposed therefore a predictive model for these performance structures that took into account both demands; this model accounted for 72% of total pause time variance whereas the linguistic structures alone accounted only for 56%.

The question that arose naturally for sign language was the following: Can a formal model of the linguistic structure of a sign sentence alone explain the results obtained during the production of a text in ASL (the durations of the pauses found by Grosjean and Lane, 1977, for example) or does the signer, like the speaker, need to make a compromise between respecting the linguistic structure and balancing the length of the constituents? Grosjean, Grosjean, and Lane (1979) reanalyzed the pause distributions obtained by Grosjean and Lane (1977) and found that the model of performance structure better predicted the durations of pauses in ASL than the syntactic structure of the sign utterance alone. (The model accounted for 72% of total variance in pause time whereas the linguistic structure accounted for 61%.) A subsequent study by

Grosjean, Battison, Teuber, and Lane (1979a) invoked four different experimental tasks in order to study performance structure in ASL; parsing of sentences, reading at reduced speed (in order to encourage pausing), relatedness judgments for pairs of signs, and sign recall. These four different approaches produced very similar performance structures—structures that reflect at one and the same time the linguistic structure of the sentence and the need to produce constituents of approximately equal length. The authors conclude that performance structures have their roots in the organization of language in general and not in some property specific to the production modality whether oral or visual.

Grosjean (1978) concludes his synthesis, therefore, by proposing that despite the numerous differences that exist between sign language and oral language (production modality, role of breathing in production, etc.) these languages share, at least in part, a common underlying production mechanism, which is influenced by such factors as the rate of output of the utterance, the semantic novelty of the message, the syntactic structure of the sentence, and the necessity to produce groups of words or signs of approximately equal length. Further study of this common mechanism may lead to its integration into a general model of language production, clearly revealing those apsects that are common to the two modalities and those that are unique to each.

THE PERCEPTION OF SIGN LANGUAGE

Although a number of perceptual tasks have been used by sign language investigators (Bellugi et al., 1975; Lane et al., 1976; Stungis, 1978) their aim was more to demonstrate the psychological reality of the structural organization of the language or to study the memorization of the language than to clarify the processing of the visual signal from the moment it is detected by the retina to the moment the word or utterance is understood by the observer.

The few studies that do exist have only touched upon the scope of this vast domain of research. Grosjean (1977), for example, studied the perception of rate among English listeners and ASL observers. He showed that the function that relates physical rate to apparent rate for the listener and the observer is linear in log–log coordinates. But the two power functions, determined for a comparable range of stimulus rates (about 3 to 1) have different exponents: 1.9 for English and 1.6 for ASL. This means that when a speaker and a signer double their rate, a listener will perceive a fourfold increase in the speaking rate whereas an observer will perceive a threefold increase in the signing rate. These results, confirmed with subjects who know neither the oral language nor the sign language in question, may be explained by the modality difference between the two languages but this remains to be demonstrated experimentally.

Reef, Lane, and Battison (1978) were interested in another aspect of the perception of sign language, the visual persistence of signs. Erwin and Hershenson (1974) and Erwin (1976a, 1976b) showed that when one asks a subject to react as quickly as possible to the onset of a stimulus and then to react to the end of the same stimulus, the difference in the reaction times is in general greater than the duration of the stimulus. This difference is called the visual persistence of the stimulus. When the stimulus can be encoded linguistically, visual persistence is shorter than when the stimulus is not readily codified in linguistic terms. Erwin (1976a, 1976b) attributes the duration of the visual persistence to an iconic short-term memory that persists while visual information is being encoded and disappears only when that encoding is finished. The hypothesis advanced by Reef et al. (1978) was therefore the following: For users of ASL the visual persistence of signs should be shorter than that of handshapes impossible in ASL, because the latter are not codable linguistically, but this difference should not appear for subjects who are unacquainted with ASL. Their results confirm the hypothesis. On the average, the visual persistences of real signs and of nonsigns were identical for naive subjects but significantly different for the users of ASL. Deaf signers gave shorter visual persistences for the signs than for the nonsigns, thus suggesting that the first were encoded more rapidly than the second. The authors conclude that visual persistence reflects stimulus encoding and can be used to study the cognitive processes involved in the perception of sign language.

The process of recognition for signs presented individually also interested Grosjean, Teuber, and Lane (1979c). In a prior study (Grosjean, 1979), ASL users had been asked to measure the durations of a certain number of signs. This task created no particular problem, but they always placed the onset of the sign (that is to say, the moment at which they started timing) at a point when the location had hardly been reached, the handshape was not fully formed, and the movement had hardly begun. What visual cues were the observers relying on to decide that a sign had actually begun? This was the question that Grosjean et al. (1979c) sought to answer. The approach they used was to present a sign repeatedly, increasing its duration with each presentation, measured from the beginning of the sign, from 28 msec to 744 msec. The subjects were to accomplish three tasks after each presentation: copy what they had just seen, guess the sign that had been presented, and give an estimate of their confidence in that guess (along a scale of 1 to 5).

This experiment showed, first, that the formational parameters of a sign are not all copied correctly at the same instant. The orientation of the hand, its configuration, and the location of the sign are copied correctly much sooner than the movement of the sign. This finding is explained by the fact that movement is distributed over time and is associated with the inherent duration of the sign; it is therefore normal that it should be the last parameter to be copied correctly.

When we examine the moment at which a parameter is used correctly in a guess, similar results are obtained. Movement is again the last parameter to be guessed correctly and it is movement, as a result, that triggers the correct identification of the sign. The authors conclude that the on-line processing of a sign does not consist of an all-or-none operation but rather that observers narrow in on the sign parameter by parameter.

An analysis of the errors made by the subjects when they were guessing the signs leads to the same conclusion. Sixty percent of all the errors involved only one parameter (usually movement); 28% of the errors concerned two parameters (movement once again played the major role), and as might be expected, very few errors involved three or four parameters (these results closely resemble those obtained by Crittenden, 1974, in his study of identification of signs by subjects learning ASL). The error data confirm that observers narrow in on the sign by using the information given by the different parameters, and as movement is the last parameter to be identified, it is involved in the greatest number of erroneous guesses.

Grosjean, Teuber, and Lane (1979) then studied the factors that account for the identification time of signs. They noticed at the outset that only the first half of the sign proved critical for its identification. This finding illustrates very clearly the temporal redundancy of sign language at the lexical level. Further, the time necessary to identify a sign was not constant across signs: On the average, a sign was identified in 400 msec and the range was from 200 msec (for the sign LIKE) to 600 msec (COW). How can we explain this range of some 400 msec? Two factors, the duration of the sign and the number of alternative signs with the same place of articulation, did not account for the variation. However, place of articulation, the number of hands used in the sign, frequency of occurrence of the sign, the use of visual and bodily indices in articulation of the sign and the existence of other signs that differ from the stimulus sign in only one parameter—which is to say, minimal pairs—all played a role in sign identification. Research is now underway to compare lexical access and lexical storage in English and American Sign Language with words and signs occurring in the context of sentences.

The on-line processing of sign can be approached in quite a different way: with a shadowing task, such as that used in oral language studies undertaken by Miller and Isard (1963), Rosenberg and Jarvella (1970), and Marslen-Wilson (1975). Marslen-Wilson proposes, for example, that the on-line processing of spoken language is not serial, as Bever and Hurtig (1975) would contend, but rather that it is interactive and parallel. The phonetic analysis of the linguistic signal, its lexical analysis, and the construction of syntactic and semantic representations all take place concurrently. Information at any given level is accessible to all levels and modifications of internal representations at each level are on-going in a parallel and interactive fashion. This perspective of on-line processing of the signal is sharply opposed to that of other psycholinguists who maintain that signal processing is conducted principally in an additive and serial fashion. An extreme interpretation of the latter position would be as follows: Lexical units remain in short-term memory until the end of the clause and are then integrated in order to construct a semantic representation of the clause. By using a shadowing task with selectively disrupted stimuli, Marslen-Wilson (1975) was able to show that restoration errors produced by subjects were not only phonetic but also syntactic and semantic, thus indicating an interactive and parallel analysis at several levels.

McIntire and Yamada (1976) undertook a similar study with ASL in order to find out whether such interactive and parallel processing was modality invariant. They asked two sign language users to tell several stories, which were videotaped and then presented to deaf subjects who attempted to shadow the stories as closely as possible. The shadowing performances were recorded and the shadowing lag between the stimulus and the response tapes was calculated. Marslen-Wilson had found a latency varying from 200 to 800 msec for an oral language (English) and McIntire and Yamada report a similar range for a sign language (ASL). But what is even more interesting are the types of errors that were made by the subjects, errors that tend to support the hypothesis of parallel interactive processing of linguistic information. First, no error yielded an ungrammatical sequence in ASL, which led the investigators to conclude that syntactic and semantic processing was ongoing throughout the task. For example, many personal pronouns were omitted during shadowing but only in those cases where the linguistic structure allowed it (the referent having already been established). There were also numerous additions, but once again their presence did not lead to lack of grammaticality. And what is perhaps even more important is that numerous errors of semantic substitution occurred, such as to leave the meaning of the sentence in which one sign was substituted for another largely unchanged (e.g., the sign OK was replaced by the sign FINE). This type of substitution would be impossible if the observer merely copied the stimulus sentence: It suggests that decoding is proceeding at all linguistic levels (phonetic, semantic, syntactic) during on-line processing.

We should note also that errors of elaboration were also found—that is the addition of several signs that add information to the base message. These errors suggest that the signer/observer again is not limiting himself to a simple copying of the signal but that he has understood the meaning of the incoming stimuli and can embellish the story in a logical manner. McIntire and Yamada (1976) conclude therefore that, whatever the modality of the language, oral or visual, the message is processed simultaneously and interactively at all levels of analysis. Mayberry (1977) also used a shadowing task to determine the importance of facial expression in the processing of sign. Although the data concerning this question were not clear-cut—native ASL subjects shadowed equally well under the face-in and face-out conditions (in the latter condition fleshtones were Chromakeyed out), less well under the face-out with poor signal-to-noise ratio, and least well under the face-in with poor signal-to-noise ratio—Mayberry reports that the errors subjects made were semantically correct and that they made frequent dialectal and synonym substitutions, thus confirming the results reported by McIntire and Yamada.

Although studies of sign language perception are still few in number, they tend to show that after a peripheral analysis differing from that of oral language the processing of the message in the two modalities follows a similar route, which takes the form of interactive and parallel analysis.

MEMORY FOR SIGN LANGUAGE

Although only a few studies of memory in sign language have been conducted, they all show that the strategies adopted by deaf subjects are very similar to those used by hearing subjects in oral language. Bellugi and her collaborators (Bellugi et al., 1975; Bellugi & Siple, 1974) have studied the short-term memory of lists of signs of varying length (three to seven signs) with ASL users. Conrad (1962, 1970) and Sperling and Speelman (1970), among others, had shown that when words and letters are presented visually to hearing subjects for memorization and later recall, the errors of recall that are made are phonetic in nature, not visual or semantic. Thus, among the erroneous responses obtained for the stimulus written C, there were more responses of Z than O (which is visually close to C), and for the word *bee* more errors were found that were due to phonetic resemblance with the word (e.g., *pea*) than semantic resemblance (e.g., *wasp*). How does all this work out in sign language? How do users of ASL store signs in short-term memory? Are they encoded in terms of parameters of sign formation or in terms of some other system (a global visual representation of the signs, a coding of their meaning, a translation of the signs into oral language and memorization in terms of the latter, etc.)?

The study by Bellugi et al. (1975) undertook to answer these questions. They asked two groups of eight subjects each, one composed of hearing students, the other of deaf students (all of the latter had learned ASL as a native language) to participate in a memory experiment with word lists (for the hearing) and sign lists (for the deaf). The lists, with three to seven items, were presented aurally and visually at the rate of one word or sign per second. The recall task after each list required the subjects to recall the words or signs in the order presented (in English). The authors found curves of serially ordered recall that were similar for the two groups; both groups showed recency and primacy effects but the memory span for the deaf in signs (4.9 items) was one item shorter than for the hearing subjects in words (5.9 items). The authors explained this difference by the smaller primacy effect found among the deaf; the rehearsal of the signs at the start of the list takes more time than that of words and this reduces the number of items that can be memorized at the start of the list. (Bellugi & Fischer, 1972, and Grosjean, 1979, indeed showed that the rate of sign production is less than that of spoken words.)

The recall errors of the hearing subjects turned out, as expected, to be largely phonetic. For example, the word *vote* was replaced by *boat, peas* by *knees*, etc. In the same way, the errors of the deaf subjects almost all showed visual similarity with the sign stimuli. For a stimulus sign articulated with two hands, the substitution in recall had the same number of hands involved. Further, the majority of the errors preserved the parameter values of the sign stimuli save one, thus creating minimal pairs. For example, a frequent error of the sign HOME was the sign YESTERDAY. In ASL these two signs share the same place of articulation, hand-orientation, and movement but differ in handshape. Other errors distinguished the sign stimulus from its recall along other formational parameters; for example, SOCKS became STAR, an error primarily of orientation; and BIRD became NEWSPAPER, an error in place of articulation. An evaluation of the errors made by the hearing subjects in English and the deaf subjects in ASL confirm that these errors were indeed acoustic in the former case and visual in the latter. Bellugi et al. (1975) conclude that short-term memory errors in sign-language provide further evidence of the existence of formational parameters in the structure of signs (see the earlier section on linguistic description and psychological reality).

Poizner, Bellugi, and Tweney (1979) pursued the work on the recall of signs by running three experiments that examined short-term encoding processes for different aspects of signs. Experiment 1 compared short-term memory for lists of formationally similar signs with memory for matched lists of random signs, (for example, TAPE, CHAIR, NAME, EGG, etc. which all share the same place of articulation and which are made with two hands in contact as opposed to random lists of the type RUSSIA, APPLE, PRESIDENT, SENTENCE, which differ from each other on most parameters.) Just as the acoustic similarity of words interferes with short-term memory for word sequences, the formational similarity of signs had a marked, debilitating effect on the recall of sequences of signs. In a second experiment, the authors evaluated the effects of the semantic similarity of signs on short-term memory: semantic similarity (e.g., AMERICA, RUSSIA, ENGLAND, SCOTLAND or CHERRY, LEMON, CABBAGE, TOMATO) produced a weak, adverse effect on the short-term recall of sequences of signs. And in the third experiment, they studied the role that the iconic value of signs played in short-term recall. The results showed that greater iconicity has no reliable effect on recall, but there was no testing of iconically homogeneous lists. The authors conclude that further support is provided for the conclusion that deaf signers code signs in short-term memory in terms of linguistically significant formational parameters. The semantic and iconic information of signs, however, seem to have little effect on short-term memory.

In a recent study, Poizner, Newkirk, Bellugi, and Klima (in press) leave aside the recall of basic sign forms and investigate the coding and remembering of morphologically complex signs. They wanted to find out whether inflected verbs are remembered as holistic units or in terms of a base and an inflection. Ten basic ASL verbs and eight inflected forms of each verb were used. Forms were inflected for referential indexing, numerosity, and temporal aspect. Several types of lists (all four signs long) containing a varying number of inflected forms and basic signs were presented. Subjects viewed each list and immediately afterwards tried to recall, in sign, each item in the correct serial position. An analysis of the error patterns suggests that signers do indeed remember signs in terms of base and inflection. For example, in their recall, subjects deleted inflections, recalling only basic signs, and added inflections to basic signs presented alone. Also, subjects transposed inflections across basic signs, recalling the basic signs in the correct serial position. And in addition, recombinations occurred in which the recalled inflection maintained the meaning, but differed in form from the presented inflection. This last result clearly indicates that the errors of recombining morphological elements within lists were not due simply to subjects misremembering movements similar in form but rather implies a more abstract encoding of inflections. Poizner et al. (in press) conclude that subjects were indeed encoding inflections and basic signs as independent units that constitute the building blocks for a morphological system of a combinatorial nature.

How are signs stored in long-term memory? Are they stored according to their formational parameters (as in short-term memory) or rather according to semantic traits (as for words)? In order to answer this question, Siple, Fischer, and Bellugi (1977) undertook a recognition study with signs and words using deaf subjects.

The experimenters asked their subjects to observe a list of 160 lexical items composed of signs and written words and presented on a television screen. At the end of the presentation, the subjects were to wait a half hour before seeing a second list of items (the recognition list); this list differed from the first in the following way: Half of the words and signs were new, and among these some differed from the original signs in one parameter only (for example, BIRD and NEWSPAPER) whereas others were entirely different. Furthermore, the items that had been presented previously were presented either in their original language (whether ASL or English) or in the other of the two languages. The subjects were asked to indicate if the items were present in the original list and, if so, in which language they had originally appeared, ASL or English.

The results showed that the ASL items were stored in long-term memory in the same way as the lexical items from English, specifically according to their semantic traits. Although the formational parameters of a sign play an important role in short-term memory these parameters are not utilized in the organization of long-term memory. The subjects in the present experiment were rarely misled when the new signs resembled the old in every formational respect but one. (Similar findings are reported by Liben, Nowell, & Posnansky, 1978.)

Battison, Lane, and Grosjean (1978) were equally interested in memory for signs but in the context of sentences. The psycholinguistics of oral languages is rich in studies that show the importance of syntax in the recall of isolated sentences. For example, Johnson (1965, 1968) found a strong correlation between the importance of a syntactic break (for example, the break between the noun phrase and the verb phrase) and the transitional probability of an error in recalling the word following the break given correct recall of the word preceding the break. A different approach (Suci, Ammon, & Gamlin, 1967) consisted in presenting a sentence followed immediately by one of the words of the sentence. The subject was to state as rapidly as possible the words in the sentence that followed the probe word given by the experimenter. The results demonstrated once again the role of syntactic structure in the recall of sentences. Response latency was always longer when the probe word and the response word lay on either side of an important syntactic break and shorter when they surrounded a minor break within a major constituent.

The study by Battison et al. (1978) asked whether comparable results would be obtained for sentences in ASL, that is, whether the syntactic structure of the signed sentence would play a role in its memorization. Moreover, they were interested in the possibility of replicating the following finding for spoken language (Grosjean et al., 1979b; see the earlier section on production of sign language): When the major constituents of a sentence, the noun phrase or the verb phrase, are unequal in length, processing measures are better predicted by a performance model that embraces linguistic structure and a tendency to balance the constituents than they are by linguistic structure alone. Balanced sentences, wherein the noun phrase was as long as the verb phrase, and unbalanced sentences where the noun phrase was much shorter, were presented to deaf native users of ASL, and each syntactic break in the sentence was probed in the method of Suci et al. (1967). The results obtained were in the expected direction. For the balanced sentences, the correlation between order of the syntactic break and reaction time was r = .86, indicating the importance of syntax in the recall of sentences of ASL. But when the noun phrase and the verb phrase differed in length, the syntactic structure of the sentence was no longer able to predict reaction time (r = .14). Instead accurate prediction required the model of performance structure that took into account the surface structure of the sentence and the balancing tendency mentioned earlier; the performance model predicted the results with a correlation of r = .88 for the balanced sentences and r = .70 for the unbalanced sentences. These results are entirely comparable to those obtained in spoken language. Dommergues and Grosjean (1979) replicated the study by Johnson (1965) using balanced sentences and unbalanced sentences. They found that errors of recall were better predicted by the duplex model of Grosjean et al. (1979b) than by the syntactic structure alone.

Our account of studies of memory in sign language must end here. In view of the results reported previously, it is likely that forthcoming studies will provide further evidence of parallel processes in the two language modes, visual and oral. How far does this parallelism extend? When a signed sentence is understood, is its meaning stored in long-term memory without any trace of the original syntactic structure (see the results of Sachs for English, 1967)? Are elements of meaning integrated with one another? Brewer, Caccamise, and Siple (1979) adapted the Bransford and Franks (1971) paradigm and showed that subjects receiving manually coded English integrated semantic information from the linguistic stimuli. Although the experiment still needs to be run with native users of ASL, one would expect similar results. Is inferred meaning added to this core meaning (Bransford, Barclay, & Franks, 1972)? And is the message thus enriched, integrated in turn with already existing knowledge (Bransford & Johnson, 1972)? In view of the initial results obtained by Bellugi and others, it would seem likely that future research will reveal that all these operations apply equally to sign language memory.

CONCLUSIONS

We would like to recapitulate here the aspects of encoding and decoding that are specific to the language modality on the one hand and common to all languages, oral or visual, on the other. Although this conclusion can be rooted in only a small number of studies which are, furthermore, concerned primarily with ASL and English, we believe that it will prove useful insofar as these results may ultimately be extrapolated to other oral and sign languages.

Differences in modality seem to be most apparent in the first steps of decoding—receptor systems, feature detectors, preperceptual storage, primary and secondary recognition systems (see the model of speech decoding in Massaro, 1978), and in the last steps of encoding—morphophonemic rules, phonetic and phonological rules, motor commands to muscles, articulation of utterance, (see the model of speech production in Fromkin, 1971).

But at a deeper level of language processing, oral and visual languages seem to be processed in much the same way. Production rate in sign language and in oral language can serve as an example. The phonetic rate of English and of ASL (measured in signs and words per minute) is quite different but speakers of the two languages produce an identical number of propositions per minute thus yielding a similar information rate in a given time. Another example concerns the change of rate in the two languages: signers and speakers adopt different strategies in modifying rate but in the end cover comparable ranges when they speed up and slow down. Thus, because of the different modalities—visual and auditory—signed and spoken languages are necessarily characterized by different peripheral traits but at a deeper level of analysis the two languages have numerous points in common. We will mention only a few. First, communication in sign language is as rapid and as effective as in oral language. Next, the two types of languages are organized in hierarchical units that play a role in encoding and decoding. Distinctive features at the phonological level, morphological units at the morphological and lexical levels, constituents, propositions, sentences at the syntactic level—all these units are truly functional in the production and perception of language. In addition, it would appear that speakers and signers have in common an underlying production mechanism influenced by such factors such as the rate of production, the semantic novelty of the message, the syntactic structure of the sentence and the need to output segments of approximately equal length. Also the processing of the message in the two modalities takes the form of an interactive and parallel analysis. Finally, signs and words are stored in short-term memory according to their formational or phonetic parameters, whereas in long-term memory they are stored according to their meaning.

Although still in its infancy, the psycholinguistics of sign language has not only made headway in uncovering the processes invoved in the production, perception, and memorization of manual languages, but it has also begun to isolate those aspects of encoding and decoding that are specific to the modality of communication (oral or visual) and those that are common to all languages, whatever their modality of perception and production. In this it is helping to frame a general model of linguistic performance.

ACKNOWLEDGMENTS

The preparation of this chapter was funded in part by grant numbers BNS 768 2530, National Science Foundation, and RR 07143 Department of Health, Education and Welfare. The author wishes to thank Harlan Lane for translating the chapter from French and Robbin Battison, Howard Poizner, Patricia Siple, Jim Stungis, and Hartmut Teuber for their comments and suggestions.

REFERENCES

Baker, C. What's not on the other hand in American Sign Language. In *Papers from the 19th Regional Meeting of the Chicago Linguistics Society.* Chicago: The University of Chicago Press, 1976.

Baker, C. Regulators and turn-taking in American Sign Language discourse. In L. Friedman (Ed.), *On the other hand: New perspectives on American Sign Language.* New York: Academic Press, 1977.

Baker, C. & Padden, C. Eye blinking behavior in a visually monitored language. In P. Siple (Ed.), *Understanding language through sign language research.* New York: Academic Press, 1978.

Battison,R. Phonological deletion in American Sign Language. *Sign Language Studies,* 1974, *5,* 1–19.

Battison, R. *Lexical borrowing in American Sign Language.* Silver Spring, Md.: Linstok Press, 1978.

Battison, R., Lane, H., & Grosjean, F. *Probed recall latencies reflect both within clause and across clause boundaries in American Sign Language.* Working paper, Northeastern University, Boston, 1978.

Bellugi, U., & Fischer, S. A comparison of sign language and spoken language. *Cognition,* 1972, *1,* 173–200.

Bellugi, U., Klima, E., & Siple, P. Remembering in signs. *Cognition,* 1975, *3,* 93–125.

Bellugi, U., & Siple, P. Remembering with and without words. In F.Bresson, (Ed.), *Current problems in psycholinguistics.* Paris: Centre National de la Recherche Scientifique, 1974.

Bever, T., & Hurtig, R. Detection of a nonlinguistic stimulus is poorest at the end of a clause. *Journal of Psycholinguistic Research,* 1975, *4,* 1–7.

Bode, L. Communication of agent, object, and indirect object in signed and spoken languages. *Perceptual and Motor Skills,* 1974, *39,* 1151–1158.

Bransford, J., Barclay, J., & Franks, J. Sentence memory: A constructive versus interpretive approach. *Cognitive Psychology,* 1972, *3,* 193–209.

Bransford J., & Franks, J. The abstraction of linguistic ideas. *Cognitive Psychology,* 1971, *2,* 331–350.

Bransford, J., & Johnson, M. Contextual prerequisites for understanding: Some investigations of comprehension and recall. *Journal of Verbal Leaning and Verbal Behavior,* 1972, *11,* 717–726.

Brewer, L., Caccamise, F., & Siple, P. Semantic integration in the adult deaf. In the *Proceedings of the Model Secondary School for the Deaf Research Conference.* Washington, D.C.: Gallaudet College, 1979.

Chomsky, N., & Halle, M. *The sound pattern of English.* New York: Harper & Row, 1968.

Conrad, R. An association between memory errors and errors due to acoustic masking of speech. *Nature,* 1962, *193,* 1314–1315.

Conrad, R. Short-term memory processes in the deaf. *British Journal of Psychology,* 1970, *61,* 179–195.

Crittenden, J. Categorization of cheremic errors in sign language reception. *Sign Language Studies,* 1974, *5,* 64–71.

D'Andrade, R. U–Statistic hierarchical clustering. *Psychometrika,* 1978, *43,* 59–67.

Dommergues, J. Y., & Grosjean, F. *Performance structures in the recall of sentences.* Working paper, Northeastern University, Boston, 1979.

Erwin, D. Further evidence for two components in visual persistence. *Journal of Experimental Psychology: Human Perception and Performance,* 1976, *2,* 191–209. (a)

Erwin, D. The nature of information extraction from visual persistence. *American Journal of Psychology,* 1976, *89,* 659–667. (b)

Erwin, D., & Hershenson, M. Functional characteristics of visual persistence predicted by a two-factor theory of backward masking. *Journal of Experimental Psychology,* 1974, *103,* 249–254.

Fischer, S. Two processes of reduplication in the American Sign Language. *Foundations of Language,* 1973, *9,* 469–480.

Fischer, S. Influences on word-order change in American Sign Language. In C. Li (Ed.), *Word order and word order change.* Austin: The University of Texas Press, 1975.

Fromkin, V. The non-anomalous nature of anomalous utterances. *Language,* 1971, *47,* 25–52.

Fromkin, V. Slips of the tongue. *Scientific American,* 1973, *229,* 109–117.

Garrett, M. The analysis of speech production. *Psychology of Learning and Motivation,* 1975, *9,* 133–177.

Grosjean, F. The perception of rate in spoken and sign languages. *Perception and Psychophysics,* 1977, *22,* 408–413.

Grosjean, F. *Cross-linguistic research in the perception and production of English and American Sign Language.* Paper presented to the Second National Symposium on Sign Language Research and Teaching, Coronado, Calif., October, 1978.

Grosjean, F. A study of timing in a manual and spoken language. American Sign Language and English. *Journal of Psycholinguistic Research,* 1979, *8,* (4), 379–405.

Grosjean, F., Battison, R., Teuber, H., & Lane, H. *Performance structure in American Sign Language.* Working paper, Northeastern University, Boston, 1979. (a)

Grosjean, F., Grosjean, L., & Lane, H. The patterns of silence: Performance structure in sentence production. *Cognitive Psychology,* 1979, *11,* 58–81. (b)

Grosjean, F., & Lane, H. Pauses and syntax in American Sign Language. *Cognition,* 1977, *5,* 101–117.

Grosjean, F., Teuber, H., & Lane, H. *When is a sign a sign? The on-line processing of gated signs in American Sign Language.* Working paper, Northeastern University, Boston. 1979. (c)

Hoemann, H. The development of communication skill in deaf and hearing children. *Child Development,* 1972, *43,* 990–1003.

Hoemann, H., & Florian, V. Order constraints in American Sign Language. *Sign Language Studies,* 1976, *11,* 121–132.

Johnson, N. The psychological reality of phrase structure rules. *Journal of Verbal Learning and Verbal Behavior,* 1965, *4,* 469–475.

Johnson, N. Sequential verbal behavior. In T. Dixon, and D. Horton (Eds.), *Verbal behavior and general behavior theory.* Englewood Cliffs, N.J.: Prentice-Hall, 1968.

Jordan, I. A referential communication study of signers and speakers using realistic referents. *Sign Language Studies,* 1975, *6,* 65–103.

Kegl, J., & Wilbur, R. When does structure stop and style begin? Syntax, morphology and phonology vs. stylistic variations in American Sign Language. In *Papers from the 12th Regional Meeting of the Chicago Linguistic Society.* Chicago: The University of Chicago Press, 1976.

Klatt, D. Linguistic uses of segmental duration in English: Acoustic and perceptual evidence. *Journal of the Acoustical Society of America,* 1976, *59,* 1208–1221.

Lane, H., Boyes-Braem, P., & Bellugi, U. Preliminaries to a distinctive feature analysis of handshapes in American Sign Language. *Cognitive Psychology,* 1976, *8,* 263–289.

Liben, L., Nowell, R., & Posnansky, C. Semantic and formational clustering in deaf and hearing subjects' free recall of signs. *Memory and Cognition,* 1978, *6,* 599–606.

Liddell, S. *An investigation into the syntactic structure of American Sign Language.* Doctoral dissertation, University of California, San Diego, 1977.

Marslen-Wilson, W. Sentence perception as an interactive parallel process. *Science,* 1975, *189,* 226–228.

Massaro, D. An information-processing model of understanding speech. In D. Gerver & H. Sinaiko (Eds.), *Language interpretation and communication.* New York: Plenum, 1978.

Mayberry, R. *Facial expression, noise and shadowing in American Sign Language.* Paper presented at the First National Symposium on Sign Language Research and Teaching, Chicago, 1977.

McCall, E. *A generative grammar of sign.* Masters Thesis, University of Iowa, Iowa City, 1965.

McIntire, M., & Yamada, J. *Visual shadowing: An experiment in American Sign Language.* Paper presented to the Linguistic Society of America, Philadelphia, Pennsylvania. 1976.

Miller, G., & Isard, S. Some perceptual consequences of linguistic rules. *Journal of Verbal Learning and Verbal Behavior,* 1963, *2,* 217–228.

Miller, G., & Nicely, P. An analysis of the perceptual confusions among some English consonants. *Journal of the Acoustical Society of America,* 1955, *27,* 339–352.

New England Sign Language Society. Sign Language research and linguistic universals. In J. Stillings (Ed.), *U/Mass Occasional Papers in Linguistics. Vol. II.* University of Massachusetts, Amherst, 1976.

Newkirk, D., Klima, E., Pedersen, C., & Bellugi, U. Linguistic evidence from slips of the hand. In V. Fromkin (Ed.), *Slips of the tongue and hand.* Proceedings of the 12th International Congress of Linguistics, Vienna, 1979.

Oléron, P. *Communication et syntaxe dans le langage gestuel des sourds.* Working paper, Laboratoire de Psychologie Génétique, Université René Decartes, Paris, 1978.

Poizner, H., Bellugi, U., & Tweney, R. *Processing of formational, semantic and iconic information of signs from American Sign Language.* Working Paper, the Salk Institute, La Jolla, California. 1979.

Poizner, H., Newkirk, D., Bellugi, U., & Klima, E. Short-term encoding of inflected signs from American Sign Language. To appear in the *Proceedings of the Second National Symposium on Sign Language Research and Teaching.* Silver Spring, Md: National Association of the Deaf, in press.

Reef, S., Lane, H., & Battison, R. *Visual persistence in handshapes in American Sign Language: An exploratory study.* Working paper, Northeastern University, Boston, 1978.

Rosenberg, S., & Jarvella, R. Semantic integration as a variable in sentence perception, memory, and production. In G. Flores d'Arcais & W. Levelt (Eds.), *Advances in psycholinguistics.* Amsterdam: North Holland, 1970.

Sachs, J. Recognition memory for syntactic and semantic aspects of connected discourse. *Perception and Psychophysics,* 1967, *2,* 437–442.

Schlesinger, I. The grammar of sign language and the problem of language universals. In J. Morton (Ed.), *Biological and social factors in psycholinguistics.* Urbana: University of Illinois Press, 1970.

Shepard, R. Analysis approximities: Multidimensional scaling with an unknown distance function. *Psychometrika,* 1962, *27,* 125–140, 219–246.

Shepard, R. Psychological representation of speech sounds. In E. Davis and P. Denes (Eds.), *Human communication: A unified view.* New York: McGraw-Hill, 1972.

Siple, P., Fischer, S., & Bellugi, U. Memory for nonsemantic attributes of American Sign Language Signs and English words. *Journal of Verbal Learning and Verbal Behavior,* 1977, *16,* 561–574.

Sperling, G., & Speelman, R. Acoustic similarity and auditory short-term memory experiments and a model. In D. Norman (Ed.), *Models of human memory,* New York: Academic Press, 1970.

Stokoe, W. Sign language structure: An outline of the visual communication system of the American deaf. *Studies in Linguistics,* Occasional Papers No. 8, 1960.

Stokoe, W. Linguistic description of sign. *Languages Monograph Series in Language and Linguistics,* 1966, *19,* 243–250.

Stungis, J. *Identification and discrimination of handshape in American Sign Language.* Working paper, Northeastern University, Boston, 1978.

Suci, G. Ammon, P., & Gamlin, P. The validity of the probe-latency technique for assessing structure in language. *Language and Speech,* 1967, *10,* 69–80.

Tweney, R., & Heiman, G. The effect of sign language grammatical structure on recall. *Bulletin of the Psychonomic Society,* 1977, *10,* 331–334.

Tweney, R., Heiman, G., & Hoemann, H. Psychological processing of sign language: Effect of visual disruption on sign intelligibility. *Journal of Experimental Psychology: General,* 1977, *106,* 255-268.

Tweney, R., Liddell, S., & Bellugi, U. *The perception of grammatical boundaries in American Sign Language.* Working paper, Bowling Green University, Ohio, 1978.

Wickelgren, W. Distinctive features and errors in short term memory for English vowels. *Journal of the Acoustical Society of America,* 1965, *38,* 583-588.

Wickelgren, W. Distinctive features and errors in short term memory for English consonants. *Journal of the Acoustical Society of America,* 1966, *39,* 388-398.

4 The Acquisition of Sign Language

Robert Hoffmeister
Ronnie Wilbur
Boston University

The study of sign language is intriguing from many perspectives. It holds promise of providing new insights into the structure of human language and communication systems, the nature of human perception, memory and production mechanisms, and the relationship between language, meaning, and culture. The study of sign language acquisition has an important additional dimension, as it is quite clear that information gained from research in this area has the power to influence the techniques and educational approaches used with young deaf children. In fact, until recently, the majority of research investigations on sign language were comparisons of educational effectiveness, with a major goal being the determination of whether or not knowledge of sign language affects speech and speechreading abilities. Studies of signing deaf children compared to nonsigning deaf children were often confounded by parental deafness—those children who signed from an early age had deaf parents, while those who were oral from an early age had hearing parents. Such research often failed to consider the psychological, linguistic, and cognitive skills of the children being studied.

In actuality, only about 10% of all deaf children have deaf parents. Although a minority of the deaf population, they are nonetheless the advantaged. They appear to have normal psychological, cognitive, linguistic, and familial development (Furth, 1966; Moores, 1977; Schlesinger & Meadow, 1972). They are generally superior socially and academically to their counterparts with hearing parents. In fact, they are four times more likely to continue their studies into a college program (Stevenson, 1964). Such information engendered arguments among the experts as to whether this superiority was due to their knowledge of sign language or their parents' better acceptance of the children's deafness. As the study of language itself has broadened to include the communicative context in which it is used and learned, the question of knowledge versus acceptance has been rendered moot. Deaf children of deaf parents are brought up in an environment paralleling that of hearing children of hearing parents, save the language difference. As this fact has been recognized throughout the psycholinguistic community, a concomitant acceptance of sign language usage in the educational system has been observed (Jordan, Gustason, & Rosen, 1976).

With the increasing acceptance of sign language, many hearing parents have begun to use signing systems based on English (see Wilbur, 1976, 1979 a for details). Deaf children of hearing parents represent a distinct research population from deaf children of deaf parents, in that the language being learned is quite different in morphology and syntax. (A third group, not dealt with in depth here, comprises hearing children of deaf parents, who learn both spoken English and sign language.)

Table 4.1 summarizes the available studies of deaf children of deaf parents. Knowledge of how deaf children acquire a visual language system from hearing parents is virtually nonexistent. Table 4.2 presents children who have been studied longitudinally but only six of whom have been exposed to a formalized visual language. The number of children studied and the total time of observation is still extremely small for both groups. The similarities

TABLE 4.1
Data Reported for Deaf Children of Deaf Parents
(Longitudinal Studies)

Child	Ages of Observation	Hours of Videotapes	Year(s) Reported	Investigator
Ann, 1	8–34 mos.	12 hours	1972	Schlesinger & Meadow
Karen	31–79 mos.	6 1/4 hours	1972	Schlesinger & Meadow
Ann, 2	31 mos.	1 hour	1973	Boyes-Braem
FF	12–21 mos.	2 hours	1974	McIntyre
Sonia	24–46 mos.	6 1/2 hours	1972	Lacy
Pola	?	7 hours	1972	Lacy
Alice, 1	25–54 mos.	20 hours	1978a	Hoffmeister
Thomas	43 mos.	14 hours	1978a	Hoffmeister
Carol	27–36 mos.	6 hours	1977	Ashbrook
Suzanne	27–36 mos.	1 hour	1977	Ashbrook
Anne	25–32 mos.	6 hours	1978b	Hoffmeister
Alice, 2	27–88 mos.	10 hours	1977	Maxwell
Arturo	1 day–4 mos.	4 hours	1978	Maestas y Moores[a]
Bradley	4–6 mos.	4 1/2 hours	1978	Maestas y Moores[a]
Donna	14–16 mos.	4 1/2 hours	1978	Maestas y Moores[a]
Elizabeth	14–19 mos.	4 hours	1978	Maestas y Moores[a]

[a]Pilot study.

TABLE 4.2
Data Reported for Deaf Children of Hearing Parents
(Longitudinal Studies)

Child	Ages of Observation	Hours of Videotapes	Year(s) Reported	Investigator
Ruth	34–75 mos.	37 hours	1972	Schlesinger & Meadow
Marie	40–70 mos.	12 hours	1972	Schlesinger & Meadow
Elsbeth	24–46 mos.	11 hours	1978	Schlesinger
Sergei	29–53 mos.	7 hours	1978	Schlesinger
Josette	51–76 mos.	17 hours	1978	Schlesinger[a]
Kathy	29–32 mos.	4 1/2 hours[b]	1977	Goldin-Meadow & Feldman
Chris	38–42 mos.	1 1/2 hours[b]	1977	Goldin-Meadow & Feldman
Donald	29–54 mos.	5 1/2 hours[b]	1977	Goldin-Meadow & Feldman
David	34–46 mos.	4 hours[b]	1977	Goldin-Meadow & Feldman
Tracy	49–51 mos.	1 hour[b]	1977	Goldin-Meadow & Feldman
Laurent	28–34 mos.	4 hours	1978	Hoffmeister & Goodhart
Matthew	12 to 15 mos.–25 mos.	N/A	1978	Stoloff & Dennis

[a]Other children were mentioned by Schlesinger (1978) but no data were attributed to them.
[b]Estimated.

63

between the two groups of children should lead us to a greater understanding of the impact of deafness on language development and the feasibility of using the visual channel as a pedagogical tool. This chapter is broken into two parts, one for each group.

DEAF CHILDREN OF DEAF PARENTS

Studies of the acquisition of ASL (Ashbrook, 1977; Bellugi & Klima, 1972; Boyes-Braem, 1973; Hoffmeister, 1975, 1978a, 1978b, 1978c; Kantor, 1977; Lacy, 1972a, 1972b; McIntire, 1977; Wilbur & Jones, 1974) indicate that children learning ASL pass through developmental stages similar to those reported for children learning spoken languages. For example, Bellugi and Klima (1972), Ashbrook (1977), and Hoffmeister (1978a) report that the full range of semantic relations found with children learning English (Bloom, 1970) is expressed by children in the early stages of ASL acquisition. Wilbur and Jones (1974) report similar findings for hearing children of deaf parents who are learning both ASL and English.

It appears that a deaf child's first sign may emerge 2 to 3 months earlier than a hearing child's first spoken word (Boyes-Braem, 1973; McIntire, 1974; Wilbur & Jones, 1974). Similarly, in hearing children of deaf parents, the child's first sign may emerge several months before the same child's first spoken words (Wilbur & Jones, 1974). In addition, the child's spoken vocabulary complements his sign vocabulary, with only a small overlap of words that are spoken and signed (Wilbur & Jones, 1974). This indicates that the child is not simply learning spoken words to correspond to signs already known, nor signs to correspond to spoken words already known, at least not in the initial stages (the opportunity for differential usage of signs and speech is probably substantially involved in this difference).

One further comparison that has been made is that of vocabulary size. McIntire (1974) reports a vocabulary of about 20 signs at age 10 months, the age at which a hearing child is likely to produce its first spoken word. McIntire also reports two-sign utterances at 10 months (two spoken word utterances generally begin about 18 months) and three-sign utterances at 18 months. Schlesinger (1978) reports first signs at approximately 12 months, and she observed attempts at signs at approximately 10 months.

These comparisons of the "first" sign to the "first" spoken word must be considered with caution. There is, of course, considerable difficulty in determining when a child produces the first word, because what may be intelligible to parents who are with the child constantly may not be intelligible to an outside observer. The previous comparisons should be approached with caution for another reason: The number of children studied to date is extremely small. Considerably more documentation is needed for all of these comparisons, but should the differences just noted be confirmed, the earlier emergence of signs is of considerable interest. It is possible that the earlier emergence and growth of signs is attributable to greater control of the hand muscles as compared to the oral muscles.

Phonological Acquisition

The study of the acquisition of phonology in ASL has been limited primarily to the acquisition of handshape. Boyes-Braem (1973) presents a model of handshape complexity based on considerations of anatomy and motor development. Within this model, A is considered the unmarked handshape, and the others are described in terms of the addition of features, where other handshapes are simply described as extended fingers, opposed thumb, or contact with thumb.

McIntire (1974, 1977) modified the Boyes-Braem model, eliminating the distinctions that appear irrelevant to early development (such as the distinction between A and S). She reported four stages of handshape development affected by: (1) opposition of the thumb; (2) extension of one or more fingers; and (3) contact of a finger with the thumb. In the first stage, only one of the hands requires a finger to make contact with the thumb. At this initial stage, the child can produce the following handshapes: 5, S, L, A, G, C, and baby O, in which an O handshape is made with only the thumb and index finger rather than with all the fingers. The second, third, and fourth stages include handshapes that involve touching a finger to the thumb, or more than one of the factors previously mentioned. Stage 2 includes, B, F, and adult O. Stage 3 includes I, Y, D, P, 3, V, H, and W, some of which include extension of the weaker finges (ring finger and pinky). The fourth stage includes 8, 7, X, R, T, M, N, and E, some of which involve crossing fingers.

The interaction of distinctive features and context has been shown to be of critical importance in acquiring spoken language. Hearing children appear to develop strategies that aid them in acquiring the rules of phonemic production. For example, children may be able to produce certain phonemes in isolation or in specific positions (i.e., initial or final consonants) within words but cannot produce the same phoneme in all possible positions (Smith, 1973; Menn, 1976; Ingram, 1974, 1976). In the acquisition of spoken segments, it has become necessary to distinguish between: (1) discriminating sounds perceptually, (2) pronouncing sounds correctly; and (3) using sounds appropriately.

These distinctions are undoubtedly relevant to the study of manual language. We might expect to find modification of a handshape depending on the environment in which it occurs (type of motion, orientation, location). For example, a child who can produce the S handshape in a sign like WORK (both hands in S shape, dominant one taps back of nondominant wrist) might not be able to produce that same handshape in the sign CHANGE because of the difference in motion (twisting wrist) and contact (wrist to wrist). Thus McIntire's stages are relevant primarily for the acquisition of handshapes within single signs, usually simple lexical items (as opposed to the more complex classifiers) although an interaction in complex forms does occur (Kantor, 1977). Within multisign utterances, assimilations, reductions, etc. may occur. The syntactic and semantic components of the child's development must also be investigated for its influence on phonological development. Although Kantor (1977) has reported one such investigation, much research remains to be done in this area.

Syntactic Acquisition

Studies of syntactic acquisition, like those of phonological acquisition, are few in number. Lacy (1972a, 1972b) and Hoffmeister, Ellenberger, and Moores (1975) investigated the beginning stages of acquisition of negation by deaf children of deaf parents. Lacy (1972b) reports from his longitudinal investigation that the earliest forms of negation were NO (a sign that appears to be derived from the fingerspelled N-O) and the negative headshake (which is more frequent). The negative headshake could occur either in linear order with manual signs, or simultaneously with a sign or sign sequence. In later stages, the use of NO decreased, and the two signs NOT and CAN'T (not a contraction of CAN NOT, but a suppletive form in ASL) were used internally in sentences. As in the acquisition of spoken English, the form for "can't" was acquired before the positive form "can." These developmental stages appear to parallel those reported by Bellugi (1967) in her study of the acquisition of negation by hearing children learning English.

Hoffmeister and Moores (1973) investigated the development of specific reference in deaf children learning ASL. In doing so, they distinguished between formal and informal means of indicating specific reference. The formal mechanisms are the citation forms of the signs THIS (dominant G hand points to palm of nondominant B hand) and THAT (dominant Y hand palm down on nondominant B hand, palm up). They considered pointing with the G hand to be an informal procedure for indicating reference. This investigation of pointing led to a more extensive study and analysis reported in Hoffmeister (1978a) and discussed separately subsequently.

Fischer (1973) reports on the acquisition of verb inflection by two deaf children of deaf parents, Shirley and Cory. Fischer divided the data into arbitrary 6-month stages. For Cory, she analyzed five stages, Stage Zero (age 2), Stage I (age 2½), Stage II (age 3), Stage III (age 3½), and Stage IV (age 4). For Shirley, there were four, starting from Stage I (same age) on up. Fischer included in her study aspects of verb inflection related to the phonological realization of verb agreement. She divides the verbs into three classes: (1) locational (verbs that can be made at an agreement point other than body anchor verbs); (2) reversing verbs (those that reverse or modify hand orientation toward agreement point); and (3) directional verbs (those that move between two agreement points). Looking at the phonological realizations, Fischer reports that at Stage Zero Cory showed no inflections at all and verbs that should have been inflected were modified to an uninflected form. At Stage I for both children, Fischer observed only locational verbs, with nonlocational verbs incorrectly modified to be locational (i.e., directional verbs became locational). At Stage II, the children indicated regular overgeneralization of the verb inflection rule (parallel to hearing children first correctly producing *came*, then later incorrectly producing *camed*). Here, verbs made on the body that are not in any of the above three classes and that were correctly produced at Stage I are now incorrectly made into locational verbs. Reversal also appears at this stage and is overgeneralized. The beginning of directional verbs was also observed at this stage. By Stage III, both girls clearly knew which verbs inflected in which ways, although at Stage IV, Cory was still making occasional overgeneralizations.

In an initial report of the development of ASL word order in deaf children of deaf parents, Hoffmeister (1978c) provides supporting evidence for the verb development observed by Fischer (1973) cited previously. Basic S–V, V–O, and S–V–O orderings were used even when the children used verbs which could be modulated for subject, object, and/or location. Even at Stage IV, when children began to shift sentence constituents, modulated verbs were "backed up" by pointing. The effect of redundancy in ASL on the acquisition process is still under investigation.

Semantic Acquisition

Initial reports of the acquisition of ASL began as descriptions of sign-by-sign acquisition. Schlesinger and Meadow (1972) report that the two deaf children of deaf parents they observed began formalized recognizable signs at 12 months of age. By 19 months they had a vocabulary of well over 100 signs and were using connected language. The youngest child, Ann, used a small set of signs that had multiple functions. That is, she used signs for reference, request, comment, etc. and in some cases individual signs had the impact of a full sentence.

In Schlesinger and Meadow's (1972) description of Karen at 34 months, the data indicate that she has acquired the typical semantic relationships of children her age. She exhibits sentences that have actions produced with either overt agents or objects. She expresses possession, location, and nomination. At this age she has both internal and external negatives. The only unusual development is that instead of a predictable agent–object relation Karen expressed this relation only through three term utterances where action was present (Schlesinger, 1978).

As mentioned previously, semantic relations expressed by children in the early stages of ASL acquisition have been investigated by a number of researchers. Aside from the conclusion that the development of these semantic relations appears to parallel that in spoken language acquisition, one other interesting finding comes from Ashbrook (1977). She originally separated semantic relations expressed through a sequence of signs (as one would do through a sequence of spoken words) from those expressed simultaneously within a complex sign (e.g., agent expressed by verb agreement with that referent point in space, thus one sign starting at that point indicates both agent and action). Her intent was to see if some developmental difference in expression type might exist. In fact, she found no such developmental difference. Thus in the children's language, as in the adult language, both expressions are possible. Comprehensive determination of what governs these choices in the adult language, and their corresponding development in children, still remains to be conducted.

Another type of semantic study (although they do not specifically call it one) is that of Ellenberger and Stayaert (1978). Their primary interest was in the representation of action by one child between the ages of 43 and 71 months. They reported the following developmental trends: (1) a decrease in the use of pantomime or gestures along with signs which indicate action; (2) a gradual increase in the use of abstract symbols and a decrease in the use of iconic, re-enactments of events; (3) when telling stories, a shift from the role of actor to that of narrator; (4) the development of the ability to establish referents in space which can be incorporated into the action sign; and (5) an increasing skill in the use of signs that can incorporate information about participants in the action (including classifiers in the verbs, for example).

Recent Extensive Investigations

This section includes two completed studies, Kantor (1977) and Hoffmeister (1975, 1978a), which exemplify in-depth acquisition studies, and a third ongoing study (Maestas y Moores, 1978), which attempts to investigate the earliest interactions. These studies provide unique perspectives on the structure and acquisition of ASL, and consequently require separate and extended discussion. Kantor's study is cross-sectional and investigates classifier development. Hoffmeister's study is longitudinal and traces the development of various systems in ASL that appear to be based on the pointing gesture. Hoffmeister's study was conducted as part of a larger investigation at the University of Minnesota (Ellenberger, 1977; Hoffmeister, 1975; Hoffmeister et al., 1975; Hoffmeister, Moores, & Best, 1974; Hoffmeister, Moores, &

Ellenberger, 1975a, 1975b; Moores & O'Malley, 1976; Morgan, 1975; O'Malley, 1975). Maestas y Moores' (1978) is longitudinal, covers birth to 18 months, and includes one deaf couple who also use Spanish.

The purpose of Kantor's (1977) study was to obtain data on the developmental stages that deaf children pass through in acquiring the adult form of classifiers. The description of classifiers laid out in Kegl (1976a, 1976b) and Kegl and Wilbur (1976) was treated as the adult form to be learned. Within this model of classifiers, classifier signs are linguistically complex, requiring syntactic, semantic, and phonological information for appropriate choice and function. If they are linguistically complex, and if there is any relationship between linguistic complexity and case/order/age of acquisition, then one might expect that classifiers would take longer than other signs for deaf children to learn, although this relationship is not necessarily so direct (Wilbur, 1979b). They may also require different strategies because of the interaction of phonological, syntactic, and semantic components on their proper use.

Kantor conducted a cross-sectional study, using nine children aged 3-11 years. All children were congenitally, profoundly deaf with deaf parents. They were presented with a story specifically designed for elicitation of classifiers, signed by a native user of ASL on videotape, after which they were asked to retell and discuss the story with a deaf houseparent. This interaction was videotaped for later analysis. The children also were given imitation and comprehension tasks to provide a complete picture of their abilities.

The results of this investigation can be more easily discussed in light of Kantor's (1977) model of classifier use. (It is derived from a more general model of development suggested by M. Bernstein.)

The use of a classifier in any utterance can be illustrated in the following way:
1. There is a proposition to express.
2. If the environment requires a classifier, substitute one and attach it to the verb.

Does require substitution   Does not require substitution

| ↓

| use citation form

↓

3. What is the appropriate form
a. semantically (what are the properties of the noun, i.e., is it taller than it is wide etc.?)
b. phonologically (what are the parameters of the actual sign?)
c. syntactically (where does it move; what are the agreement points?) [p. 48].

The first step in classifier usage, then, is the syntactic recognition that one is needed. Kantor found that even the youngest children in the study were making this recognition, and only one or two real violations of the conditioning environments for classifier usage occurred. If a classifier was not actually used, then either: 1) deletion occurred such that no form was used; or (2) the citation form of the verb was used without the element which would have conditioned the classifier (e.g., without verb agreement or without the directional preposition, this information being simply omitted). If a classifier did occur, it was likely that other modifications also occurred.

The remaining steps required for total mastery of the classifier system do not come until much later, in the sense that proper substitution of a classifier in one environment did not ensure that the same classifier would be substituted in another environment, and phonological modifications occurred as a result of the differences in syntactic environments. Similarly, handshapes used appropriately in simple signs (such as 3 in the numeral, or V in the sign SEE) were not used correctly in the classifier forms in a consistent manner.

From the types of errors the children made, their relative performance on the three different tasks, and the changes in abilities over age, Kantor (1977) concluded:

1. The late acquisition of classifiers confirms Kegl and Wilbur's (1976) and Kegl's (1976a, 1976b) description of them as a system of great complexity.
2. Classifiers are not acquired as lexical items per se but rather as a complex syntactic process. This is evidenced by several instances of appropriate classifier usage in some environments and inappropriate usage in others.
3. Classifiers begin to emerge around age three, but are not completely mastered as a set of rules until 8 or 9 years old;
4. The deaf child's acquisition of segments is not simply a matter of incremental ability to control the weaker digits of the hand. Rather, it is a complex interaction of the various components of the language.
5. There is an influence of syntactic and phonological environments operating on the acquisition of rules in ASL similar to the effect of environment on spoken-language rule acquisition as described by Smith (1973) and Menyuk (1977);
6. The notion of function as described by Smith (1973), Ingram (1976), and Menn (1976) is applicable to the acquisition of segments in ASL.
7. The domain of application for a rule widens as the child matures in much the same way it does in hearing children as described by Menyuk (1977).
8. The earliest handshapes in initial use of classifiers correspond to the stages of development suggested by Boyes-Braem (1973) and McIntire (1977).
9. The order of feature acquisition corresponds to the hierarchy suggested by Wilbur and Jones (1974) with the addition of orientation. On the basis of developmental stages within the acquisition of simple single signs, Wilbur and Jones (1974) suggested that the order of acquisition of parameters would be

location, movement, and handshape. Kantor found that orientation appears to share the final stage with handshape, giving: location, movement, hand-shape/orientation.

Thus Kantor's study confirms a number of important issues regarding the adult description of ASL (such as the complexity of classifiers) and questions about the acquisition of signs by children (developmental stages that display an interaction of various components of the grammar).

Hoffmeister's (1975, 1978a) study identifies various functions that pointing can serve in adult ASL, such as demonstrative pronoun, determiner, part of the possessive system (with the B hand), reflexive (with the A hand); it also seems to indicate plural and specific reference. Hoffmeister names the point-ing gesture POINT. His observations indicate that the POINT forms the basis of several developmental stages. For example, the early two sign productions consist of two POINTs: If a child wishes to indicate that a particular toy is his, this possessor–possessed relationship might be a sequence of two POINTs, one to the toy, the other to the child himself. He also found that the first three-sign utterances consisted of three POINTs: "Let's you and me go downstairs" POINT (to addressee) POINT (to self) POINT (down). Subsequent develop-ments in the three-sign stage included one sign and two POINTs, two signs and one POINT, and finally three non-POINT signs. Hoffmeister's intention was to show that the POINT was part of the developmental sequence of ASL and that the child learning ASL used pointing gestures in a manner which was linguistically constrained and functional within a system while a hearing child's pointing gestures would not be. Agreement points can be established in space for reference to nonpresent objects and persons, which represents a greater linguistic abstraction than pointing to visibly present objects (see Wilbur, Chapter 2 in this volume, 1979a). And in fact, Hoffmeister found that a developmental sequence was present, such that the "concrete" pointing was acquired earlier than the abstract pointing. The significance for child lan-guage studies is easy to demonstrate. In Wilbur and Jones (1974), sequences of a noun sign followed by or preceded by a pointing gesture were observed, which it was naively assumed were there because the child lacked the linguistic ability to say what he wanted and chose to point instead, hoping to be understood. Locative POINTs were not separated from object reference POINTs; the distinction was not considered. In analysis, it was incorrectly decided that POINTs did not count. In retrospect, it is quite clear that the earliest two-sign utterances were combinations of sign and POINT, and that such sequences occurred at least a month earlier than two non-POINT signs together. The POINT signs obeyed the same type of constraints Hoffmeister observed, but at that time, of course, they had not been noticed.

Hoffmeister's study, as indicated previously, was part of a larger study. In all, some 500 hours of videotape were collected on about 10 deaf children of deaf parents for periods ranging up to about 5 years duration. For his investigation of the role of pointing, Hoffmeister chose one child, named Alice, and backed up his findings by selectively sampling the data of other children. Alice's productions were divided into arbitrary units of 1000 utterances each, giving the following stages and ages: Stage I (29 months), Stage II (38 months), Stage III (45 months), Stage IV (50 months), and Stage V (52 months). Stages I to IV are remarkably similar in age to those reported by Fischer (1973): Stage I (30 months), Stage II (36 months), Stage III (42 months), and Stage IV (48 months). Bear in mind that Fischer decided on her stages by 6-month age intervals (not developmental sequences) and Hoffmeister arrived at his by total output of utterances. Neither of these reports is intended to convey the concept of developmental stage by use of the word "stage" in their units of investigation (i.e., they do not mean stage in the same sense that Brown (1973) uses it to refer to a range of linguistic development from mean length of utterance 1.0 to 2.0).

In the expression of semantic relations, Hoffmeister reports that at Stage I, the use of a POINT and a *noun* for Demonstrative + Entity ("that book") or POINT and an *adjective* for Demonstrative + Attribute ("that [is] red") constitute 56.3% of all semantic relations expressed. By Stage II, this had decreased to 24.3%, by Stage III to 12.8%, and by Stages IV and V, about 5%.

At Stage I, the POINT is used to indicate agent, patient, locative, object-possessed, and possessor, and it is used syntactically as a demonstrative. All these POINTs must be directed at a real-world object or person visibly present in the environment. In the initial stage, these pointing gestures are constrained to the signer, the addressee, and third-person objects present in the room. Also in the early part of Stage I, the possessor–possessed relationship is represented by a POINT to the object followed by a POINT to self, using the G hand for pointing. Later in Stage I, the adult B hand begins to replace the G hand when referring to the possessor (but with considerable alternation between G and B). The possessed object again must be present in the room. When using the B hand to indicate the possessor, the child may "back up" this production with an additional G hand POINT, just to be sure the message has been correctly received. Also present in Stage I is the possessive construction N + N (as in "Mommy sock"). Plurals at this stage are indicated by repeated POINTs to the same object (i.e., "lamps" might be represented by pointing several times to a lamp), also sometimes accompanied by the sign MANY/MUCH or a numeral.

In Stage II, the POINT may now be made with a Y hand, which we label here THAT (even though it was not produced like the adult citation form, with the nondominant B hand, palm up). Sometimes, the POINT with G hand would be used as a back-up for THAT. Occasionally, THAT would actually touch the real-world object it was referring to, and then the POINT would be aimed at the object (but not contacted). In the possessive construction at this stage, the possessor may now be a third person (not just a signer and addressee), and a new development, the use of HAVE, is seen: CAT HAVE LEG "the cat has a leg." For plurals, a continuous POINT to many pictures is used to mean "all," pointing to two objects, each with a different hand, is used to mean "both of them," and two fingers on one hand is used also to mean "both of these" (this latter is not necessarily the V hand, but is the precursor of the adult dual pronoun). In Stage II, Hoffmeister also observed the POINT used to establish a particular location, after which the verb was inflected to agree. (Stage II was also when Fischer first observed verb inflections.)

In Stage III, Hoffmeister reports that developments were primarily in areas other than the POINT, with complex and conjoined sentences appearing. The signed English possessive affix 'S appears in Alice's signing, correctly from the beginning, reflecting the influence of her schooling on her signing. In this stage, the requirement of having a real-world referent for each pronoun is starting to fade. Alice set up her G hand as a substitute for SUN (definitely the wrong classifier) and then refers to her finger with the other hand.

In Stage IV, full control of all two and three unit semantic relations is observed. All possible forms of the possessive are correctly produced. The reflexive is begun, with the POINT again used as a back-up. (For further details on this aspect, see Hoffmeister, 1978a). In Stage IV, the adult dual pronoun made with the V hand appears. Finally, although Alice began to use reference to nonpresent objects in Stage III, the remaining control is established here in two ways. In one form, a real-world object present in the room is used to substitute for another object not present. Thus, Alice points to a lamp near her while referring in her conversation to another lamp in her room. In the other form, arbitrary points in space are established, and the verb is moved between them, with some use of classifiers if needed, and with the back-up of the familiar POINT just in case.

By Stage V, Alice has mastered adult use of the POINT, possessive, plural, reflexive, and verb agreement in terms of establishing arbitrary points in space.

All of the studies of sign language acquisition previously discussed have concentrated on the later development of syntactic properties. In a recent ongoing study, Maestas y Moores (1978) is investigating aspects of mother–child interaction in deaf mothers and their deaf children. She is following five children from as early as birth to approximately 18 months. Preliminary results indicate that parents go to great lengths in order to maximize the visual attention and message reception of their children. Many of the first signs are formed on the child's body (rather than appropriately on the adult's). Other areas of analysis included in the study are signing style, modality (speech, signs, or combinations), use of fingerspelling, egocentric signing, and cross-modal communication. The use of manual communication and its effects on the development of speech will also interact with the study, particularly because most deaf parents have been brought up to believe that there is a negative relation between use of signs and development of speech. Finally, a unique feature of the Maestas y Moores study is the inclusion of a deaf Spanish family. The parents appear to move easily between mouthing Spanish and English words while using ASL signs.

DEAF CHILDREN OF HEARING PARENTS

Detailed longitudinal reports of the acquisition of sign language in deaf children of hearing parents are not available because hearing parents usually do not have extensive access to sign language when their child is first identified as deaf. Recently, more parents of very young deaf children have had the opportunity to learn sign language and use this mode when interacting with their children. However, because hearing parents have such a short period of time to learn a sign system, most have opted for a manual coding of English rather than for American Sign Language. When delivered in conjunction with speech, Schlesinger (1978) refers to this as bimodal presentation and acquisition as opposed to bilingual acquisition. The term bilingual acquisition is reserved for deaf children of deaf parents who acquire a spoken language after they have acquired ASL.

The first two deaf children of hearing parents to be studied for their acquisiton of sign language were Ruth and Marie, age 34 months and 40 months respectively. Their parents did not use a sign system until Ruth was 17 months and Marie was 36 months old. Shortly after these children began learning signs, 36 months for Ruth and 42 months for Marie, the test of comprehension described in Fraser, Bellugi, and Brown (1963) was administered. Both children appeared able to comprehend the contrasts of subject/object, present progressive/past, singular/plural, and affirmative/negative. In addition, subsequent observation indicated that Marie could also use appropriately the "S" sign inflections for past tense, plural, present progressive, and possessive. Schlesinger (1978) indicates in a follow-up report that five other deaf children of hearing parents are obtaining similar success in acquiring sign language. All the children she studied appeared to follow Slobin's (1973) operating principles of "pay attention to the order of words" and "to the end of words." These are important in learning manually coded English because inflections are separate sign segments attached or juxtaposed to signs. All of the children appeared to acquire the appropriate linguistic modulations by age six.

In a recent report, Matthew, a young deaf child whose mother and teacher began using signs when he was 12 months old, displayed the early emergence of signs also seen in deaf children of deaf parents (Stoloff & Dennis, 1978). Matthew was combining signs at 18 months and was rapidly expanding his vocabulary. This child's success with signed English underscores the potential of a visual language when presented to young deaf children.

A very important point of the studies of Schlesinger and Meadow (1972), Schlesinger (1978) and Stoloff and Dennis (1978) is that the child's vocabulizing does not appear to decrease when signs are learned but actually increases in frequency. The above authors claim that these children may actually fade signs, or use speech when no sign exists or when they have not learned the equivalent sign process.

The only detailed longitudinal study that described a deaf child's language in linguistic terms is that of Laurent (Goodhart, 1978; Hoffmeister & Goodhart, 1978; Hoffmeister, Goodhart, & Dworski, 1978). At 29 months, Laurent had only 9 months of sign exposure; he was nonetheless capable of expressing two and three-term semantic relationshps expected of normal hearing children and of deaf children of deaf parents at the same age. In addition he expanded agents and patients using adjectives and/or determiners as part of the expanded noun phrase. Because Laurent's mother was presenting a combination of ASL and signed English, Laurent produced a number of signed sequences that are common to both systems. For example, at 29 months he used verb modulations similar to those in ASL as in BUG++ (bugs; pluses indicate repetitions) POINT (toward the ceiling) # fly = Y (up toward the ceiling) # "these bugs flew to the ceiling," and ASL plural production in POINT (that/eggs) EGG^{+6} (repeated 6 times) POINT (that/eggs) EGG^{+2} POINT (those/eggs)$^{+2}$ EGG, where the repeated signs indicate reference to more than one.

In addition to the just-mentioned processes Laurent also developed compound signs by simultaneously producing parameters of two signs as in $\frac{FISH}{BOAT}$ "boat in the shape of a fish" (where the FISH handshape and orientation is performed with the up and down motion of the sign BOAT). Laurent also used the POINT, which is the foundation of ASL development, in all possible roles. In the same manner as Alice, he modulated old forms for new functions using the POINT for his initial modulations. By 36 months, Laurent, for the most part, is equivalent to Alice's development of language in terms of complexity, quantity, and quality of linguistic knowledge. That this was all accomplished in a period of less than a year, with parents who were just beginning to learn sign language, is encouraging.

SUMMARY

It is no doubt obvious that language when presented in a visual mode can be acquired easily and in the same quantity and quality as language presented in an oral-aural mode. Apparently it is sufficient to present a model that has internal consistency. These investigations indicate that children are powerful learning agents. Deaf parents may have inferior educational backgrounds and generally lower socioeconomic standing, and they are not part of everyday hearing society, but their deaf children are the most intact psychologically and socially, and the most advanced in terms of language development when compared with other deaf children. However, when given the tools to communicate comfortably, deaf children of hearing parents may also achieve the psychological, social, and linguistic status of deaf children of deaf parents. Schlesinger (1978) points out that this may come about not only from the advent of using signs, but also from the fact that parents of deaf children may then communicate and interact more like parents of normal hearing children. That is, they may treat their children as children, accept them as children, love them as children, and reduce the trauma and separation that deafness creates.

These studies are only the beginning in the effort to understand and compile information that truly elaborates the potential development of young deaf children. Because language is one of the major obstacles to learning for deaf children, these reports indicate that ASL and signed languages may allow the potential of deaf children to finally be realized.

REFERENCES

Ashbrook, E. *Development of semantic relations in the acquisition of American Sign Language.* Unpublished manuscript, Salk Institute for Biological Studies. La Jolla, Calif., 1977.

Bellugi, U. *The acquisition of negation.* Unpublished doctoral dissertation, Harvard University, 1967.

Bellugi, U., & Klima, E. The roots of language in the sign talk of the deaf. *Psychology Today,* 1972, *76,* 61–64.

Bloom, L. *Language development: Form and function in emerging grammar.* Cambridge: MIT Press, 1970.

Boyes-Braem, P. *A study of the acquisition of the DEZ in American Sign Language.* Working paper, Salk Institute for Biological Studies, La Jolla, Calif., 1973.

Brown, R. *A first language: The early stages.* Cambridge: Harvard University Press, 1973.

Ellenberger, R. *Sequential aspects of American Sign Language phonology.* Paper presented at the Annual Meeting of the Linguistic Society of America, 1977.

Ellenberger, R., & Stayaert, M. A child's representation of action in American Sign Language. In P. Siple (Ed.), *Understanding language through sign language research.* New York: Academic Press, 1978.

Fischer, S. *The deaf child's acquisition of verb inflection in American Sign Language.* Paper presented to the Annual Meeting of the Linguistic Society of America, San Diego, 1973.

Fraser, C., Bellugi, U., & Brown, R. Control of grammar in imitation, comprehension, and production. *Journal of Verbal Learning and Verbal Behavior,* 1963, *2,* 121–135.

Furth, H. *Thinking without language.* London: Collier-MacMillian, 1966.

Goldin-Meadow, S., & Feldman, H. The development of language-like communication without a language model. *Science,* 1977, *197,* 401–403.

Goodhart, W. *An analysis of the syntactic behavior of a deaf child of hearing parents.* Unpublished manuscript, Boston University, 1978.

Hoffmeister, R. *The development of location in a deaf child of deaf parents.* Unpublished manuscript, Research, Development, and Demonstration Center in Education of the Handicapped, University of Minnesota, 1975.

Hoffmeister, R. *The acquisition of American Sign Language by deaf children of deaf parents: The development of the demonstrative pronouns, locatives, and personal pronouns.* Unpublished doctoral dissertation, University of Minnesota, 1978. (a)

Hoffmeister, R. *An analysis of possessive constructions in the ASL of a young deaf child of deaf parents.* Unpublished manuscript, Temple University, 1978. (b)

Hoffmeister, R. *Word order acquisition in ASL.* Paper presented at the Third Annual Boston University Conference on Language Development, Boston, 1978. (c)

Hoffmeister, R., Ellenberger, R., & Moores, D. *Sign language development in deaf children of deaf parents.* Paper presented at the Fifty-Third Annual Convention of the Council for Exceptional Children, Los Angeles, 1975.

Hoffmeister, R., & Goodhart, W. *A semantic and syntactic analysis of the sign language behavior of a deaf child of hearing parents.* Paper presented at the MIT Sign Language Symposium, Cambridge, 1978.

Hoffmeister, R., Goodhart, W., & Dworski, S. *Symbolic gestural behavior in deaf and hearing children.* Paper presented at the American Speech and Hearing Association Conference, San Francisco, 1978.

Hoffmeister, R., & Moores, D. *The acquisition of specific reference in a deaf child of deaf parents.* Report #53, Research, Development, and Demonstration Center in Education of the Handicapped, University of Minnesota, 1973.

Hoffmeister, R., Moores, D., & Best, B. *The acquisition of sign language in deaf children of deaf parents.* Research report No. 65, Research, Development, and Demonstration Center in Education of the Handicapped, University of Minnesota, 1974.

Hoffmeister, R., Moores, D., & Ellenberger, R. *The parameters of sign language defined: Translation and definition rules.* Research report No. 83, Research, Development, and Demonstration Center in Education of the Handicapped, University of Minnesota, 1975. (a)

Hoffmeister, R., Moores, D., & Ellenberger, R. Some procedural guidelines for analyzing American Sign Language. *Sign Language Studies,* 1975, *7,* 121-137. (b)

Ingram, D. Phonological rules in young children. *Journal of Child Language,* 1974, *1,* 49-64.

Ingram, D. *Phonological disability in children.* New York: Elsevier-Holland Publishing Co., 1976.

Jordan, I., Gustason, G., & Rosen, R. Current communication trends at progams for the deaf. *American Annals of the Deaf,* 1976, *121,* 527-532.

Kantor, R. *The acquisition of classifiers in American Sign Language.* Unpublished master's thesis, Boston University, 1977.

Kegl, J. *Pronominalization in American Sign Language.* Unpublished manuscript, MIT, Cambridge, 1976. (a)

Kegl, J. *Relational grammar and American Sign Language.* Unpublished manuscript, MIT, Cambridge, 1976. (b)

Kegl, J. & Wilbur, R. When does structure stop and style begin? Syntax, morphology, and phonology vs. stylistic variation in American Sign Language. In S. Mufwene, C. Walker, and S. Steever (Eds.), *Papers from the Twelfth Regional Meeting, Chicago Linguistic Society.* Chicago: The University of Chicago Press, 1976.

Lacy, R. *Development of Pola's questions.* Unpublished manuscript, Salk Institute for Biological Studies, La Jolla, 1972. (a)

Lacy, R. *Development of Sonia's negations.* Unpublished manuscript, Salk Institute for Biological Studies, La Jolla, 1972. (b)

Maestas y Moores, J. *Patterns of interaction between infants and deaf parents: An ethnographic pilot study.* Unpublished manuscript, University of Minnesota, 1978.

McIntire, M. *A modified model for the description of language acquisition in a deaf child.* Unpublished master's thesis, California State University, Northridge, 1974.

McIntire, M. The acquisition of American Sign Language configurations. *Sign Language Studies,* 1977, *16,* 247–266.

Maxwell, M. *A deaf child's invention of signs.* Working paper, Salk Institute for Biological Studies, La Jolla, 1977.

Menn, L. *Pattern, control, and contrast in beginning speech: A case study in the development of word form and word function.* Unpublished doctoral dissertation, University of Illinois, Urbana-Champaign, 1976.

Menyuk, P. *Language and maturation.* New York: Academic Press, 1977.

Moores, D. *Educating the deaf: Psychology, principles, and practice.* Boston: Houghton-Mifflin, 1977.

Moores, D., & O'Malley, P. *Pronominal reference in American Sign Language.* Research, Development, and Demonstration Center in Education of the Handicapped, University of Minnesota, 1976.

Morgan, A. *The process of imitation in deaf children of deaf parents.* Unpublished master's thesis, University of Minnesota, 1975.

O'Malley, P. *The grammatical function of indexic reference in American Sign Language.* Unpublished manuscript, Research, Development, and Demonstration Center in Education of the Handicapped, University of Minnesota, 1975.

Schlesinger, H. The acquisition of bimodal language. In I. M. Schlesinger (Ed.), *Sign language of the deaf: Psychological, linguistic, and sociological perspectives.* New York: Academic Press, 1978.

Schlesinger, H., & Meadow, K. *Sound and sign: Childhood deafness and mental health.* Berkeley: University of California Press, 1972.

Slobin, D. Cognitive prerequisites for the development of grammar. In C. Ferguson and D. Slobin (Eds.), *Studies in child language development.* New York: Holt, Rinehart & Winston, 1973.

Smith, N. *The acquisition of phonology: A case study.* London: Cambridge University Press, 1973.

Stevenson, E. A study of the educational achievement of deaf children of deaf parents. *California News,* 1964, *80,* 143.

Stoloff, L., & Dennis, Z. Matthew. *American Annals of the Deaf,* 1978, *123,* 452–459.

Wilbur, R. The linguistics of manual language and manual systems. In L. Lloyd (Ed.), *Communication assessment and intervention strategies.* Baltimore: University Park Press, 1976.

Wilbur, R. *American Sign Language and sign systems.* Baltimore: University Park Press, 1979. (a)

Wilbur, R. Theoretical phonology and child phonology: Argumentation and implications. In D. Goyvaerts (Ed.), *Phonology in the 1970s.* Ghent: Story-Scientai, 1979. (b)

Wilbur, R., & Jones, M. Some aspects of the bilingual/bimodal acquisition of sign language and English by three hearing children of deaf parents. In M. LaGaly, R. Fox, & A. Bruck (Eds.), *Papers from the Tenth Regional Meeting, Chicago Linguistic Society.* Chicago: Chicago Linguistic Society, 1974.

5

Cerebral Asymmetry for Sign Language: Clinical and Experimental Evidence

Howard Poizner
The Salk Institute for Biological Studies

Robbin Battison
Northeastern University

The study of sign languages offers an unusual opportunity for insight into the nature of language processing, because they utilize a sensory modality different from that of spoken languages. The value of such study becomes immediately apparent in the area of the functional organization of the human brain. The literature on cerebral asymmetry of people with normal hearing clearly indicates that the two hemispheres do not subserve the same behavioral functions; instead, the left hemisphere (for right-handers) is specialized for language processes and the right hemisphere primarily for visual-spatial processes. Sign languages display both complex language structures and complex spatial relations; in fact, Poizner and Lane (1978) have found that both the particular way in which American Sign Language (ASL) uses spatial location linguistically and the psychophysical properties of those locations constrained their perception. Because of these dual constraints on its perception, for each of which one hemisphere shows predominant functioning, sign language offers a valuable opportunity for refining our concept of cerebral asymmetry. In addition to illuminating the relative importance of linguistic and visual-spatial properties in determining cerebral asymmetries, research on the lateralization of sign language bears on developmental issues in the organization of the brain and on competing theories of cerebral asymmetry. In order to focus these issues, we first review the literature on cerebral asymmetry in the normally hearing, then the clinical literature on lateralization of sign, and finally examine experimental evidence from studies of cerebral asymmetry in the deaf.

CEREBRAL ASYMMETRIES IN
THE NORMALLY HEARING

Currently, at least five broad lines of evidence converge to suggest that the left hemisphere predominates for spoken language functions and the right hemisphere primarily for visual-spatial functions in normally hearing people who are right-handed. First, brain lesions that produce aphasias (language disorders resulting from brain damage unaccountable by defects of sensory or motor systems) are primarily located in the left cerebral hemisphere (Geschwind, 1970). On the other hand, lesions in comparable portions of the right hemisphere seem to produce subtle visual-spatial deficits and a loss of musical ability (Milner, 1968, 1971). Second, the two halves of the brain differ in their anatomy. Geschwind and Levitsky (1968) found that in 65 of 100 adult brains a portion of the upper surface of the left temporal lobe (the *planum-temporale*—a language-mediating area) was about one-third larger than the corresponding area on the right. Both Wada (cited in Geschwind, 1970), and Witelson and Pallie (1973) have found these differences present in infant brains at birth. Third, chemical anesthesia of the left hemisphere produces a loss of speaking ability while anesthetizing the right hemisphere produces no such effect (Wada & Rasmussen, 1960). Fourth, patients with complete surgical division of their forebrain commissures (split-brain patients) show corresponding differences in the function of the hemispheres (Gazzaniga & Sperry, 1967; Gazzaniga, 1970). Split-brain subjects could *name* a visually or tactually presented object only if the sensory information reached the left hemisphere (each hemisphere receives such input only from the contralateral visual field or hand). The right hemisphere appeared to have no control over speech production mechanisms although it seemed to possess superior capacities in perceiving and manipulating certain kinds of spatial relationships.

Finally, normal (i.e. non–brain-damaged) subjects also generally confirm this pattern of hemispheric asymmetry. Experimental procedures for studying lateralization in normals have typically relied upon two techniques, dichotic listening and visual hemifield presentation, as discussed in the following section. However, tactual (Witelson, 1974), temporal (Murphy & Venables, 1969) and manual discriminations (Kimura, 1973b, 1973c, 1976) have also been studied and electrophysiological recordings taken. The electrophysiological work provides further converging evidence for the lateralization of both receptive and productive language functions in the left cerebral hemisphere (see especially Wood, Goff, & Day, 1971; McAdam & Whitaker, 1971; Buchsbaum & Fedio, 1969). Interestingly also, cerebral asymmetries in auditorily evoked responses to certain speech sounds appear to be present at birth (Molfese, Freeman, & Palermo, 1975).

Subjects show a consistent right-ear advantage under dichotic listening conditions (simultaneous presentation of different auditory stimuli, one to each ear) for words and nonsense syllables (Studdert-Kennedy & Shank-weiler, 1970; Kimura, 1967). However, certain nonspeech sounds (e.g. musical melodies) elicit a left-ear advantage (Kimura, 1964, 1973a). Kimura has attributed the obtained ear advantages to the prepotency of the contralateral auditory pathways over the ipsilateral ones during dichotic stimulation (Milner, Taylor, & Sperry, 1968) in conjunction with cerebral dominance.

The visual modality provides yet another avenue with which to investigate cerebral asymmetries. Evidence from the visual modality both confirms the basic findings reported previously and clarifies the differing functions of each hemisphere. The visual system is so arranged that visual information from one side of a central fixation point is directly transmitted to the contralateral hemisphere, the ipsilateral hemisphere receiving the input only via the corpus callosum. Under tachistoscopic presentations that preclude eye movements, visual stimuli can be directed to either cerebral hemisphere.

The left hemisphere has proven dominant in processing written as well as spoken language. Right visual-field advantages occur for identification of tachistoscopically presented words (Hines, 1976) and mirror-images of words (Isseroff, Carmon, & Nachson, 1974), for judgments of inclusion of words in a conceptual category (Gross, 1972), for identification of digits (Geffen, Bradshaw, & Wallace, 1971), of individual letters (Bryden, 1965, 1966), of letter sequences varying in familiarity and orientation (Bryden, 1970), and for making name matches to letters which can be either physically identical or share the same name (Geffen, Bradshaw, & Nettleton, 1972; Cohen, 1972).

The right hemisphere, on the other hand, has proven superior for processing spatial, nonverbal material. Left visual-field advantages have been found for facial recognition (Rizzolatti, Umilta, & Berlucchi, 1971), stereoscopic depth perception (Durnford & Kimura, 1971) blackened cells of a matrix (Gross, 1972), line orientation (Fontenot & Benton, 1972), enumeration of dots and forms (Kimura, 1966), and for recognizing random geometric shapes of low association value (Hellige & Cox, 1976).

A wealth of data, then, from brain-injured and commissurotomized patients, and from physiological and behavioral studies in various sensory modalities with normals, come together to demonstrate left-hemisphere dominance for verbal material and right-hemisphere dominance for certain visual-spatial and musical material. Interpretations of the functional differences of the hemispheres have taken primarily one of three opposing views. The first school of thought attributes left hemispheric specialization to speech functions, and right hemispheric specialization to nonspeech ones (Liberman, 1974). Left hemispheric specialization is thus due to the specific linguistic mechanisms of spoken language.

A second school attributes left hemispheric specialization more generally to processes requiring analysis of the internal structure of a stimulus, the right hemisphere being predisposed for integrative gestalt-like functions (Bever,

Hurtig, & Handel, 1976; Bryden & Allard, 1976; Nebes, 1974). This group considers general symbolic manipulation processes, of which speech is only a particular instance, to be in the domain of the left hemisphere. Kimura (1976, 1973b, 1973c) has recently proposed yet a third view of cerebral asymmetry. The symbolic language functions of the left hemisphere are considered to be a secondary consequence of specialization of the left hemisphere for skilled motor activities that lend themselves readily to communication. In this view, the control of the speech apparatus is not fundamentally different from control of certain other kinds of skilled motor sequences.

It is reasonable to expect that the study of sign languages can shed substantial light on the issues and competing theories of cerebral dominance that we have surveyed heretofore. Is left-hemisphere dominance specific to spoken language, or does it underlie any symbolic analysis, or does it mediate the integration of skilled motor sequences? The latter two views would seem to predict that manual, like spoken, language processing is left-lateralized; the former does not.

CEREBRAL ASYMMETRIES IN THE DEAF

Clinical Evidence

Although the first case of pathological language impairment in a deaf person was not reported until 1896 by Grasset, the history of inquiry into the subject goes back 18 years earlier, when Hughlings-Jackson proposed that "No doubt, by disease of some part of the brain, the deaf-mute might lose his natural system of signs which are of some speech value to him [1878, p. 312]." One hundred years later, a review of his remarkably tentative statement seems in order. At that time, it is likely that no one would have accepted, as is done now, that sign languages are natural languages in the formal linguistic sense, with quite complex grammatical structures. It was so different, after all: manual rather than spoken, visual rather than aural; iconic rather than arbitrary, and surely simple, because it was clearly used only by uneducated and isolated people (Battison [1978] examines some of these suppositions). Sprinkled throughout the earliest case reports are the authors' thoughts on sign languages: They were "primitive" and "international" (Critchley, 1938), "primitive" and "affective" (Tureen, Smolik, & Tritt, 1951), "a highly developed form of pantomime" (Burr, 1905). All of the earliest cases erroneously refer to deaf people as "deaf mutes" or even "deaf and dumb." Indeed, deafness seems to be regarded as some kind of disease: "She married a deaf-mute and this illness complicated the first pregnancy" (Douglas & Richardson, 1959 [p. 69]). We would like to suggest that these judgments affected every aspect of gathering language samples from these patients: lines of inquiry, methods of interrogation, and the evaluation of results. Without adequate linguistic knowledge of the language their deaf patients used, these case histories become suspect and unreliable.

The evidence on every theoretically interesting point remains scanty. Unfortunately, few of the 11 reported cases of pathological language impairments in signers (9 deaf, 2 hearing) give us reliable information about the language backgrounds and linguistic behaviors of these subjects. Because normative studies on deaf sign language communication have only recently approached the sophistication of analyses of spoken languages, there is a preliminary question to be answered before evaluating the linguistic behavior of deaf aphasics: How can we define an error in signing, and best arrive at a description of the impairment? This issue is more subtle than it seems. One of the reasons it is difficult to make judgements about sign language errors is the tremendous variance noted for sign language behavior. With deaf people, there can be no assumption of a premorbid communicative baseline because of variance introduced by several physical, psychological, and social variables. The etiology of the hearing loss, its severity, and the age of onset will affect primary language acquisition. Residual hearing might or might not be exploited in language development, and early education varies greatly as to what and how deaf children learn. Sign language is not as uniformly introduced, used, or regarded as spoken language. A deaf person may start learning it as an infant from signing parents, or learn it upon first encountering other deaf children in school (which may or may not incorporate signing into instructional situations), or gestural habits might not develop until later in life, even into adulthood. A person might sign or speak, or do both simultaneously, depending on the situation. In addition, the signer might model the sign language on the syntax and morphology of an oral language (e.g. Sign English used in the United States), or might use it in a separate grammatical tradition (e.g. American Sign Language). In an extreme case, a sign system will act as a manual cipher on a spoken language by assigning distinct hand configurations to each letter of the alphabet and literally spelling words and sentences in the air, letter by letter. Disorders of signing systems heavily based on spoken languages are not especially revealing, because the patient's signing may be mediated by knowledge of the spoken language. Clear interpretation of disorders of signing systems due to brain damage is possible only for the congenitally deaf patient who natively learned an autonomous sign language (e.g. American Sign Language), a language typically used by the deaf among themselves. Most of the reported cases of disorders of manual signing, however, have occurred in persons who did not learn an autonomous sign language as a first language and, indeed, who did not clearly even learn such a language fluently. Unfortunately, in the absence of material recorded prior to the brain injury, the investigator is forced to rely on the subjective reports of family and friends in order to reconstruct prior communication habits; there is no evidence that this is a reliable procedure. With these caveats in mind, let us examine the case histories.

Grasset reported in 1896 the case of a right-handed male patient, age 50, who suffered a left hemisphere lesion "due to thrombosis of certain branches of the left sylvian [p. 281]." This patient apparently had no comprehension difficulty and suffered a mild paresis of the right arm; remarkable, however, was his inability to produce fingerspelling or writing with his right hand. His left-handed fingerspelling was unimpaired; signing abilities were not mentioned. Although the report suggests an absence of other practic disturbances, the impairment is surely peripheral not central, since the left hand was completely unimpaired.

The patient reported by Burr (1905) was a 56 year-old woman who had been deafened early in childhood; she suffered a tumor in the left hemisphere, complicated by hemorrhaging and thrombosis, which created a softening that involved "almost the entire white matter of the hemisphere [p. 1107]." Unfortunately the patient's handedness was not reported, but the patient suffered from a general intellectual deterioration, including loss of language functions, making an evaluation of organization of the brain for language impossible.

With the entrance of Critchley's (1938) case on the records, we have a bit more evidence but no resolution of any of the issues. His patient, a 42 year-old right handed male, was postlingually deafened; of his lesion we know only that it was a left-sided cerebral vascular accident (CVA). Critchley tells us that there was no hemianopia and no apraxia; the patient's speech was dysarthric and ungrammatical. His expressive fingerspelling was impaired, while signing was intact. Three things of note here: Signing was not the patient's primary communication medium; the testing was conducted with an interpreter; not a single detail is given on the testing of signs. Interestingly, Critchley contributes to a terminological confusion when he labels the impairment as "dactylological apraxia," having already maintained that there was no apraxia present.

Leischner (1943) presents what seems to be an ideal case: a 64 year-old congenitally deaf man, apparently right-handed, who acquired sign language natively from his deaf parents (and presumably also from his two elder deaf brothers). This patient did not have any instruction in speech until age eight, and thus it is safe to presume that his signing skills were primary, and were not based on speech, as was the case with Critchley's (1938) patient. Testing was complicated by the Czech-German bilingual status of the family, with most of the testing being conducted in Czech Sign Language, which has no fingerspelling adjunct (Hartmut Teuber, personal communication), and written tests of Czech. The patient suffered damage to the left angular and supramarginal gyri and some white matter underneath; some softening was noted in the right hemisphere.

The practic tests administered to the patient showed little or no impairment, although the patient seemed free to choose which hand would respond. Much of the language evaluation depended upon information supplied by the patient's daughter and son, who acted as interpreters for the testing. His habit of reinforcing his signing with morphologically uninflected spoken words was continued after his CVA, with the following difference: Substitution of irrelevant words from the same semantic category as the intended word. He would thus apparently make more sense with his signs, and his words would not match what he was signing. The report additionally seems to indicate that some of his signs were inappropriate substitutions, but correctly executed; there is not a clear distinction made in the text between words and signs. When his signs were impaired, his daughter judged that he seemed to be only indicating the movement of the intended sign, and not executing the full movement required. This was especially true of required finger movements (some signs might require flexion or extension of the digits). Unfortunately, there are no examples or descriptions of his sign formational impairments. The patient showed difficulty in understanding his son and daughter in Czech Sign Language and showed perseverated responses to questions. His ability to produce the numbers, alphabet, and days of the week in sequence was impaired.

Yet another left hemisphere CVA was reported by Tureen, Smolik, and Tritt (1951). This 43-year-old congenitally deaf right-handed male had a left subcortical neoplasm involving the second and third frontal convolution; surgical removal of the posterior portion of the second frontal convolution was performed. The patient's signing and speaking abilities were lost and recovered simultaneously. Fingerspelling was the most impaired communication system. Although the authors claim that there was no apraxia involved, like Critchley (1938), they provide a label for the impairment: apraxia and agnosia for fingerspelling[p. 242]. Of his signing all that is reported is that he was unable to read or produce signs during certain periods of his impairment, even when he was able to read written English. No descriptions of his signing are given, possibly because the interpreter only knew fingerspelling.

Douglas and Richardson (1959) reported on a 21-year-old congenitally deaf, right-handed woman who suffered a post-partum left CVA involving the fronto-parietal regions. She had two older deaf siblings from whom she had learned sign language, although judgments of those who knew her rated her fingerspelling as her superior skill; it is difficult to interpret the statement that her "basic sign language skills, although adequate for most of her needs, were probably somewhat limited in versatility [p. 71]." In any event, signing was apparently more impaired than fingerspelling, displaying sign-finding difficulty, paraphasia, and formational errors; no description is given.

The patient reported by Sarno, Swisher, and Sarno (1969) was a 69-year-old congenitally deaf right-handed male who experienced a cerebral infarct resulting in left front-parietal damage. This man apparently was not taught sign until the age of seven, having been taught written and spoken English until that age. Sarno, Swisher, and Sarno ranked his expressive impairments as worst in speaking, next worst in fingerspelling and writing, and least in signing. Receptively, his reading of print and signs was better than reading fingerspelling or lip movements. They report no limb apraxia. Unfortunately, no sign errors are reported, although "his wife reported he was much less proficient than he had been prior to his stroke [p. 406]."

Two cases involving hearing signers have surfaced recently. Meckler, Mack, and Bennett (1971) discuss a 19-year-old left-handed son of deaf parents who sustained a left-sided traumatic contusion, apparently involving the parietal lobe. The authors note the absence of apraxia in the unaffected left limb; however, the patient was globally aphasic, with apparently greater retention of signing skills over fingerspelling, both being better preserved than speech. Hamanaka and Ohashi (1974) report a 56-year-old right-handed male CVA patient who experienced difficulty in using a syllabically based gestural code for Japanese, used by him and by his deaf wife in her profession as a Geisha; the site of the lesion is not mentioned, nor are there any unequivocal localizing signs.

Battison and Padden (1974) and Battison (1979) discuss a 70-year-old right-handed male who had been deafened at the age of 6. Thrombosis produced an occlusion of the left middle cerebral artery. The subject was first interviewed 2 years after the initial result; speaking, signing, fingerspelling, and writing were all dysfluent, with hesitations, substitutions, formational errors, and perseverations; he showed no oral apraxia. Kimura, Battison, and Lubert (1976) administered a test of manual apraxia, which had been run on a number of hearing patients (Kimura & Archibald, 1974); although the patient was able to imitate static hand postures (handshapes), imitation of meaningless gestures presented some difficulty, his scores falling below those of three deaf controls matched for age and education. Thus some part of his difficulty in producing signs may be related to a more general practic disturbance. This patient had not signed from infancy, and this may be the cause of a reversal of a pattern noted with Leischner's (1943) earlier patient. When communicating in signs and speech simultaneously (a behavior which is unfortunately often elicited automatically in the presence of a hearing investigator), he would produce the correct word and an incorrect sign: for example, correctly saying "communicate" but making the sign DO (DO and the target sign COMMUNICATE use the same handshapes, but different movements, locations, and orientations of the hands: a possible formational confusion); the confusion may be a semantic one, as in correctly saying "hour" but signing YEAR; or an error based on an English phonological representation, correctly saying "principal" but signing PRACTICE. These errors cannot be regarded as conclusive that his signing is more impaired than his speech, but indicative that, in some situations at least, his primary language is English and his signing skills may be built on that (hearing second-language signers frequently make mistakes of the type "principal"/PRACTICE).

His writing is much more impaired than his signing, yielding error patterns typical of hearing agraphia: perseveration, agrammatism, word substitutions based on phonological similarities. His fingerspelling productions resemble his written productions, although fingerspelling alone cannot be regarded as a natural communicative task for this man. One interesting finding was that his right versus left-handed unimanual fingerspelling productions appeared to be dissimilar in quality: right-hand productions appeared to be fluent nonsense, whereas left-hand productions tended to be dysfluent but communicative.

Additional observations on the forms of the signs produced in both free and elicited conversations showed a number of other error patterns in his expressive language: not maintaining the required tension in his muscle actions that would ensure that the sign reached its articulation targets (reminiscent of Leischner's patient); inappropriate substitutions (e.g. ARMY for RUSSIA; NOTICE for READ); some occasional spatial confusions (as when reporting opposing team scores in sports); reversion to a dialect form of a sign that was learned earlier in life, denying knowledge of the more standard form, which he had known and used. Especially crucial for the issue of sign language and lateralization, however, are the following observations: Although fingerspelling alone, like his writing, was severely impaired, when unable to recall a particular sign, he would begin to fingerspell when normal signers would have been expected to provide rather common signs (e.g. ALSO, SPORTS, MAGAZINE). He sometimes would make inappropriate alternations between the right-handed role and the left-handed role in a two-handed sign. Although this might result in a left-hander's version of a sign (which might or might not be appropriate to a situation), on a few occasions it resulted in a sign that had, for example, the spatial orientation of a right-handed version of a sign, but the movement was produced by the left hand, leaving the mildly paretic right arm inert. In short, the two-handed nature of a large part of the sign lexicon creates opportunities for left and right limb confusions and alternations, but also, especially in the case of fingerspelling, allows for independent evaluation of the language productions of the two limbs. Much more work is needed to explore these particular issues.

Battison (1979) also describes the first occurrence of a right hemisphere CVA: a 68-year-old male, prelingually deafened, with atherosclerotic cardiovascular disease suffered an apparent embolism and consequent left hemiparesis. The subject had been left-handed until forced by his schoolteachers to write with his right hand; he continued to use his left hand for other skilled tasks, such as using tools. He had been exposed to signing from at least age 4 (entry into residential school), and perhaps before (through contact with a deaf sister 10 years his senior).

This right hemisphere patient was severely impaired in comprehension and production of signs, fingerspelling, and writing; no history of speech could be established. His history of mixed handedness and aphasic impairment both suggest that his right hemisphere was dominant for language; this is supported by the notable lack of disturbance of affect, facial expression, and paralinguistic gestures, which would normally accompany right hemisphere damage in a right-hander. Tests of both oral and manual praxis could not be evaluated because he was unable to imitate oral or manual gestures without a sustained model; his imitations of signs suffered from this also. Both in sign imitation, and in eliciting the sign names for objects, he would characteristically either try to place and mold his plegic left fist into the correct position (reminiscent of the patient in Sarno et al. 1969), or simply make a one-handed sign as if the other hand were present and in its correct position (this is done by normal signers when one hand is occupied nonlinguistically). He rarely produced spontaneous signing and never produced more than a two-sign string in the limited testing periods available.

Summary of Clinical Studies

How well does the evidence to date on pathological language impairments in deaf signers address the questions proposed in the introduction? Eight of the nine cases were unilateral left CVA's in apparent right-handers. One right CVA caused impairments for a patient with a history of left hand preference. Unfortunately, these cases of pathological disruption of signing do not bear directly on issues of the organization of the brain of the deaf for independent sign systems such as American Sign Language, because the sign systems used by these patients may well have been based in large part on the structure of spoken languages. The fact that damage to the dominant hemisphere of each patient disrupted both sign and spoken language does not imply that these areas of the brain mediate the production or comprehension of sign languages such as ASL; rather, the representation of language in the brain for these patients may have been determined by structures of spoken language. In only one case was the patient congenitally deaf of deaf parents, with the patient learning sign language as a first language (Leischner, 1943), but even this case was not ideal for interpretation.

Furthermore, there is not enough linguistic description of the signing behavior of these patients to make any conclusive comparisons regarding the degree of impairment across communication modalities. Apart from this, the patterns of linguistic errors are similar for signing and speaking aphasics; production is disfluent; there are hesitations, misarticulations, and word- or sign-finding difficulties; language is agrammatic; there are paraphasias and neologisms; subjects sometimes monitor and correct their production, while at other times they seem oblivious to errors; a reversion to earlier learned language forms has been reported; errors of substitution, omission, and perseveration are found; comprehension is affected as well as production. The two cases presented by Battison (1979), however, also suggest that there may be some error patterns in deaf aphasics that would be unique to the gestural mode: having different qualities of impairments on the left and right hands, inappropriately switching from left- to right-handed language production, and showing a lack of coordination of the left and right hands in producing the spatial and movement target patterns. These issues bear further investigation.

Finally, regarding the third hypothesis advanced by Kimura (1973b, 1973c, 1976) that the left hemisphere may be specialized not for symbolic functions per se, but for the ability to form movement sequences, there appears to be supportive evidence from the one patient available for testing so far (Kimura et al., 1976). The signer, in addition to having impairments of signing and fingerspelling, was impaired in his ability to copy meaningless gestures of comparable complexity to moving signs. Whether this finding will be consistently supported by later cases, and whether the hypothesis can be enriched in order to explain more particulars of impairments in signing and speaking aphasia, are open issues.

Future investigations need be careful to clearly separate asymmetries for signed systems based on spoken languages from those that are not. Because the incidence of sign aphasia is low, and the proportion of the deaf population having deaf parents is also low, clinicians are still awaiting the most clearly interpretable sign aphasia cases. The ideal case would involve a congenitally, profoundly deaf monolingual signer, who had deaf parents and who learned an independent sign language as a first and only language. Furthermore, good videotaped records of the linguistic functioning before brain injury would exist, and a fluent, preferably native, signer would conduct all language testing. The patient and his or her family would also have undergone thorough handedness testing. Finally, the brain lesion in this case would be well localized, with the brain later available for detailed examination. Without such cases, interpretation of the clinical data is most difficult.

EXPERIMENTAL EVIDENCE

Investigating the lateralization of sign within the paradigms used for other visual material is complicated by the difficulty of capturing movement in the very brief exposure necessary to (initially) stimulate one hemisphere exclusively. Except for Poizner, Battison, and Lane (1979), investigators have

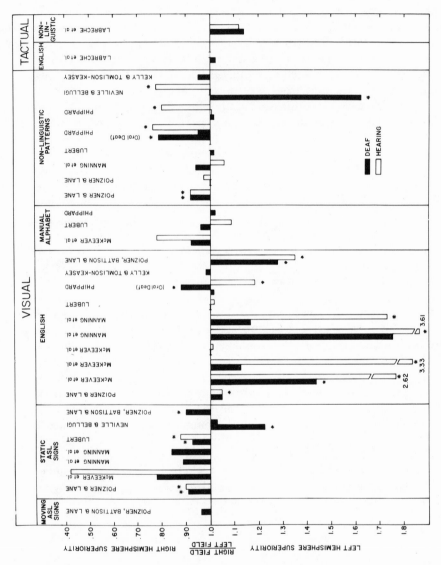

FIG. 5.1.

presented static line drawings or photographs of signs tachistoscopically to visual hemifields. Interpretation of the experimental literature is complicated not only by this factor, but also by methodological difficulties such as a lack of control of the language background of the deaf subjects: clearly native ASL signers are needed for research of this sort.

To date, only a handful of experimental studies exists on the lateralization of function in the deaf. Figure 5.1 summarizes these studies, including data from hearing controls where available, and from multiple experimental conditions within each study. The figure presents right field/left field ratios, taken from accuracy or speed of responding. Ratios of subject performance in the two visual fields help to normalize scores from different studies for differences in accuracy or response speed. Ratios greater than 1.0 reflect left-hemisphere advantages (LHA's) in all cases, ratios less than 1.0 reflect right-hemisphere advantages (RHA's); asterisks indicate statistically significant field differences. Figure 5.1 divides the experimental results by type of task and by stimulus modality. Laterality ratios are displayed for the visual presentation of static ASL signs, for ASL signs with movement, for printed English, for (static) manual alphabet handshapes, and for nonlinguistic visual patterns. Ratios are also displayed for tactually presented nonlinguistic shapes and English letters. The hatched bars represent ratios of deaf subjects and the open bars, ratios of hearing controls. Some general patterns clearly emerge from the figure. First of all, both deaf and hearing subjects tend to show RHA's to signs presented statically. Secondly, both deaf and hearing subjects tend to show LHA's to printed English, with hearing subjects often showing larger asymmetries than the deaf. The figure further shows that manual alphabet handshapes tend to elicit only weak lateral asymmetries whereas the various nonlinguistic visual patterns tend to elicit more right hemisphere involvement.

Let us take a closer look at these studies. Lubert (1975) required deaf and hearing subjects to match four kinds of tachistoscopically presented stimuli to items on a choice board: English letters, photographs of ASL signs, photographs of manual alphabet handshapes, and dot stimuli to be enumerated. Unfortunately, the hearing subjects did not show a LHA to the English letters, complicating interpretation of the responses to the signs. However, both the deaf and the hearing subjects showed significant RHA's to the ASL signs, and showed no lateral differences to the other three tasks.

FIG. 5.1. (Opposite page) Right field/left field ratios of deaf (hatched bars) and of hearing subjects' performance to both linguistic and nonlinguistic stimuli from nine studies. The ratios from Kelly and Tomlinson-Keasey (1977) and from Poizner and Lane (1979) are computed from the inverse of subjects' reaction times; all other ratios are derived from mean accuracy rates. (See text for results from Neville [1977] who used electroencephalographic testing.)

McKeever, Hoemann, Florian, and Van Deventer (1976) evaluated cerebral asymmetries to printed English, to manual alphabet handshapes, and to line drawings of ASL signs with congenitally deaf and hearing subjects who knew sign language. The hearing subjects showed reliable LHA's to two of three tasks employing English material whereas the deaf subjects showed a reliable LHA to one of these three tasks (and no lateral differences on the other two). Both groups, furthermore, showed a tendency for a RHA for the manual alphabet handshapes and for the ASL signs, although recognition scores were almost three times as high for the former, for both groups. The authors then pooled the results for the two manual tasks and found a significant RHA for the hearing subjects but only a trend in that direction for the deaf. The authors conclude that auditory experience appears to be a major determinant of the functional asymmetry of the brain. However, this conclusion does not seem warranted. Because the high recognition scores for the manual alphabet handshapes were pooled with the low recognition scores of the ASL signs, the authors evaluated asymmetries, not for ASL, but for handshapes that are a cipher on the English alphabet. Also, because only linguistic visual stimuli were presented, generalizations regarding asymmetries for general visual-spatial processing in the deaf are difficult to make. Furthermore, deaf and hearing subjects used different response modes, so that their results are not strictly comparable.

Manning, Goble, Markman, and LaBreche (1977) performed two experiments on cerebral asymmetry in the deaf. In the first, they bilaterally presented English words, line drawings of signs, and random geometric shapes to five groups of hearing-impaired subjects, and one group of normally hearing subjects. Three of the five hearing-impaired groups were deaf, with groups varying in age of onset of deafness; the other two groups comprised hard of hearing subjects. The hearing subjects showed a significant LHA for the words, as expected. Although all hearing impaired groups were more accurate to words in the right-visual field, this LHA reached significance only for two of the five groups. The deaf and hard of hearing groups showed no visual field differences to the signs and no group showed visual field differences to the geometric forms. The authors found no reliable effect of age of onset of deafness on lateral asymmetries. In the second experiment, they bilaterally presented English words, photographs of signs, and words plus signs to congenitally deaf subjects. Normally hearing subjects also viewed the English words. The response mode was the same across groups and tasks with subjects matching words or signs to pictures of objects on a choice board. The hearing subjects showed a significant LHA for the words; the deaf subjects showed a significant interation of stimulus type with visual field, tending to be more accurate to words in the right visual field, and tending to be more accurate to signs in the left visual field. Interestingly, in the bilateral words condition, the deaf were almost twice as accurate as the hearing to words in the left visual field, but werê only one and a quarter times as accurate to words in the right visual field. In the combined word-sign condition, the deaf showed a strong tendency toward a LHA for the words and little or no visual field differences to the signs. These results indicate that deaf subjects show smaller asymmetries to English words than do normally hearing subjects, although the deaf also tend to have a LHA for English. The results also indicate a trend toward better right hemisphere processing of statically presented signs by the deaf. Although Manning et al. selected their deaf subjects from schools for the deaf, they make no mention of the language background of their subjects, leaving it unclear how many of their signers learned ASL natively. Unfortunately, they also used some signs that were not bilaterally symmetric about the midline of the body. Assuming a right-handed signer, the hands and arms would be closer to the fixation point in the right visual field than in the left visual field. Because retinal acuity increases the closer the image is to the fovea, subjects should have seen signs in the right visual field more clearly than the signs in the left visual field, yielding a LHA on this basis.

LaBreche, Manning, Goble, and Markman (1977) tested hemispheric asymmetry in the deaf and hearing for the tactual perception of English letters and nonlinguistic shapes. Subjects tactually explored pairs of stimuli simultaneously with both hands. They matched the shapes to choices on a response board, and wrote or fingerspelled responses to letters. Neither deaf nor hearing subjects showed lateral asymmetries to the English letters, whereas both groups showed a tendency towards right hand superiority for shapes. No differences emerged between the deaf and hearing groups.

Phippard (1977) had deaf and hearing adolescents match presented stimuli to response items on a choice board. She ran two groups of deaf subjects; one had received exclusively oral training (training in speaking and lipreading with no use of manual communication), the other had received training in both manual and oral communication. Both groups viewed English letter stimuli and variously oriented lines presented unilaterally to a visual field. In addition, the deaf subjects with manual communication training also viewed manual alphabet handshapes and human faces. Hearing controls viewed the English letters, oriented lines and human faces. As predicted, the hearing subjects yielded reliable LHA's to the English letters and RHA's to the lines and faces. Interestingly, the group of orally trained deaf subjects showed RHA's to both the English letters and the oriented lines. However, the deaf subjects with manual communication training showed no visual field differences to any of the four tasks.

Phippard reasonably suggests that the RHA to the English letters of the orally trained group might be due to visual matching strategies encouraged by the matching response requirements of the task. The fact that the orally trained deaf showed RHA's and the manually trained group showed no asymmetries, however, remains unexplained. These results suggest reduced asymmetries in this manually plus orally trained group of subjects for non-linguistic as well as English stimuli. Unfortunately, no ASL stimuli were presented, so no evaluation was made of lateral asymmetry for sign.

Kelly and Tomlinson-Keasey (1977) asked deaf children in the third, fourth, and fifth grade levels to decide as rapidly as possible whether pairs of words or pairs of pictures were the same or were different. They presented both high and low imagery words and concrete and abstract pictures. The children responded faster to the high imagery words and to both the concrete and abstract pictures when presented in the left visual field on both same and different trials. Responding was slightly faster to the low imagery words presented in the right visual field overall. However, the only statistically significant visual field difference to emerge was a RHA for high imagery words for same trials.

Although the authors conclude that deaf children do not demonstrate the same lateral specialization as do normally hearing people, the design of the experiment precludes such an interpretation. In the first place, subjects used a matching response, and as the authors point out, had the subjects used a verbal response, the results could have been quite different. Even more fundamentally, such an interpretation is unwarranted because hearing controls were not run on the same task. Only if normally hearing children showed a different pattern of visual field differences to the word and picture stimuli, using the same response mode, could asymmetries in the deaf be compared to those in the normally hearing.

Neville (1977) presents the first report of electroencephalographic testing of lateral asymmetry in the deaf. She presented line drawings of common objects unilaterally to a visual field for recognition by deaf and hearing children. Neither group was reliably more accurate to pictures presented in one visual field than in the other. Data for the hearing children, however, did show reliable evoked potential differences suggesting right hemisphere dominance in this task. Overall, the evoked potentials of the deaf showed no lateral asymmetries. Neville then separated her deaf subjects into two groups—those that reported signing at home with their parents, and those who reported communicating with their parents through other means. She found a significant interaction between superior hemisphere and subject group for the evoked potential data: Hearing subjects tended to show right hemisphere superiority, whereas the deaf who reported signing with their parents tended to show left hemisphere superiority (no analysis of a main effect of left hemisphere dominance for these signers was reported). Deaf subjects who reported not signing at home with their parents showed no lateral differences.

Neville and Bellugi (1978) presented congenitally deaf native signers with both unilateral and bilateral line drawings of ASL signs and dot localization tasks; hearing controls were also run on the unilateral dot localization task. The deaf subjects identified the line drawings of signs by making the appropriate sign; subjects pointed to one of 20 dots in a response matrix to indicate the location of a presented dot in the dot localization tasks. The deaf subjects not only showed a significant LHA to the unilateral sign task, but showed an even larger LHA to the unilateral dot localization task; no visual field differences occurred to signs or dots bilaterally presented. The hearing subjects showed the expected RHA to the unilateral dot localization task.

The authors interpret the LHA for both the identification of unilaterally presented (static) signs and for localizing dots in space as perhaps indicating that the left hemisphere of deaf signers functions both for linguistic and certain nonlinguistic visual-spatial processing. They further speculate that the right hemisphere of congenitally-deaf native signers may be specialized for some functions that the left hemisphere of hearing people is dominant for, such as the perception of temporal order.

The studies on sign lateralization reviewed previously used static representations of signs which normally incorporate movement. It is unclear which hemisphere would predominate in any reconstruction process of the movement. The right hemisphere of split-brain patients has been shown to surpass the left in the ability to reconstruct a complete stimulus from fragmentary information. This was so in matching arcs of circles to the complete circle (Nebes, 1971), in matching fragmented geometric forms to their unfragmented condition (Nebes, 1972), and in perceiving forms comprised of dots that were variously spaced (Nebes, 1973). On the other hand, reconstruction of linguistic stimuli might require analytic processing, a purported left hemisphere function. The presentation of signs that do not incorporate movement or of actually moving signs would avoid confounding dominance for ASL with dominance for any reconstruction process. Poizner and Lane (1979) used the former approach. Both congenitally deaf, native ASL signers and normally hearing subjects unfamiliar with sign identified four kinds of stimuli: signed numbers from ASL that incorporate no movement in citation form, handshapes never used in ASL, Arabic digits corresponding to the signed numbers, and random geometric forms. Stimuli were tachistoscopically presented to a visual hemifield and subjects manually responded as rapidly as possible to specified targets; the response mode here was the same across groups and tasks. The hearing subjects showed a LHA to the Arabic digits in this experimental paradigm, as expected. Both the deaf and the hearing subjects showed significant RHA's to the signs and to the non-ASL hands. Neither group had reliable visual field differences to the geometric forms, and the deaf subjects showed a trend towards a LHA for the Arabic digits.

Poizner, Battison, and Lane (1979) explored, for the first time, cerebral asymmetry for actually moving signs. Movement of the hands, arms, and fingers is integral to sign (Klima & Bellugi, 1979; Bellugi, Klima, & Siple, 1975; Grosjean, 1979; Stokoe, Casterline, & Croneberg, 1965) and must be incorporated in any definitive evaluation of lateralization for sign language.

Poizner et al. simulated movement through the sequential presentation of still photographs taken at strategic points of a sign. Stimulus durations (max. 167 msec) were kept under eye movement latency (so that stimuli could initially stimulate one or the other hemisphere exclusively) by exposing each sign for only a few frames of film. Congenitally deaf native signers viewed three types of stimuli presented to one visual hemifield or the other: English words, signs portrayed statically, and signs portrayed with movement. Hearing subjects viewed the English words, and showed the expected LHA in identifying these stimuli. Deaf subjects showed a significant LHA to the words, a significant RHA to the signs presented statically, and no lateral differences to the signs presented with movement (deaf subjects signed responses to both sets of signs).

Poizner et al. (1979) classified the kinds of motions used in the signs they presented with movement and the motions normally incorporated in the signs they presented statically, as being either simple or complex. Simple movements were defined as movements in single, straight lines, whereas complex movements were the other kinds of movement used at the lexical level in ASL. Interestingly, subjects tended to show RHA's to signs incorporating simple movements, irrespective of whether the signs were presented statically or with motion; subjects further tended to show either reduced asymmetry or LHA's to signs with complex movements, providing further evidence for the importance of movement in determining cerebral asymmetry for ASL. The shift from right dominance to a more balanced hemispheric involvement with the change from static to moving signs is consistent with Kimura's position that the left hemisphere predominates in the analysis of skilled motor sequencing. The results also indicate that ASL may be more bilaterally represented than is English.

Conclusions

What then may we conclude from the experimental literature on cerebral asymmetry in the deaf? Although methodological difficulties limit interpretations of several studies, certain points emerge. First of all, the deaf do show cerebral asymmetries. Significant visual field advantages emerged in more than one study for signs presented statically, for printed English, and for certain nonlinguistic forms. Thus, auditory experience does not seem a necessary condition for the development of cerebral specialization, although the deaf showed a smaller asymmetry for printed English than did hearing controls in every study reported. The direction of this asymmetry, however, was the same as in hearing subjects, towards an LHA. Whether this reduced asymmetry for English in the deaf comes from poorer facility with English, lack of auditorily recoding printed English, or from having learned English as a second language, is unclear at this time.

In general, we also observe more right hemisphere than left hemisphere involvement in the perception of ASL signs presented statically although considerable variability exists. Apparently, processing the complex spatial properties of these signs primarily invokes the right hemisphere. Other evidence exists that the spatial processing requirements of a task can override purported analytic requirements (such as naming) in yielding right hemisphere advantages to linguistic material. For example, Japanese has two kinds of nonalphabetic symbols, *kana* and *kanji*, the former phonetic symbols for syllables, the latter nonphonetic symbols for lexical morphemes (Sasanuma, Itoh, Mori, & Kobayashi, 1977). Subjects show a LHA for *kana* words, and a RHA for *kanji* words (Hatta, 1977; Sasanuma et al. 1977) and the expected RHA for a nonlinguistic visual-spatial discrimination (Sasanuma & Kobayashi, 1978).

The McKeever et al. (1976) study of asymmetries in deaf and hearing subjects provides further evidence that the visual-spatial nature of linguistic stimuli can determine cerebral asymmetries. Their hearing subjects, who knew sign, showed a RHA in vocally identifying manual alphabet stimuli, but these same subjects had also shown a LHA in vocally identifying English words in the same experimental paradigm. In this case, the spatial processing required for the manual alphabet handshapes seemed to have overridden both the naming requirements of the task and the verbal response mode to yield the RHA. Similarly, Bryden and Allard (1976) found that hemispheric asymmetries depend on the typeface of the lettering. Print-like lettering yielded the typical LHA, while certain script-like material reliably yielded a RHA, even with subjects vocally identifying single letters. Finally, the blind show a left-hand RHA in the tactual reading of Braille (Hermlin & O'Connor, 1971).

Further research is clearly needed to more definitely specify the nature of cerebral asymmetries in the congenitally deaf during the perception of both linguistic and nonlinguistic stimuli. Some investigators have found similar patterns of cerebral asymmetry in the deaf and hearing (LaBreche et al., 1977; Lubert, 1975; Poizner et al., 1979; Poizner & Lane, 1979), others have found reduced asymmetries in the deaf (Phippard, 1977), whereas still others have found opposite asymmetries in the deaf and hearing (Neville, 1977; Neville & Bellugi, 1978). Only one experiment has dealt with signs that actually move (Poizner, Battison, & Lane, 1979), yielding a different pattern of lateral asymmetry from signs presented statically. Because movement is critical to sign languages and temporal variables now seem critical in determining cerebral asymmetries (Halperin, Nachson, & Carmon, 1973; Kimura, 1976;

Robinson & Solomon, 1974), the effects of various linguistic movements on cerebral asymmetries, in both native signers and in hearing people who do not know sign, needs to be be a focal point of future experimental research.

ACKNOWLEDGMENTS

This work was supported in part by National Institutes of Health Grant No. NS09811 and by National Science Foundation Grant No. BNS78-07225 to The Salk Institute for Biological Studies, and by National Science Foundation Grant No. BNS76-82530 to Northeastern University.

REFERENCES

Battison, R. *Lexical borrowing in American Sign Language.* Silver Spring, Md.: Linstok Press, 1978.

Battison, R. *Linguistic aspects of aphasia in deaf signers.* Unpublished manuscript, Northeastern University, 1979.

Battison, R., & Padden, C. *Sign language aphasia: A case study.* Paper presented at the 49th Annual Meeting of the Linguistics Society of America, December, 1974, New York.

Bellugi, U., Klima, E. S., & Siple, P. Remembering in signs. *Cognition,* 1975, *3,* 93–125.

Bever, T. G., Hurtig, R. R., & Handel, A. B. Analytic processing elicits right ear superiority in monaurally presented speech. *Neuropsychologia,* 1976, *14,* 175–181.

Bryden, M. P. Tachistoscopic recognition, handedness, and cerebral dominance. *Neuropsychologia,* 1965, *3,* 1–8.

Bryden, M. P. Left-right differences in tachistoscopic recognition: Directional scanning or cerebral dominance? *Perceptual and Motor Skills,* 1966, *23,* 1127–1134.

Bryden, M. P. Left-right differences in tachistoscopic recognition as a function of familiarity and pattern orientation. *Journal of Experimental Psychology,* 1970, *84,* 120–122.

Bryden, M. P., & Allard, F. Visual hemifield differences depend on typeface. *Brain and Language,* 1976, *3,* 191–200.

Buchsbaum, M., & Fedio, P. Visual information and evoked responses from the left and right hemispheres. *Electroencephalography and Clinical Neurophysiology,* 1969, *26,* 266–272.

Burr, C. W. Loss of the sign language in a deaf mute from cerebral tumor and softening. *New York Medical Journal,* 1905, *81,* 1106–1108.

Cohen, G. Hemispheric differences in a letter classification task. *Perception and Psychophysics,* 1972, *11,* 139–142.

Critchley, M. Aphasia in a partial deaf mute. *Brain,* 1938, *61,* 163–169.

Douglas, E., & Richardson, J. C. Aphasia in a congenital deaf mute. *Brain,* 1959, *82,* 68–80.

Durnford, M., & Kimura, D. Right hemisphere specialization for depth perception reflected in visual field differences. *Nature,* 1971, *231,* 394–395.

Fontenot, D. J., & Benton, A. L. Perception of direction in the right and left visual fields. *Neuropsychologia,* 1972, *10,* 447–452.

Gazzaniga, M. S. *The bisected brain.* New York: Appelton-Century-Crofts, 1970.

Gazzaniga, M. S., & Sperry, R. W. Language after section of the cerebral commissures. *Brain,* 1967, *90,* 131–148.

Geffen, G., Bradshaw, J. L., & Nettleton, N. C. Hemispheric asymmetry: Verbal and spatial encoding of visual stimuli. *Journal of Experimental Psychology,* 1972, *95,* 25–31.

Geffen, G., Bradshaw, J. L., & Wallace, G. Interhemispheric effects on reaction time to verbal and nonverbal visual stimuli. *Journal of Experimental Psychology,* 1971, *3,* 413–422.

Geschwind, N. The organization of language and the brain. *Science,* 1970, *170,* 940–944.

Geschwind, N., & Levitsky, W. Human brain: Left-right asymmetries in temporal speech region. *Science,* 1968, *161,* 186–187.

Grasset, J. Aphasie de la main droite chez un sourd muet. *Le Progrès Médical,* 1896, *4,* 169.

Grosjean, F. A study of timing in a manual and a spoken language: American Sign Language and English. *Journal of Psycholinguistic Research,* 1979, *8,* 379–405.

Gross, M. M. Hemispheric specialization for processing of visually presented verbal and spatial stimuli. *Perception and Psychophysics,* 1972, *12,* 357–363.

Halperin, Y., Nachson, I., & Carmon, A. Shift of ear superiority in dichotic listening to temporally patterned nonverbal stimuli. *Journal of the Acoustical Society of America,* 1973, *53,* 46–50.

Hamanaka, T., & Ohashi, H. Aphasia in pantomimic sign language. *Studia Phonologica* VIII, 23–35. Institute for Phonetic Sciences, University of Kyoto, 1974.

Hatta, T. Recognition of Japanese kanji in the left and right visual fields. *Neuropsychologia,* 1977, *15,* 685–688.

Hellige, J. B., & Cox, R. J. Effects of concurrent verbal memory on recognition of stimuli from left and right visual fields. *Journal of Experimental Psychology: Human Perception and Performance,* 1976, *2,* 210–221.

Hermlin, B., & O'Connor, N. Functional asymmetry in the reading of braille. *Neuropsychologia,* 1971, *9,* 431–435.

Hines, D. Recognition of verbs, abstract nouns, and concrete nouns from the left and right visual half-fields. *Neuropsychologia,* 1976, *14,* 211–216.

Hughlings-Jackson, J. On affectations of speech from disease of the brain. *Brain,* 1878, *1,* 304–330.

Isseroff, A., Carmon, A., & Nachson, I. Dissociation of hemifield reaction time differences from verbal stimulus directionality. *Journal of Experimental Psychology,* 1974, *103,* 145–149.

Kelly, R. R., & Tomlinson-Keasey, C. Hemispheric laterality of deaf children for processing words and pictures visually presented to the hemifields. *American Annals of the Deaf,* 1977, *122,* 525–533.

Kimura, D. Left-right differences in the perception of melodies. *Quarterly Journal of Experimental Psychology,* 1964, *16,* 355–358.

Kimura, D. Dual function asymmetry of the brain in visual perception. *Neuropsychologia,* 1966, *4,* 275–285.

Kimura, D. Functional asymmetry of the brain in dichotic listening. *Cortex,* 1967, *3,* 163–178.

Kimura, D. The asymmetry of the human brain. *Scientific American,* 1973, *228,* 70–78. (a)

Kimura, D. Manual activity during speaking-I. Right-handers. *Neuropsychologia,* 1973, *11,* 45–50. (b)

Kimura, D. Manual activity during speaking-II. Left-handers. *Neuropsychologia,* 1973, *11,* 51–55. (c)

Kimura, D. The neural basis of language qua gesture. In H. Whitaker & H. A. Whitaker (Eds.), *Studies in neurolinguistics* (Vol. 2). New York: Academic Press, 1976.

Kimura, D., & Archibald, Y. Motor functions of the left hemisphere. *Brain,* 1974, *97,* 337–350.

Kimura, D., Battison, R., & Lubert, B. Impairment of nonlinguistic hand movements in a deaf aphasic. *Brain and Language,* 1976, *3,* 566–571.

Klima, E. S., & Bellugi, U. *The signs of language.* Cambridge: Harvard University Press, 1979.

LaBreche, T. M., Manning, A. A., Goble, W., & Markman, R. Hemispheric specialization for linguistic and nonlinguistic tactual perception in a congenitally deaf population. *Cortex,* 1977, *13,* 184–194.

Leischner, A. Die aphasie der taubstummen. *Archiv für psychiatrie und nervenkrankheiten,* 1943, *115,* 469–548.

Liberman, A. M. The specialization of the language hemisphere. In F. O. Schmitt & F. G. Worden (Eds.), *The neurosciences: Third study program*. Cambridge: MIT Press, 1974, 43–56.

Lubert, B. J. *The relation of brain asymmetry to visual processing of sign language, alphabetic and visuo-spatial material in deaf and hearing subjects*. Unpublished masters thesis, University of Western Ontario, 1975.

Manning, A. A., Goble, W., Markman, R., & LaBreche, T. Lateral cerebral differences in the deaf in response to linguistic and nonlinguistic stimuli. *Brain and Language*, 1977, *4*, 309–321.

McAdam, D. W., & Whitaker, H. A. Language production: Electroencephalographic localization in the normal human brain. *Science*, 1971, *172*, 499–502.

McKeever, W. F., Hoemann, H. W., Florian, V. A., & Van Deventer, A. D. Evidence of minimal cerebral asymmetries for the processing of English words and American Sign Language stimuli in the congenitally deaf. *Neuropsychologia*, 1976, *14*, 413–423.

Meckler, R., Mack, J., & Bennett, R. *Sign language aphasia in a non-deaf mute*. Paper presented at the American Academy of Neurology, 1971.

Milner, B. Visual recognition and recall after right temporal-lobe excision in man. *Neuropsychologia*, 1968, *6*, 191–209.

Milner, B. Interhemispheric differences in the localization of psychological processes in man. *British Medical Bulletin*, 1971, *27*, 272–277.

Milner, B., Taylor, L., & Sperry, R. W. Lateralized suppression of dichotically presented digits after commissural section in man. *Science*, 1968, *161*, 184–185.

Molfese, D. L., Freeman, R. B., & Palermo, D. S. The ontogeny of brain lateralization for speech and nonspeech stimuli. *Brain and Language*, 1975, *2*, 356–368.

Murphy, E. H., & Venables, P. H. Effects of ipsilateral and contralateral shock on ear asymmetry in the detection of two clicks. *Psychonomic Science*, 1969, *17*, 214–215.

Nebes, R. D. Superiority of the minor hemisphere in commissurotomized man for the perception of part-whole relations. *Cortex*, 1971, *7*, 333–347.

Nebes, R. D. Dominance of the minor hemisphere in commissurotomized man in a test of figural unification. *Brain*, 1972, *95*, 633–638.

Nebes, R. D. Perception of dot patterns by the disconnected right and left hemisphere in man. *Neuropsychologia*, 1973, *11*, 285–290.

Nebes, R. D. Hemispheric specialization in commissurotomized man. *Psychological Bulletin*, 1974, *81*, 1–14.

Neville, H. Electroencephalographic testing of cerebral specialization in normal and congenitally deaf children: A preliminary report. *Language Development and Neurological Theory*. New York: Academic Press, Inc., 1977.

Neville, H. J., & Bellugi, U. Patterns of cerebral specialization in congenitally deaf adults: A preliminary report. In P. Siple (Ed.), *Understanding language through sign language research*. New York: Academic Press, 1978.

Phippard, D. Hemifield differences in visual perception in deaf and hearing subjects. *Neuropsychologia*, 1977, *15*, 555–561.

Poizner, H., Battison, R., & Lane, H. L. Cerebral asymmetry for perception of American Sign Language: The effects of moving stimuli. *Brain and Language*, 1979, *7*, 351–362.

Poizner, H., & Lane, H. L. Discrimination of location in American Sign Language. In P. Siple (Ed.), *Understanding language through sign language research*. New York: Academic Press, 1978.

Poizner, H., & Lane, H. L. Cerebral asymmetry in the perception of American Sign Language. *Brain and Language*, 1979, *7*, 210–226.

Rizzolatti, G., Umilta, C., & Berlucchi, G. Opposite superiorities of the right and left cerebral hemispheres in discriminative reaction time to physiognomical and alphabetic material. *Brain*, 1971, *94*, 431–442.

Robinson, G. M., & Solomon, D. J. Rhythm is processed by the speech hemisphere. *Journal of Experimental Psychology*, 1974, *102*, 508–511.

Sarno, J., Swisher, L., & Sarno, M. Aphasia in a congenitally deaf man. *Cortex*, 1969, *5*, 398–414.

Sasanuma, S., Itoh, M., Mori, K., & Kobayashi, Y. Tachistoscopic recognition of *Kana* and *Kanji* words. *Neuropsychologia*, 1977, *15*, 547–553.

Sasanuma, S., & Kobayashi, Y. Tachistoscopic recognition of line orientation. *Neuropsychologia*, 1978, *16*, 239–242.

Stokoe, W. C., Casterline, D. C., & Croneberg, C. G. *A dictionary of American Sign Language*. Washington, D.C.: Gallaudet College Press, 1965. [Reprinted 1976, Linstok Press, Silver Spring, Md.]

Studdert-Kennedy, M., & Shankweiler, D. Hemispheric specialization for speech perception. *Journal of the Acoustical Society of America*, 1970, *48*, 579–595.

Tureen, L., Smolik, E., & Tritt, J. Aphasia in a deaf mute. *Neurology*, 1951, *1*, 237–244.

Wada, J., & Rasmussen, T. Intracarotid injection of sodium amytal for the lateralization of cerebral speech dominance. *Journal of Neurosurgery*, 1960, *17*, 266–282.

Witelson, S. F. Hemispheric specialization for linguistic and nonlinguistic tactual perception using a dichotomous stimulation technique. *Cortex*, 1974, *10*, 3–17.

Witelson, S. F., & Pallie, W. Left hemisphere specialization for language in the newborn. *Brain*, 1973, *96*, 641–646.

Wood, C. C., Goff, W. R., & Day, R. S. Auditory evoked potentials during speech perception. *Science*, 1971, *173*, 1248–1251.

6
Some Sociolinguistic Aspects of French and American Sign Languages

James Woodward
Gallaudet College

THE RELATIONSHIP BETWEEN FRENCH AND AMERICAN SIGN LANGUAGES

The relationship between French Sign Language (FSL) and American Sign Language (ASL) can best be described utilizing the concepts of continuum and creolization.

The Continuum Between French and American Sign Languages

No one denies that French and American Sign Languages are related. Empirical studies also show that FSL and ASL are undergoing similar linguistic changes. Woodward (1976a) found that FSL and ASL cognates are undergoing at least 18 types of similar historical changes. In 92.6% of the cases, French signers used older forms more often than American signers. Woodward and De Santis (1977a, 1977b) demonstrated that both FSL and ASL are undergoing Negative Incorporation (see Regional Variation in ASL Grammar) and two-hand to one-hand shift. French signers had categorical absence of Negative Incorporation with the sign GOOD, whereas American signers had categorical presence of Negative Incorporation for the sign GOOD. French signers utilized more of the older two-handed signs on the face than American signers. In another study by De Santis (1977), French signers used older signs on the elbow more frequently than American signers.

Creolization of French and American Sign Languages.

Although it is possible to see a continuum of historical change in certain processes in French and American Sign Language, one should not jump to the conclusion that FSL and ASL are nearly identical. Glottochronological procedures (cf. Gudschinsky, 1964) show extremely large lexical differences between modern FSL and modern ASL, even though they have been separated for only 160 years. As Hymes (1971) points out, glottochronology has many problems but has been useful in arguing for possible earlier creolization of a language (cf. Hymes, 1971; Frake, 1971; Southworth 1971). Hymes (1971) states, "The glottochronological distinctiveness of pidgins and creoles was first discovered by Hall (1959), who showed that Neo-Melanesian had diverged from its base language, English, at a rate far exceeding that normally found. Whereas glottochronology normally errs in the direction of underestimating the time-depth of divergence between languages, here it greatly overestimates the time-depth [p. 198]."

Signs are comparable to words in oral languages and rates of change of basic signs in a sign language are comparable to what has been found for oral languages (cf. Gudschinsky, 1964). For example, Gejl'man (1957) found a 97.5% rate of cognates (a hypothetical range of 14–130 years at 90% confidence) for 70 pairs of Russian signs in a real 122-year time span. Woodward (1976b) in an analysis of 423 ASL signs from before 1918 showed a 99% rate of cognates and a hypothetical time span of 5–41 years, where the actual time span is at least 58 years. Woodward (1976b) also performed a glottochronological analysis of a 1913 film of Hotchkiss, who as a young boy signed often with Clerc, who brought FSL to the U.S. There was a 99.6% rate of cognates for 251 pairs of signs. This is a hypothetical time separation of 9 years, where the time span is at least 63 years.

However, when we compare modern FSL and modern ASL with an actual separation of around 160 years, we find a totally different picture. Woodward (1976b) found that with 872 modern FSL and modern ASL signs the rate of cognates wss only 57.3%. This would hypothetically date the arrival of FSL in America between 584 A.D. and 802 A.D. with a 90% level of confidence. This is a 1000–1200 year discrepancy. Even limiting the analysis to words chosen from the Swadesh word list, Woodward (1976b) found only a 61% rate of cognates between modern FSL and moder ASL. This would hypothetically date the arrival of FSL in the U.S. between 504 A.D. and 1172 A.D. at a 90% level of confidence.

These great differences may be explained through creolization, because massive changes occurring in the process of creolization can happen much faster than natural internal language change. The presence of fairly substantial amounts of restructurings like metathesis also support the theory of early creolization of FSL upon its arrival in the United States.

THE LANGUAGE SITUATION
IN THE U.S. DEAF COMMUNITY

Contrary to the hearing ethnocentric view of deaf people as isolated pathological individuals, deaf people in industrial and some nonindustrial nations
form thriving communities. In the United States, the deaf community is held
together by such factors as self-identification as a deaf community member
(Markowicz & Woodward, 1978; Padden & Markowicz, 1976) language
(Croneberg, 1965; Meadow, 1972; Woodward & Markowicz, 1975), endogamous marital patterns (Fay, 1898; Ranier, Altshuler, & Kallman, 1963), and
numerous national, regional, and local organizations and social structures
(Meadow, 1972). Not all hearing impaired individuals belong to the deaf
community; in fact, audiometric deafness, the actual degree of hearing loss,
often has very little to do with how a person relates to the deaf community
(Padden & Markowicz, 1976).Attitudinal deafness, self-identification as a
member of the deaf community, and identification by other members as a
member appear to be the most basic factors determining membership in the
deaf community (Padden & Markowicz, 1976).

Research has shown that attitudinal deafness is always paralleled by appropriate language use. The language situation in the U.S. deaf community
can best be described as a bilingual diglossic continuum between American
Sign Language and English. Stokoe (1970b) first pointed out the existence of
diglossia in the deaf community, using Ferguson's (1959) classic paper on
diglossia as a model. Stokoe defined the *H* variety as Manual English and the
L variety as American Sign Language and demonstrated that Manual English
and American Sign Language have the sociolinguistic characteristics that
languages in diglossic situations have.

Signing that approaches English along the continuum serves as H in the
diglossic situation and tends to be used in formal conversations, such as in
church, the classroom, lectures, and with hearing people. Signing that approaches ASL tends to be used in smaller, less formal, more intimate conversations. Publicly, English in often considered superior to ASL, and ASL is
often regarded as ungrammatical or nonexistent. Signers generally feel that
"grammatical" English should be used instead of ASL for teaching. Much
formal grammatical description has been done on English (in its spoken or
written form), but only relatively recently has any research on ASL been
done. Some signers feel that standardization is necessary, but sign language
diglossia appears as stable as other diglossic situations.

There appears to be only one possible point of conflict between diglossia in
the U.S. deaf community and diglossia in hearing communities—how the
languages are acquired. In hearing diglossic situations, *L* is learned first at
home and *H* at school. But only 10% of the deaf population has deaf parents,
so this can't be true for the deaf community. However, if we remember that

the home is the initial locus of enculturation for hearing children and that residential schools have served as the initial locus for enculturation of many deaf children of hearing parents, this seeming problem is overcome. For we can now say that L is generally learned early in the initial locus for enculturation. To the present, many of these deaf children of hearing parents learned ASL from their peer-group deaf children from deaf parents or from older deaf children who had already been enculturated into the deaf community. This acquisition of ASL took place in informal situations. English (signed, spoken, or written) was learned in more formal classroom situations.

More recently, several researchers have added some new dimensions to the discussion of diglossia, namely: (1) an expansion of what language varieties may be considered H; and (2) the notion of a language continuum.

Meadow (1972) and Stokoe (1973) have pointed out that for some signers a formal variety of ASL (including or in addition to Manual English) may serve as H. While it is not known which groups of signers have a variety of ASL functioning in formal situations, we can hypothesize that these people are probably deaf, have deaf parents, and/or learned signs before the age of six (or that their closest associates have these characteristics), since Woodward (1973a, 1973c, 1973d, 1974) has shown that these variables are useful in predicting which people use a language closest to "pure" ASL in informal situations.

It is also possible that for some signers special varieties of Sign English exist for informal conversations. This would probably be true of signers who function primarily near the English end of the continuum.

The Sign-to-English Continuum

The notion of a language continuum in the deaf community has been pointed out by Stokoe (1972), Moores (1972), and Woodward (1972). Varieties of ASL were seen at one end of this continuum (which as Stokoe [1973] points out is probably multidimensional) and varieties of Manual English at the other. Woodward (1973c) also demonstrated that intermediate varieties along this continuum had the linguistic and sociological characteristics of a pidgin language. There is no really good definition of pidgin languages. However, it is generally agreed that pidgin languages are reduced in morphological structure, contain a partial mixture of structure of two to several languages, and contain structure common to none of the languages in the communication situation. Pidgins are not native languages of any of the users. Pidgins are primarily used in restricted social situations for communicative purposes and are not generally used for socially integrative and personally expressive functions. Generally along with this restricted use go negative attitudes toward the pidgin. More recent research has accepted this notion of a continuum with intermediate pidgin varieties.

Battison, Markowicz, and Woodward (1975) and Woodward (1973a, 1973b, 1973c, 1973d, 1974) have shown that variation along this continuum is nondiscrete, but regular, rule-governed, and describable in terms of modified scalogram analysis (Bailey, 1973; Bickerton, 1973) and variable rules (Fasold, 1970; Labov, 1969). This variation also correlates with gross social variables of whether a person is deaf or hearing, has deaf or hearing parents, learned signs before or after the age of six, and attended some or no college (Woodward, 1973a).

Unfortunately, along with this recognition of variation has come a proliferation of names—American Sign Langauge, ASL (Stokoe, 1960), Ameslan (Fant, 1972), Ameslish (Bragg, 1973), Signed English (O'Rourke, cited in Stokoe, 1970a), Siglish (Fant, 1972), [Pidgin] Sign English (Woodward, 1972, 1973c), Manual English (Stokoe, 1970a). This proliferation is unfortunate for two reasons: (1) it confuses people; and (2) it obscures the concept of a continuum and seemingly emphasizes discrete languages.

To simplify things, we might consider the use of the names given to these language varieties in sign language: Sign, Sign-English, (Manual) English. Sign could be used for the varieties of the continuum that are furthest removed from English. This would avoid the lengthy American Sign Language and also the acronym Ameslan, which so many people variously mispronounce and misspell.

Sign-English removes the terms Ameslish, Signed English, Siglish, and Pidgin Sign English, but still shows the intermediate and pidgin-like nature of these varieties. The present use of Ameslish and Siglish is somewhat misleading because it implies discrete dialects or languages. This is in direct opposition to the notion of a continuum. Ameslish and Siglish are really pidgin Sign-English varieties that are closer to and further from the Sign end of the continuum, respectively.

Manual English could be used for those sign varieties that attempt to approach English as closely as possible. Possibly Signed English could be used as the generic term for these varieties, but it might be confused with the "Signed English" (Bornstein, 1973) that was developed in the Gallaudet Preschool Project.

Whatever the final decision on names, it should be remembered that there are only two discrete language poles on the continuum: sign and (a manual representation of) English. Intermediate varieties contain various overlaps, are not discrete, but are describable in terms of current variation theory in linguistics (Woodward 1973a, 1973c, 1973d, 1974). As stated earlier, these intermediate varieties along the American Sign Language-to-English diglossic continuum have certain sociological and linguistic characteristics of pidgin languages (Woodward, 1973c; Woodward & Markowicz, 1975).

For example, Pidgin Sign English demonstrates the reductions (Samarin, 1971) and admixtures (Hymes, 1971) in morphology and phonology that are typical of pidgin languages. Pidgin Sign English retains certain grammatical characteristics of both American Sign Language and English and some of the phonological characteristics of American Sign Language, although the number of redundancies are reduced.

Deaf signers retain more American Sign Language characteristics in their Pidgin Sign English than do hearing signers who retain more English characteristics. However, due to the incapability of the visual channel to directly transmit oral phonological information, there is almost no retention of English phonology in Pidgin Sign English. Thus Hearing Pidgin Sign English production is much more reduced than Deaf Pidgin Sign English production. Hearing signers are often said to sign without expression or to mumble.

Some grammatical characteristics of Pidgin Sign English include some use of American Sign Language Verb Reduplication, the use of a copula plus uninflected verb for progressive aspect, and the use of the American Sign Language completive marker FINISH plus uninflected verb for perfective aspect. Older signers tend to use uninflected copulas, whereas some younger signers have some inflection for copulas. Pidgin Sign English also has variable use of articles and some use of American Sign Language Noun Reduplication to express plurality. There is also some use of American Sign Language Negative Incorporation and Agent-Beneficiary Directionality but also some dependence on English word order for negatives and agent-benefactive relationships.

In Pidgin Sign English phonology, there are more handshapes distinctive at the phonological level than in American Sign Language, due to the influence of English borrowings. However, places and movements are somewhat restricted for deaf signers and greatly restricted for hearing signers. No English suprasegmentals can be retained in Pidgin Sign English because of the incompatibility of the visual and oral channels. Suprasegmentals that are distinctive at the phonological level in American Sign Language are redundant in Pidgin Sign English. Deaf signers because of their American Sign Language base tend to use more of these redundancies than hearing signers who almost always come from an English base.

Charrow (1974) has added a possible new dimension to the study of Pidgin Sign English in her study of written Deaf English. Charrow suggests that Deaf English may be the written analog of Pidgin Sign English, although it is probably closer to Standard English than Pidgin English along the American Sign Language-to-English diglossic continuum. Reductions in number and tense markers as well as variable use of articles and copulas indicate similarities between Deaf English and Pidgin Sign English. Much further work, however, needs to be done before a clear relationship of Pidgin Sign English and Deaf English emerges.

MICROLINGUISTIC STUDIES OF SOCIOLINGUISTIC VARIATION IN AMERICAN SIGN LANGUAGE

In addition to the sociolinguistic variation between ASL and English, empirical studies have shown phonological, grammatical, and lexical variation within ASL due to regional, social, ethnic, and historical factors.

Regional Variation in ASL Phonology

Regional variation occurs in American Sign Language phonology, syntax, and lexicon. One example of regional variation that has been documented for ASL phonology is face-to-hand variation (Woodward, Erting, & Oliver, 1976). Certain signs that are made on the face in the Washington, D.C. area are made on the hands in some regions of the South. Seven signs that were noted to undergo face-to-hand variations were tested and found to be implicationally ordered with a 92.7% rate of acceptability. The signs in order of acceptability for face variants were MOVIE, RABBIT, LEMON, COLOR, SILLY, PEACH, PEANUT. With 45 Southern consultants there was a very high dependency relation between region and linguistic variation. New Orleans signers used more face variants than Atlanta signers who used more hand variants.

Regional Variation in ASL Grammar

American Sign Language has several verbs tht may be negated by a bound, outward-twisting movement of the moving hand(s) from the place where the sign is made. Five verbs that undergo this Negative Incorporation transformation were tested and found to be implicationally ordered with a 97% rate of acceptability. With 144 consultants, it was found (Woodward & De Santis, 1977a) that Northwestern signers (Montana and Washington state) used significantly more Negative Incorporation in their grammars than Northeastern signers (Washington, D.C., New York, and Maryland).

Regional Variation in ASL Lexicon

There are numerous variations in ASL vocabulary according to region. Very common signs such as BIRTHDAY, SHOES, GOAT, HALLOWEEN have a number of very distinct regional variants that are not formationally related.

Social Variation in ASL Phonology

De Santis (1977) researched a type of centralization that is occurring in both ASL and FSL: elbow-to-hand shift. She tested eight American signs that were noted to undergo this variation and found them to be implicationally ordered at a 96.2% rate of scalability.[1] The signs in order of acceptability for elbow variants were DOOR, BEG, WARN, HELP, GUIDE, FLAG, POOR, PUNISH. With 39 American consultants, she found a dependency relationship for sex. Males in America (as in France) tended to use the newer hand form more frequently than females, who tended to use the older elbow form more frequently.

Social Variation in ASL Grammar

Woodward (1973b) found implicational relations in quantitative differences in ASL rule usage for Negative Incorporation, Agent-Beneficiary Directionality, and Verb Reduplication for 141 signers. It was shown that the use of Agent-Beneficiary Directionality in many environments implied the use of Negative Incorporation in many environments, which in turn implied the use of Verb Reduplication in many environments. It was also found that deaf people, people with deaf parents, and people who learned signs before the age of six use more of these ASL rules in many environments, whereas hearing people, people with hearing parents, and people who learned signs after six (i.e. were enculturated into the deaf community later in life) did not approach "pure" ASL as closely.

Social Variation in ASL Lexicon

More highly educated signers will tend to use more borrowings from English in their ASL. These borrowings may be either through fingerspelling of an English word or through an initialized sign, i.e. a native ASL sign that is modified by using a handshape to represent the first grapheme of the English word. For example, some ASL signers use the sign meaning "a limited kind of enclosure" to translate either "box" or "room." Other more educated signers use this sign only to mean BOX, whereas they use the same sign with R handshapes (index and mid-fingers extended and crossed) to mean ROOM. Gradually initialized signs become slightly modified to correspond to phonological constraints in ASL. The sing FAMILY with F (index and thumb contact and rest of fingers extended and spread) is now used by many signers, many of whom may not recognize that it is a borrowing from English. (This

---

[1]Scalability is the percentage of responses that follow an ideal implication. It is calculated by dividing the total number of responses by the number of responses that follow the pattern.

happens in all languages. Very few people are aware that the word "army" was borrowed from oral French into oral English.)

Ethnic Variation in ASL Phonology

One type of ethnic (and historical) variation that occurs in ASL phonology is the change of two-handed signs on the face to one-handed signs. Eight signs that were observed to undergo this variation were tested and found to be ordered implicationally with a 92.3% scalability. With 75 consultants from the South, there was a high dependency relation between ethnic background and linguistic variation. When matched for age, Black Southern signers used more of the older two-handed variants than White signers (Woodward 1976a). The signs in order of acceptability were CAT, CHINESE, COW, DEVIL, HORSE, DONKEY, DEER, FAMOUS.

Ethnic Variation in ASL Grammar

At present, there are no empirical studies of ethnic variation in grammar. The problems in gathering sufficient syntactic data are enormous, because the only researchers doing investigations in ethnic variations have been White and hearing. Black Southern signers attempt to approach White signing in conversation with White signers and also attempt to approach English when in contact with hearing people. The phonology and lexicon of Black Southern signing are less subject to shift than grammar with outsiders.

Ethnic Variation in ASL Vocabulary

Examples of synchronic variation among Black Georgia signers include SHOELACE, TRUCK, HONKY, ZIPPER, and HAY (or WOMEN'S UNDERWEAR). The sign WHITE-PERSON is particularly interesting because it is only used by some Blacks in Louisiana and on the Eastern Shore. This suggests that there may be similarities in certain Black signs in a number of Southern states.

Historical Variation in ASL Phonology

Frishberg (1975) discusses five major processes of phonological variation in ASL: fluidity, centralization, symmetry, morphological preservation, and concentration of lexical information on the hands. Because of space limitations, the discussion is limited to several examples of centralization and fluidity.

Signs tend to be centralized toward a place near the hollow of the throat, apparently for ease in perception. Downward centralization has occurred in DON'T-CARE (forehead to nose), upward centralization in YOUNG (waist to chest), inward centralization in HAPPY (over heart to center of chest). There is a whole continuum of variation from completely unassimilated TOMATO (RED + SLICE FRUIT) to a completely assimilated TOMATO with the same handshape and movement and no trace of the first sign in the original compound (Woodward & Erting, 1975).

Historical Variation in ASL Grammar

Fischer (1975) has discussed some examples of word order changes in ASL. The traditional word order in ASL was subject–object–verb. Because of influence from English, the older order of noun adjective is changing for many signers to adjective noun.

Historical Variation in ASL Lexicon

Meanings of signs change, new signs can be added through creation or through borrowing from English. An example of meaning changes in signs is the Old French sign for BAD, which became the American sign for WORSE. ASL makes a negative incorporation of GOOD to represent the semantic bundle of features for "bad" (cf. Woodward & De Santis, 1977a). MOVIE, which did not exist in Old ASL, was created by deaf people, when movies came into being. [MOVIE has undergone some phonological changes (cf. Woodward, Erting, & Oliver, 1976)]. Borrowing from English can occur in initialized signs as discussed earlier and also through fingerspelling. Battison (1977) demonstrates that certain signs, like SOON, were originally borrowed fingerspelled words that have undergone specific phonological (and sometimes morphological) modifications and conventionalizations. SOON has all but replaced the older sign for SOON (old) in America, although SOON (old) is still used in France.

Overlap of Sociolinguistic Variation

Regional, social, ethnic, and historical variations are often interrelated. For example, Woodward and De Santis (1977a, 1977b) have shown that French signers tend to use older forms more often than American signers. In America, Southerners tend to use older forms more often than Northerners (Woodward, Erting, & Oliver, 1976). In the South, Blacks tend to use older forms more often than Whites of the same age (Woodward & Erting, 1975, Woodward, 1976a).

THE MACROSOCIOLINGUISTIC SITUATION IN
THE FRENCH DEAF COMMUNITY

French deaf people, like American deaf people have formed a community that is held together by self-identification as a deaf community member, language, endogamous marital patterns, and social organizations. One interesting difference is that in social organizations for deaf people in France, hearing people may have high offices and definitely exert more *direct* control than in U.S. organizations for the deaf. Yet, at the same time, many of these hearing people in France cannot or will not sign with deaf people. In contrast, most hearing people in the U.S. who are involved in deaf organizations can and must sign. (We are naturally excluding hearing controlled educational establishments, such as Gallaudet College.)

The language situation in the French deaf community, as in the U.S. deaf community, is a bilingual diglossic continuum (between French Sign Language and Manual French). The *H* varieties (Manual French) approach French word order more closely and use a larger amount of fingerspelling and borrowed initialized signs than do the *L* varieties (FSL). In initial collections of data, varieties approaching Manual French were generally signed to me, even though I had tried to explain that I was only interested in conversational FSL used among deaf people. It seems that Manual French tends to be used in formal situations, especially with hearing people who sign.

While no in-depth studies of grammatical variation between FSL and Manual French have been completed, there appear to be systematic variations between the two poles. One example of this variation can be seen from various observed translations of the sentence, "You give me" as follows:

1. GIVE	2. YOU ME GIVE	3. YOU	ME	GIVE
inward	inward	initial-		outward
direction	direction	ized V		direction
"pure"	intermediate	"pure"		
FSL	variety	Manual French		

The agent beneficiary relationship is expressed through directionality in "pure" FSL and by word order in "pure" Manual French. The intermediate variety makes use of both directionality and word order. Note also that the Manual French variety used an initialized *V* with the sign for you (*vous*), whereas the other varieties did not.

We might also expect other intermediate varieties. For example, between 1 and 2, we might find:

YOU   GIVE   ME.
       inward
       direction

and between 2 and 3, we might find:

YOU   ME   GIVE.
             outward
             direction

From the previous example, it also seems reasonable to hypothesize that intermediate varieties along the FSL continuum may have pidgin-like characteristics. In addition to the just-mentioned admixtures, there is a great reduction of nonmanual expression in varieties approaching Manual French as compared with varieties approaching FSL.

One major difference between signing in the French deaf community and in the American deaf community is that, as late as 1976, FSL had not been subjected to the influence of *modern* artificially created systems designed to represent the oral language. This is in contrast to ASL, which has received heavy pressure from artificially created systems of signing designed to represent English (see Bornstein, 1973). Thus, the FSL continuum may exhibit certain characteristics that have no parallel in the ASL continuum or vice-versa.

MICROLINGUISTIC STUDIES OF
SOCIOLINGUISTIC VARIATION IN
FRENCH SIGN LANGUAGE

Empirical studies of variation in FSL have only discussed variations in FSL phonology. In all probability, it will also be possible to find systematic sociolinguistic variation in grammar and lexicon.

Regional Variation in FSL Phonology

One type of regional (and historical) variation that occurs in FSL (and ASL) phonology is the change of two-handed signs on the face to one-handed signs (Woodwood & De Santis, 1977b). Nine signs that were observed to undergo this variation were tested and found to be ordered implicationally: Two-handed MOUSTACHE implies two-handed CAT implies CHINESE implies GLASSES implies COW implies RABBIT implies DONKEY implies HORN implies DEER. With 60 consultants from Paris, Toulouse, Albi, and Marseille, there was a high dependency relation between region and linguistic variation. Signers from Toulouse used fewer of the older two-handed signs than signers from other cities.

Social Variation in FSL Phonology

De Santis (1977) and Woodward and De Santis (1977a) have documented dependency relationships between phonological variation in FSL and sex. De Santis (1977) discusses a type of centralization that is occurring in both ASL and FSL: elbow-to-hand-shift. She tested four French signs (and eight American signs) observed to undergo this variation and found them to be implicationally ordered at 99.2% rate of scalability. The use of an elbow tab with DOOR implied the use of an elbow tab with FLAG, which implied elbow HELP, which implied elbow POOR. With 60 consultants, it was found that males tended to use the newer hand form more frequently than females, who tended to use the older elbow form more frequently.

Woodward and De Santis (1977a) studied Negative Incorporation in both French and American Sign Languages and came to the conclusion that Negative Incorporation could be described as a phonological process of assimilation in FSL as compared to a grammatical process in ASL. Woodward and De Santis found that Negative Incorporation did not occur with GOOD in FSL, but otherwise the ordering was the same: HAVE implies LIKE implies WANT implies KNOW. With 60 French signers, it was found that female signers use more Negative Incorporation than male signers. Females are thus using newer forms more than males for Negative Incorporation. Because Negative Incorporation in FSL is still a type of assimilation for French signers, it is a type of language change. Unassimilated forms are older and assimilated are newer.

But now we have an interesting situation. In one study, females use the older form (De Santis, 1977); in another, males use the older form (Woodward & De Santis 1977a). De Santis (1977) believes like Labov (1972) the important issue is not that women or men are leading linguistic change, but that sex differentiation can play an important part in language change.

Historical Variation in FSL Phonology

One example of historical variation that has been documented for FSL (and ASL) phonology is the change of two-handed signs on the face to one-handed signs (Woodward & De Santis 1977b). Nine signs that were noted to undergo two-handed to one-handed variation were tested and found to be implicationally ordered with a 94.4% rate of scalability. The signs in order of acceptability for two-handed variants were MOUSTACHE, CAT, CHINESE, GLASSES, COW, RABBIT, DONKEY, HORN, DEER. With 60 consultants, there was a dependency relation for age. French signers above the age of

47 all categorically used two-handed signs. Younger French signers also tended to use many two-handed variants, however, a significant number of signers also used newer, one-handed variants. This slight age differentiation shows that even though there is a signficant difference based on age, the two-to-one change in hands is only incipient for French signers; it is well on the way for American signers.

SUMMARY

Drawing on comparative data from American Sign Language and empirical studies of French Sign Language, this paper has discussed some of the sociolinguistic aspects of French Sign Language. The language situation in the French deaf community is a bilingual diglossic continuum between French Sign Language and Manual French. The *H* varieties (Manual French) approach French word order more closely and use a larger amount of fingerspelling and borrowed initialized signs than do the *L* varieties (FSL). It also seems reasonable to hypothesize that intermediate varieties along the FSL continuum may have pidgin-like admixtures and reductions.

Empirical microlinguistic studies of variation in FSL have shown systematic regional, social, and historical variations in FSL phonology. Signers from Toulouse use fewer two-handed facial signs than signers from Paris, Albi, and Marseille (Woodward & De Santis, 1977b). Males use newer hand forms more frequently than females, who tend to use older elbow forms more frequently (De Santis, 1977). On the other hand, female signers use more Negative Incorporation than male signers (Woodward & De Santis, 1977a). Although the shift of two-to-one handed signs on the face is only incipient for French signers, there is still a significant dependency relationship of linguistic variation and age. French signers above the age of 47 all categorically used two-handed variants. Younger French signers also tended to use many two-handed variants, however, a significant number of signers also used newer, one-handed variants.

The sociolinguistics of sign language is an interesting new field of inquiry for researchers interested in the nature of language. Research can presently be continued and expanded by cooperation between present hearing linguists and deaf linguistic consultants. However, to achieve the best results, native deaf signers must also be trained as linguists.

ACKNOWLEDGMENTS

Research on which this paper is based was supported in part by NEH Research Grant RO-21418-75-196 from the National Endowment for the Humanities, Research Grants GS-31349 and SOC-74-14724 from the National Science Foundation, and Research Grant NS-10302-01 from the National Institute of Mental Health.

REFERENCES

Bailey, C. *Variation and linguistic theory.* Washington, D.C.: Center for Applied Linguistics, 1973.

Battison, R. *Lexical borrowing in American Sign Language: Phonological and nonphological restructuring.* Doctoral dissertation, University of California, San Diego, 1977.

Battison, R., Markowicz, H., & Woodward, J. A good rule of thumb: Variable phonology in American Sign Language. In R. Shuy & R. Fasold (Eds.), *Analyzing variation in language.* Washington, D.C.: Georgetown University Press, 1975.

Bickerton, D. The structure of polypectal grammars. *Georgetown University, Monographs in Language and Linguistics,* 1973, *25,* 17–42.

Bornstein, H. A description of some current sign systems designed to represent English. *American Annals of the Deaf,* 1973, *118,* 454–463.

Bragg, B. Ameslish: Our national heritage. *American Annals of the Deaf,* 1973, *118,* 672–678.

Charrow, V. *Deaf English: An investigation of the written English competence of deaf adolescents.* Doctoral dissertation, Stanford University, 1974.

Croneberg, C. The linguistic community. In W. Stokoe, D. Casterline, & C. Croneberg (Eds.), *A Dictionary of American Sign Language.* Washington, D.C.: Gallaudet College Press, 1965.

De Santis, S. *Elbow to hand shift in French and American Sign Languages.* Paper presented at the annual NWAVE conference, Georgetown University, Washington, D.C., 1977.

Fant, L. *Ameslan.* Silver Spring, Md.: National Association of the Deaf, 1972.

Fasold, R. Two models of socially significant linguistic variation. *Language,* 1970, *46,* 551–563.

Fay, A. *Marriages of the deaf in America.* Washington, D.C.: Volta Bureau, 1898.

Ferguson, C. Diglossia. *Word,* 1959, *15,* 325–340.

Fischer, S. Influences on word order change in American Sign Language. In C. Li (Ed.), *Word order and word order change.* Austin: University of Texas Press, 1975.

Frake, C. Lexical origins and semantic structure in Philippine Creole Spanish. In D. Hymes (Ed.), *Pidginization and creolization of languages.* Cambridge: Cambridge University Press, 1971.

Frishberg, N. Arbitrariness and iconicity: Historical Change in American Sign Language. *Language,* 1975, *51,* 696–719.

Gejl'man, I. *The manual alaphabet and the signs of the deaf and dumb.* Moscow: Vseojuznoe Kooperativnoe Izdatel'stvo, 1957.

Gudschinsky, S. The ABC's of lexicostatistics (glottochronology). In D. Hymes (Ed.), *Language in culture and society.* New York: Harper and Row, 1964.

Hall, R. Neo-melanesian and glottochronology. *International Journal of American Linguistics,* 1959, *25,* 265–267.

Hymes, D. *Pidginization and creolizaiton of languages.* Cambridge: Cambridge University Press, 1971.

Labov, W. Contraction, deletion, and inherent variability of the English copula. *Language,* 1969, *45,* 715–762.

Labov, W. *Sociolinguistic patterns.* Philadelphia: University of Pennsylvania Press, 1972.

Markowicz, H., Woodward, J., Language and the maintenance of ethnic boundaries in the deaf community. *Communication and Cognition,* 1978, *11,* 29–38.

Meadow, K. Sociolinguistics, Sign language and the deaf subculture. In T. O'Rourke (Ed.), *Psycholinguistics and total communication: The state of the art.* Silver Spring, Md.: American Annals of the Deaf, 1972.

Moores, D. Communication: Some unanswered questions and some unquestioned answers. In T. O'Rourke (Ed.), *Psycholinguistics and total communication: The state of the art.* Silver Spring, Md.: American Annals of the Deaf, 1972.

Padden, C., & Markowicz, H. Crossing cultural boundaries into the deaf community. In F. Crammattee & A. Crammattee (Eds.), *VII World Congress of the World Federation of the Deaf.* Silver Spring Md.: National Association of the Deaf, 1976.

Ranier, J., Altshuler, D., & Kallman, F. *Family and mental health in a deaf population.* New York: State Psychiatric Institute, Columbia University, 1963.

Samarin, W. Salient and substantive pidginization. In D. Hymes (Ed.), *Pidginization and creolization of languages.* Cambridge: Cambridge University Press, 1971. Pp. 117–140.

Southworth, F. Detecting prior creolization: An analysis of the historical origins of Maratti. In D. Hymes (Ed.), *Pidginization and creolization of languages.* Cambridge: Cambridge University Press, 1971.

Stokoe, W. *Sign language structure: An outline of the visual communication system of the American deaf.* Buffalo: University of Buffalo, Occasional Paper 8, 1960.

Stokoe, W. *The study of sign language.* Arlington, Va.: Center for Applied Linguistics, 1970. (a)

Stokoe, W. Sign language diglossia. *Studies in Linguistics,* 1970, *21,* 21–41. (b)

Stokoe, W. *Semiotics and human sign languages.* The Hague: Mouton, 1972.

Stokoe, W. *Sign Language syntax and human language capacity.* Summer Institute in Linguistics, Ann Arbor, Mich., 1973.

Woodward, J. Implications for sociolinguistics. Research among the deaf. *Sign Language Studies,* 1972, *1,* 1–7.

Woodward, J. *Implicational lects on the deaf diglossic continuum.* Doctoral dissertation, Georgetown University, 1973. (a)

Woodward, J. Interrule implication in American Sign Language. *Sign Language Studies,* 1973, *3,* 47–56 (b)

Woodward, J. Some characteristics of Pidgin Sign English. *Sign Language Studies.* 1973, *3,* 39–46. (c)

Woodward, J. Some observations on sociolinguistic variation and American Sign Language. *Kansas Journal of Sociology,* 1973, *9,* 191–200. (d)

Woodward, J. A report on Montana-Washington implicational research. *Sign Language Studies,* 1974, *4,* 77–101.

Woodward, J. Black Southern signing. *Language in Society,* 1976, *5,* 211–218. (a)

Woodward, J. Signs of Change: Historical variation in American Sign Language. *Sign Language Studies,* 1976, *10,* 81–94. (b)

Woodward, J., & De Santis, S. Negative incorporation in French and American Sign Languages. *Language in Society,* 1977, *6,* 379–388. (a)

Woodward, J., & De Santis, S. Two to one it happens: Dynamic phonology in two sign languages. *Sign Language Studies,* 1977, *17,* 329–346. (b)

Woodward, J., & Erting, C. Synchronic variation and historical change in American Sign Language. *Language Sciences,* 1975, *37,* 9–12.

Woodward, J., Erting, C., & Oliver, S. Facing and handling variation in American Sign Language phonology. *Sign Language Studies,* 1976, *10,* 43–52.

Woodward, J., & Markowicz, H. *Some handy new ideas on pidgins and creoles: Pidgin sign languages.* International Conference on Pidgins and Creole Languages, Honolulu, January, 1975.

7

A Chronology of the Oppression of Sign Language in France and the United States

Harlan Lane
Northeastern University

> *What experience and history teach is this—that people and governments never have learned anything from history, or acted on principles deduced from it.*
>
> —G. W. F. Hegel

DIALECTIZATION

Speakers of a dominant language have two ways of attempting to annihilate a nondominant language: replacing it outright or dialectizing it. In the latter case, they lead the users of the nondominant language to believe that theirs is a substandard dialect of the dominant language, a "vernacular" that should not be employed for serious purposes such as education and government. It has generally been thought that the nondominant language could be dialectized only if it was related to the dominant language. Kloss (1967) contrasts the cases of Basque and Catalan:

> So the Spanish government, in trying to establish and maintain the monopoly of Castilian Spanish must [and does] try to blot out the Basque language completely, for there is no possibility that the Basques will ever lose consciousness of the fact that their language is unrelated to Spanish. The position of Catalan is quite different, because both Catalan and Spanish are Romance Languages. There is a chance that speakers of Catalan can be induced to consider their mother

tongue as a patois, with Castilian as its natural standard language. As a matter of fact this attitude to Catalan is already to be found not in Catalonia proper but in the province of Valencia and in the Balearic islands. In a similar manner, nearly all speakers of Low Saxon (Low German) and the overwhelming majority of Occitan (Provençal) speakers have lost consciousness of their linguistic identity and consider their folk speech as naturally subordinated to German and French respectively, though linguists continue to group these folk languages with other Gothic and Romance Languages. The spiritual subjugation of speakers of Sardinian, and of Haitan Creole is no less complete [p. 46].

At first it might seem improbable that people whose native language is American Sign Language (ASL) could be induced to consider their mother tongue as a patois with the majority oral language, English, as their natural standard language: The two are as unrelated as any two languages could be, as the rest of this book testifies. The same may be said of French Sign Language (FSL) and French. Nevertheless, the oral majority in each nation has, from time to time, waged such a campaign of dialectization, using educational institutions for deaf children as the vehicle for indoctrination. To achieve this goal, despite the disparity between the standard language and that to be dialectized, it was necessary to bring French and FSL (and later, English and ASL) into alignment so that the gap between them was more like that between Castilian and Catalan than between Castilian and Basque. For this purpose Signed French was invented in the 1700s and Signed English in the 1800s.

My purpose in reviewing the history of the oppression of FSL and ASL is not to impugn the motives of the proponents of dialectization or of outright replacement. Undoubtedly their overriding conscious concern was (and is) the welfare of the deaf. Even the few among them who credit the deaf with their own language believe, like the opponents of bilingual education for other linguistic minorities, that the welfare of the deaf is best served when they are assimilated in the majority and hence abandon their linguistic traditions. My purpose here is, instead, to show that "language in another mode" obeys

Progress of Dialectization

Wax		Wane
Epée's *Institution des sourds et*	1774	
muets	1779	Desloges' *Observations d'un sourd et muet*
Sicard's *Cours d'instruction*	1801	
Gallaudet and Clerc open	1817	
American Asylum		
	1821	Bébian's reform in Paris
	1830	Reforms in New York and Hartford

the same behavioral laws as spoken language in the domain of language policy, just as it does in the domains of, for example, linguistics and psycholinguistics. Thus, in the former domain, as in the latter, the study of sign language can aid us in formulating general behavioral laws.

The first attempt of an oral majority to dialectize the sign language of a minority within its borders occurred in France in the middle of the 18th century.

Epée

1774. Wax. Epée was nearly 60 when he took up the calling for which he would be recognized as the founder of education of the deaf as a field of instruction, not merely an occasional philanthropic activity or teaching experiment. After a religious career that was stopped at the deaconhood and continually hampered by disputes with the church hierarchy, and after a brief period of legal study and practice, Epée was led by chance, as he tells the story, into a household with two deaf-mute sisters.

On the one hand, Epée was impressed by the medium of communication that had grown up between two deaf sisters he was asked to instruct and he undertook to learn from them. He offered them bread and obtained the sign for *eat;* water, and obtained that for *drink;* pointing to objects nearby he learned the names they applied to each. Soon, he could hold a conversation with them. On the other hand, Epée's goal was to teach his pupils to read and write French. To accomplish this, Epée invented "methodical signs," which were designed to introduce the method or structure of French grammar into manual communication. We can term the result "Signed French." "We chose first," he explains, "the signs of the three persons singular and plural because that is easiest. Then we go on to the tenses and moods and we give to each of them signs that connoisseurs find simple and natural, hence easy to remember (1776, Part 2 [p. 35])." The connoisseurs, significantly, are his deaf pupils, as his description of how he chose tense-markers makes clear:

The pupil, though Deaf and Dumb, had like us, an idea of the past, the present, and the future, before he was placed under our tuition, and was at no loss for signs to manifest the difference.

Did he mean to express a present action? He made a sign prompted by nature, which we all make in the same case without being conscious of it, and which consists in appealing to the eyes of the spectators to witness the presence of our operation; but if the action did not take place in his sight, he laid his two hands flat upon the table, bearing upon it gently, as we are all apt to do on similar occasions: and these are the signs he learns again in our lessons, by which to indicate the present of a verb.

Did he design to signify that an action is past? He tossed his hand carelessly two or three times over his shoulder: these signs we adopt to characterize the past tenses of a verb.

And lastly, when it was his intent to announce a future action, he projected his
right hand: here again is a sign we give to him to represent the future of a verb
(Epée, 1784, translated 1860 [p. 22]).

In addition, Epée required signs for the affixes of French, for its articles,
prepositions, conjunctions, in striving to make signing into a dialect of
French. Thus *aimable* (lovable) is signed in the following way: "I make the
radical sign [for love], then the sign for an adjective, but of one terminating in
able formed from a verb: To this I must subjoin the sign for possible or
necessary (Epée, 1784, translated 1860 [p. 40])." The sign for masculine
gender (to represent the French article *un*) was the same as that for a man's
hat; the feminine (*une*) was represented by the sign for a lady's bonnet. Thus,
one observer reports, a bench (*un banc*) and a table (*une table*) came out
rather originally bedecked.

Epée also found he needed signs for various root morphemes in French. In
this case he used one of two strategies: If the meaning of the word immediately
suggested a sign to his pupils, he seized upon it. If it did not, then he analyzed
the word as a combination of simpler concepts each of which was associated
with a sign. Thus, for example, the word "believe" was analyzed as the sum of
"know" plus "feel" plus "say" plus "not see" and it was signed by executing the
corresponding four signs and that for "verb"—all, as the good abbot puts it,
"in the twinkling of an eye." Once his deaf pupils learned the written word that
corresponded to each sign, they had no difficulty in signing a written text or in
transcribing such signs into writing. Indeed, it was a matter of little importance what the written language was—Italian, Latin, Spanish, French (as long
as it was a Romance language)—since it was not a question of translating but
merely of transliterating. This was too fine a distinction to make out at the
dawn of the education of the deaf, and Epée's annual demonstrations drew
hordes of laymen, scholars, and royalty alike; the last, in 1774, was attended
by 800 people in two sittings, including a score of disciples who mastered the
Signed French and returned to their cities scattered over Western Europe—
from Copenhagen to Rome, from Amsterdam to Zurich—to found similar
schools. They took with them Epée's description of these public exercises,
Institution des Sourds et Muets; the first of many editions appeared in 1774.

Epée's school grew to 68 pupils by 1783 (Peet, 1857 [p. 295]) and when, on
his death in 1789, it was declared a National Institution for Deaf-Mutes, it
numbered over 100. With the founding of a veritable deaf enclave in the midst
of Paris, and the arrival of deaf pupils from throughout France, FSL may well
have grown by accretion. Epée's successor, the Abbé Sicard promises us a
dictionary but notes that the particular signs are not critical to his method of
instruction and, in any case, were not invented by him.

It is not I who am to invent these signs. I have only to set forth the theory of them
under the dictation of their true inventors, those whose language consists of

these signs. It is for the deaf-and-dumb to make them, and for me to tell how they are made. They must be drawn from the nature of the objects they are to represent. It is only the signs given by the mute himself to express the actions which he witnesses, and the objects which are brought before him, which can replace articulate language (Sicard, 1803 [p. xiv]).

Speaking of his celebrated deaf-and-dumb pupil, Massieu, Sicard says:

Thus, by a happy exchange, as I taught him the written signs of our language, Massieu taught me the mimic signs of his.... So it must be said that it is neither I nor my admirable master [the Abbé de l'Epée] who is the inventor of the deaf-and-dumb language. And as a foreigner is not fit to teach a Frenchman French, so the speaking man has no business to meddle with the invention of signs, giving them abstract values (Sicard, 1803 [pp. 18–19]).

Desloges

1779. Wane. Pierre Desloges, deafened by smallpox at the age of seven, wrote his *Observations* to defend Epée's position in his dispute with the Abbé Deschamps on manual versus oral instruction of the deaf. This may be the first book ever published by a deaf person, according to the publisher's preface. Desloges also wished to dispel misconceptions about the limitations of the deaf and how they communicate by a language of signs: "Like a Frenchman who sees his language attacked by a German who knows a few words of French at the most, I felt obliged to defend my own language against the false imputations [of Deschamps] (Desloges, 1779 [p. 3]). Desloges was 32 years old, a bookbinder by profession, when his work was published. He did not know Epée until then and had never studied with him.

At the start of my illness, since I had not lived with deaf-mutes, I had no other way to make myself understood than writing or my poor pronunciation. For a long time I was unaware of sign language. I only used scattered signs, isolated, without an orderly sequence and without linkages. I was quite unacquainted with the skill of combining them to sketch clearly defined scenes whereby we can represent our various ideas, communicate them to our deaf companions, and converse with them in an orderly and extended discussion. The first person who taught me this very useful skill was a deaf-mute from birth, of Italian nationality, who knew neither how to read nor write; he was a servant in the home of one of the actors in the *Comédie Italienne* (Desloges, 1779 [p. 13]).

Desloges describes later in his book how the idiosyncratic signs of the isolated deaf (in asylums or in the country) are reformed when he comes to Paris.

He meets other deaf mutes more educated than he and he learns how to combine and polish his signs which were formerly without order and without liaison. He

rapidly acquires through interaction with his comrades the skill that is sup-
posedly so difficult of painting and expressing all his thoughts, even those that
are the most independent of the senses, with as much order and precision as if he
knew the rules of the grammar. . . . there are deaf-mutes from birth, workers in
Paris, who know neither reading nor writing, and who never went to the lessons
of the Abbé de l'Epée but who were so well instructed in religion, solely through
the medium of sign, that they were judged worthy of the sacraments of the
church, even of the Eucharist and of marriage. There is no event in Paris, in
France, and in the four corners of the world that is not a topic of our conversations. We express ourselves on all topics with as much orderliness, precision and
speed as if we enjoyed the faculties of speech and hearing. (Desloges, 1779 [pp.
14–15]).

I have quoted at length from Desloges because his comments confirm that
there was in Paris, prior to Epée, a structured sign language of wide communication. It even seems probable that the two deaf sisters with whom Epée
began his efforts spoke that language and more probable yet that it was
current among the poor deaf children who formed the rapidly growing
nucleus of Epée's school. Because it appears that Epée coined signs primarily
for French function words, it is likely that some of the basic vocabulary in his
Signed French came from the prior FSL. In discussing compound signs,
Desloges mentions that "M. l'Abbé de l'Epée explains very well (*Institution
des Sourds et Muets,* p. 144) the signs necessary to render the idea of
degenerate: they are the same that my comrades employ (Desloges, 1779 [p.
57])."

Sicard

1801. Wax. The Abbé Sicard, who had come from Bordeaux to learn
Epée's methods and who had returned there in 1786 to direct a school for the
deaf, was selected as Epée's successor by a competitive examination in which
each candidate was represented by one of his deaf pupils. The Abbe's most
able pupil, Jean Massieu, was judged easily the best, so Sicard was appointed
to head the new National Institution for Deaf-Mutes at Paris. In his 1801
book, an account of how he trained Massieu, Sicard points out the limitations
of Epée's method.

I have always believed that every language has two essential parts that make up
the whole and render it suitable for representing thought: the nomenclature of
words which comprise the dictionary; and the relative value of words which
constitutes the sentence and the syntax of the language. The first can exist
totally without the second; but a language which had only the first would have
only isolated images, without linkages and without orderly development. Each
word would, in fact, depict an object but we would lack this second kind of word
in whose absence those we write, one after the other, would be deprived of that

nuance which gives them life, making of all these words one complete sentence. The language of the Mute ought to have both of these capabilities. It would be to stop in midstream to be satisfied with only the first or not to try to perfect the second. The famous inventor found in the different combinations of signs the equivalent of all ideas. Thus, all the words of the French language had their counterparts in that of the Mute.... Once the nomenclature was learned, the Deaf-Mutes need not have had any difficulty in writing words for signs and in making signs for words.... But did they understand the sense of what they were writing any more than a schoolboy would understand the sense of a passage from Tacitus given the bare and isolated meaning of each word? The Deaf-Mutes should have been taught the context provided by the French sentence, the particular syntactic role of each word, and above all that of the verb, without which there is no sentence because the verb alone expresses affirmation; they should have been taught to decompose adjectival verbs and shown that each is the juncture of an active quality and the verb *to be;* they should have been given the secret of our inversion rules [and of] parts of speech; above all, they should have been practiced in writing simple sentences and in analyzing those that are not.... There you have what is lacking in the inventor's discoveries (Sicard, 1801 [p. xxxv]).

In short, Epée did not succeed in teaching French structure and Sicard did not realize that FSL had one. To succeed where Epée had failed, Sicard emphasized the analysis of written French sentences and employed Signed French to that end. When Thomas Gallaudet came to the Institution in 1815, it was Signed French that Massieu's most accomplished pupil, Laurent Clerc, taught him. The following summer Gallaudet returned to the United States with Clerc. During the long voyage, Clerc (1816) perfected his English and "we reformed certain signs which we thought would not well suit American customs and manners (Clerc, cited in Barnard, 1852 [p. 106])."

American Asylum

1817. Wax.   During the fall and winter following their voyage to America, Gallaudet and Clerc visited many cities and state legislatures in the eastern United States to demonstrate—by Clerc's very presence and by the speeches he had prepared himself—that education of the deaf was possible, and to secure funds for the opening of the *American Asylum.* The collection of funds went quickly. The state of Connecticut gave $5000—the first legislative act of this kind in America. With $17,000 in all, the first permanent school for the Deaf in America opened a year later with seven pupils. For a little more than a decade, while Signed French was taught in Paris, Bordeaux, Rouen, and so on, Signed English was taught in Hartford—and then New York, Kentucky, Pennsylvania, and so on. Clerc taught this language not only to the seven deaf pupils with whom the Hartford Asylum opened, and to the rapidly growing numbers of pupils who came in their wake, but also to the hearing professors who left to found one school after another throughout the United States and to disseminate Signed English. In an early report of the Hartford Asylum, Gallaudet (1819) writes that: "The instructors, by a constant familiar intercourse with the deaf and dumb, and still more by means of the daily lectures on the language of signs which have been given by their ingenious and experienced associate, Mr. Clerc, have made such attainments in the acquisition of the principles of this science, that they hope very soon to become masters of their profession and thus to secure its advantage beyond the danger of loss [p. 5]."

Although the rules of English grammar were respected in the classroom, we can be sure that they were not respected outside. Two years after the founding of the Asylum, Gallaudet (1819) wrote:

A successful teacher of the deaf and dumb should be thoroughly acquainted both with their own peculiar mode of expressing their ideas by signs and also with that of expressing the same ideas by those methodical signs which in their arrangement correspond to the structure of written language. For the natural language of this singular class of beings has its appropriate style and structure. They use it in their unrestrained communication with each other, [it is marked by] great abruptness, ellipses, and inversion of expression.... To take a familiar example ... "You must not eat that fruit, it will make you feel unwell"... In [the deaf's] own language of signs, literally translated, it would be thus "Fruit that you eat, you unwell, you eat no [p. 785]."

Bébian

1821. Wane. It gradually became clear, on both sides of the Atlantic, that the effort to dialectize sign language through the schools was unsuccessful and that precious class time was lost in attempting to teach Signed English and Signed French. In Paris, Sicard had learned from Epée's attempts that merely translating a French sentence into Signed French did not assist its understanding; therefore, the meaning of each sentence was first explained in FSL. It remained only for Sicard's intellectual successor, Bébian, to propose dropping the intermediate step and using FSL as the language of the school as well as of everyday life. Bébian had come from Guadeloupe to study under Sicard. He was subsequently appointed assistant to Laurent Clerc. In the year that the American Asylum opened, Bébian published his *Essai sur les Sourds-Muets et sur le Langage Naturel* (1817). He served as chief of studies (censeur) at the Paris institution from 1819 to 1821 and on Sicard's death he published a revised version of *Manuel d'Enseignement Pratique des Sourds-Muets* (1827), which was adopted by the administrative council. He founded his own school in Paris, started a journal on the education of the deaf, and later accepted an appointment as head of the Rouen Institution. In all these endeavors, his driving purpose was to tear down the scaffolding on FSL that Epée and Sicard had erected. In his eulogy of the Abbé de l'Epée, which won a Royal Academy of Sciences competition in 1819, Bébian writes:

> M. l'Abbé de l'Epée, who insists in twenty different places in his book on the necessity of instructing deaf-mutes in their own language, sometimes denatures this language himself in order to bend it into the shape of the French language which, for that matter, he teaches according to the principles of Latin grammar. I will not dwell on the considerable number of [invented] signs inspired by decomposing words, so to speak, which were a kind of syllabic spelling by gesture, such as *surprendre = prendre sur, comprendre = prendre avec* [cum], etc. May I be permitted instead to quote two or three passages...? "It is necessary, to acquaint the deaf-mutes with the cases and to teach them their names: nominative, genitive, dative, accusative, vocative, ablative, without troubling to explain these words to them. But each case has its own set of signs, first, second, third degree, with which we descend from the first case to the sixth... As for the sign for the word *case,* it is made by rolling the two index fingers one on the other while *declining,* that is, descending, from the first to the sixth.... We call the attention of the deaf-mute to the joints of our fingers, hands, fists, elbow, shoulders, and we call them *articles* or joints. Then we write that *le, la, les, de, du, des* join words as our articles join our articulations.... Thereafter, the movement of the index finger, in the shape of a hook, becomes the systematic sign that we give to every article. We express gender by raising our hand to our hat for the masculine article and to the ear where the hair of a person of this sex would ordinarily end, for the feminine gender."
>
> It is easy to believe that these artificial abstract signs which say nothing to the mind, tossed in this way in-between the various parts of the proposition, inevitably break up its connections and consequently that it is often very difficult for a deaf-mute to reassemble the scattered elements of the thought expressed. And then what happens? Why, these same students who had written quite correctly whatever was dictated to them in sign, were sometimes at a loss to explain the simplest thoughts on their own [pp. 54–56].

New York

1830. Wane. When the New York Institution sent their director to Paris to return with a Clerc of their own, they obtained Léon Vaïsse, a hearing professor, who proceeded to introduce Bébian's methods. Their Fifteenth Annual Report in 1834 described methodical signs as "wholly discarded."

> The method of Sicard in constructing his systems of methodical signs was, first, to define or illustrate each new word by means of a group of colloquial or natural signs [as they are, not very properly, called] constituting something like a circumlocution in speech; and from a consideration of this group, to devise some brief sign, named a sign of reduction, to stand as the representative of the whole. His published dictionary, denominated by him the "theory of sign," is

composed wholly of such definitions, unaccompanied, however, by corresponding signs of reduction; and is, therefore, as we are informed by M. Degérando, far from conveying a correct idea of his practice.

Our American schools have hitherto pursued the system of Sicard, making methodical signs the great dependence in instruction. But it has been only for words of most frequent occurrence that signs, strictly methodical, have been instituted. Beyond this limit, the complex sign, the circumlocution, has been retained without reduction, while the plan of verbatim translation or dictation having been still pursued, the system has failed of that lightness, simplicity, and that adaptation to the purposes of rapid execution, which its theory presumes: It has become unwieldy in its material, and burdensome in its use; retarding the labors of the instructor, and seriously impeding the progress of the pupil.

As an instrument of instruction, therefore, methodical signs have been abandoned in the New York Institution. The means on which the principal reliance is now placed are the language of action, so far as it is in familiar use, writing, symbolic grammar, design, and the manual alphabet. The employment of words themselves, is considered preferable to that of signs instituted for the sole purpose of recalling the same word (New York Institution, 1834 [pp. 29–30]).

Likewise, a Hartford instructor, F. A. P. Barnard, later president of Columbia University, wrote in 1835:

The purpose of the school is not to teach signs but words. And the labor thus spent in defining a [methodical] sign is the very labor, and no other, required to teach a word.... Truly the system of methodical signs is an unwieldy and cumbrous machine, and a dead weight upon the system of instruction in which it is recognized [p. 389].

By 1835, Signed English was thus abandoned, not only in New York and Hartford, but in most if not all schools throughout the U.S. (Peet, 1857, p. 339) and France. At the turn of the century, the head of the American Asylum could affirm that the useless and cumbersome parts of the machinery had been removed once and for all in the 1830s and that every teacher of the deaf must master ASL. Similarly, Léon Vaïsse, returned to France, and Remy Valade-Gabel after him, kept alive the reforms inaugurated by Bébian.

Thus it appeared that the forces of dialectization were permanently routed. Interestingly, the first serious inroads of the spoken majority language in French and American Schools for the Deaf coincide roughly with the abandonment of Signed French and Signed English, as if the forces of assimilation blocked on one route were channeled into another, and more ambitious, path, to which we now turn.

Epilogue

Before leaving dialectization, we must add to the present chronology the renaissance in disseminating Signed English that is now taking place in the United States. This resurgence coincides with another: a revitalized interest in the structure (and history!) of ASL that likewise dates from the 1960s. Perhaps each was a reaction to the wave of concern for minority rights (and languages) that characterized that stormy decade. The earlier failure of dialectization has not deterred its contemporary proponents, who advocate the use of one or another version in American schools.

All versions of Signed English have in common that they utilize some signs from American Sign Language as root morphemes and then inflect them in accord with English morphology by adding invented sign suffixes for tense, number, etc. Signed English goes on to invent signs for pronouns, prepositions, conjunctions—all of the appurtenances of the well-equipped language; never mind that the time to sign a message has been doubled; that there was no need for all this apparatus, sign language having its own genius to conduct it grammatical affairs: utilizing space, direction of movement, handshapes, and facial expression, among other means. Signed English goes on to declare that the order of the signs shall be in the order of English and that the choice of signs shall reflect the semantics and even homonymy of English; no matter that often one word in English subserves several concepts for which there are several signs, so that whichever one sign is adopted, it is generally incongruous. Can modern speakers of a visual language ever be induced to believe that such a contortion of their native tongue, violating its basic principles, is in fact a language of which they speak a substandard dialect? Yes indeed. Some deaf people refer to their sign language as "low verbal," "broken language" or as "slang." A deaf friend of ours referred to her signing in ASL as "low sign"; for her, "high sign" was Signed English. Other informants have referred to ASL as "broken English," or "bad English," or "broken language."

REPLACEMENT

When a single language is the national language of the great majority, the dominant language group can aspire to impose that language on all the people. Many European governments pursued this policy of replacement in the period between the two World Wars. Kloss (1967) points out that successor states to the Turkish, Hapsburg, and Russian empires ruthlessly pursued linguistic annihilation. A crucial method was, as in dialectization, to substitute the majority for minority languages in the schools. In 1918, there were 147 Lithuanian schools in Poland; in 1941, there were two. The number of

Progress of Replacement

Wax		Wane
Pereire before Academy of Sciences	1749	
	1776	Epée's *Institution des sourds et muets par la voie des signes*
	1795	Sicard's lectures at first Normal School
Itard's *Memoirs* to the Faculty of Medicine	1807	
	1817	American Asylum founded, excludes speech
N.Y. Institution founded on British model	1817	
	1821	N.Y. Institution abandons articulation
	1821	Itard's *Treatise on diseases of the ear*
	1828	Valade-Gabel views articulation as complement. None in U.S.
	1832	Ordinaire's efforts for oralism thwarted
Mann's report	1844	
	1845	Weld and Day rebuttals
	1864	Hubbard's oral school thwarted
First oral school in U.S.	1866	
Mass. legislature creates Clarke oral school	1867	
	1868	First Conference of American Principals
A. G. Bell takes up oralist cause	1872	
First International Congress, Paris	1878	
First Convention of French Teachers, Lyons	1879	
Second International Congress, Milan	1880	
Third International Congress, Brussels	1883	
International Congress, Paris	1900	

German schools in Lithuania fell to one third in the same period. There were 2600 Ukrainian Schools in East Galatia in 1918 and 400 in 1928. There were 26 American institutions for the education of the deaf in 1867 and ASL was the language of instruction in all 26; by 1907, there were 139 schools for the deaf and ASL was allowed in none. The French figures provide a comparable glimpse of ruthless linguistic imperialism. In 1845, there were 160 schools for the deaf with FSL the accepted language; by the turn of the century, it was not allowed in a single French school. The crucial event in the linguistic revolution that concerns us here took place in the latter half of the nineteenth century, but its roots go back to the 1700s.

Pereire

1749. Wax. Pereire was born in Spain; he came to France when he was eighteen, in 1733, and fell in love with a deaf girl. He had been raised with a deaf sister, and the two women inspired him to devote his life to teaching the deaf to speak. He took a special medical course, read what was available at that time on the eudcation of the deaf, and began to instruct some young pupils with singular success. In 1749 he presented one of his pupils, and in 1751 another, to the Academy of Sciences and won its commendations, including those of Buffon, who devotes a page to Pereire in his *Natural History*. According Edouard Séguin (1866), a pioneer in the education of the handicapped, who wrote a book on Pereire's life and work and had spoken with his last surviving pupil, this teacher managed to instill in the deaf "not only a natural voice and a correct pronunciation, but even his Gascony accent [p. 18]." Louis XV conferred a pension on him, and in 1753 Pereire opened a school in Paris, which drew about a dozen students from all over Europe.

To establish initial communication with his pupils, Pereire adopted Bonet's manual alphabet, used pantomime, and invented his own syllabic signs. Believing that the latter had been stolen by the Abbé de l'Epée, and hoping to secure some income from the sale of his method or to leave it as a legacy to his children, Pereire expressly forbade his pupils to reveal his methods and never did so himself in any detail. Neverthless, Séguin (1876) managed to reconstruct the main features:

> Speech was taught by imitation with vision as a guide to the internal positions in the mouth and the external muscles of the face and neck; and, for the first known time, with touch the conductor and monitor of the innermost positions and of the organic vibrations that together produce the emission of articulated sounds. By this method, the deaf-mute of ordinary capacity could learn to speak in twelve to fifteen months [p. 54].

The pupil with whom Séguin had spoken in her declining years, Marie Marois, affirmed that touch was the principal means by which Pereire taught his pupils to speak. In his address to the Academy of Sciences, Pereire seems to confirm this:

> Deaf-mute children perceive speech by touch. This translation occurs when, speaking to a deaf person, one places his mouth against the ear, the face, or another sensitive part of the body, such as the hand. Then the air which forms speech communicates impressions to these parts of the body which are as frequent and distinct as the syllables themselves, vibrations that are sufficient without other means to give a clear perception of several articulations. Thus it is shown, as by the example of young Etavigny [before the academy] that ... the profoundly deaf are capable of distinguishing some words by this process (Pereire, cited in Séguin, 1876 [p. 53]).

In learning a new sound, the student first learned one of Pereire's manual signs, which were designed to recall to mind both the shape of the articulators in making the sound and the shape of the letter that generally denotes it. Thus the signs were useful prompts for correcting pronunciation and spelling. The pupil was not allowed to communicate in sign language, however. Once he knew how to write and sign the sound, the student learned to pronounce it, in a series of exaggerations, approximations, and repetitions like those Molière parodied in his *Bourgeois Gentilhomme.* Thus the student grasps his teacher's throat, observes his throat, jaws, tongue, teeth and lips, and follows his articulatory instructions, until the teacher's ear is satisfied. Special training was also given in the way of breathing peculiar to speech.

Beyond pronunciation training, the prospectus of his school (inserted in the academy records) states that Pereire taught his pupils "to understand the force of different parts of speech, to use them correctly whether in speaking or in writing, according to the grammar and the particular genius of the language (La Rochelle, 1882, [p. 50])." He evidently succeeded in doing just that: Marie Marois remained highly intelligent and intelligible in old age; Saboureux de Fontenai (1764) became a teacher and essayist. Jean-Jacques Rousseau often visited Pereire's school; the two were good friends, and when Rousseau worked out his scheme for natural education in *Emile,* he found a place for several of his neighbor's ideas and experiments.

Epée

1776. Wane. Epée rejects the views of Pereire, Deschamps (instructor of the deaf at Orleans), and of Heinicke (instructor at Leipzig who said, "Spoken language is the hinge upon which everything turns"). Epée (1776) wrote:

> In the first place, M. Pereire himself gives us [in the prospectus of his school] the strongest proof that we ought to exclude his method in undertaking the instruc-

tion of the deaf and dumb.... Indeed, if it takes twelve to fifteen months to teach children that he has in his own home merely what he calls the first part of his art, how much time will it take me to teach just this same part to deaf and dumb children who come to my house only two times a week. It is easy to see that, proportionately, it will take me more than seven years. And what will they know? Words that they would not understand, and a few of the most common expressions [p. 24].

Thus, Epée has a practical reason against spoken French as the vehicle of instruction for the deaf: It is so difficult to acquire that articulation training preempts education. Moreover, oral instruction can be given to only one or two pupils at a time, whereas he has 60 (1776 [p. 202]). However, he is not opposed in principle to teaching spoken French because it integrates the deaf into the majority community. "The only way to return them completely to society is to teach them to hear with their eyes and to express themselves with their voices (1779 [p. 155])." In 1784 he described his method, inspired by those of Bonet (in Spain, 1620), Amman (in Holland, 1692) and Wallis (in England, 1653), relying heavily on sight, touch, and imitation. For example, he teaches most of the vowels by writing a letter on the board, uttering "the corresponding sound" with the student's finger in the teacher's mouth, then placing *his* finger in the student's mouth while the latter imitates. Epée reports some of the achievements of his early students (one learned to read aloud the 28 chapters of the Evangel) before the force of numbers obliged him to abandon this instruction. It remained in desuetude at the National Institution for the Deaf nearly a century.

Sicard

1795. Wane.   Sicard was asked by a member of the audience at one of his lectures to the first Normal School (teacher-training college) why the intelligent Jean Massieu did not speak, and he replied, "It is possible that Massieu would learn to speak, if I had the time to teach him; but that demands long and painful efforts whose success is limited in such cases and it is appropriate only for a few mutes who would in any event use speech rarely; thus I thought it better to develop intelligence by means of sign rather than by voice (Sicard, 1795 [pp. 268–269])." Sicard, like Epée, dabbled in speech training with a few students, one of whom, he claims, was better than any Pereire could ever produce. The medium of instruction was largely sign language and when this student "was addressed in sign, he spoke somewhat more fluently (Sicard, 1795 [pp. 268–269])." In 1820, Sicard reprinted Epée's description of how to teach speech to the congenitally deaf (1784) and reaffirms that this skill would be a desirable complement to the education afforded by the Institution, but it was seen merely as a complement; replacement was unthinkable.

Itard

1807. Wax. To Jean-Marc Itard must go the credit for developing, largely independently, a systematic, principled program of oral training, which would later be instituted in France and elaborated and modified by other teachers of the deaf throughout Europe and America. Just a little over a year after writing his final report on the Wild Boy of Aveyron, Itard presented two memoirs, *On the Means of Providing Hearing to Deaf-Mutes,* and *On the Means of Providing Speech to Deaf-Mutes,* to the Society of the Faculty of Medicine. At the May meeting, he presented the six deaf-mute children, "to whom he succeeded in giving the faculties of speech comprehension and production. The Society took great satisfaction in seeing the pupils carry out their various exercises (Société, 1808)." It soon became widely accepted that Itard's methods of "physiological training of the ear" could improve the lot of the deaf.

Obviously, there was no question of training the hearing of most of the children of the National Institution for Deaf-Mutes, where Itard was resident physician. Somewhere between half and two-thirds of them were profoundly deaf. Initially, Itard saw only vaguely how to characterize those who could benefit from this instruction. After some years of experimenting with oral education, however, he arrived at a classification of hearing losses into five broad diagnostic categories based on the pupil's residual ability to understand speech. These categories are described in his classic *Treatise on Diseases of the Ear and Hearing* (1821), which for many medical historians marks the beginning of otology. In the first category are those more fortunate children who can understand speech if it is addressed to them directly, loudly, and slowly. They generally acquire speech later in life than their peers with normal hearing, but they can be educated by the same means, if somewhat more slowly. In the second category are those children who fail to distinguish voiced consonants from their voiceless counterparts. Thus, *beau* sounds like *peau, don* like *ton,* and so on. They can, however, distinguish all the vowels. They find speech difficult to learn and conversation impossible. In general they cannot go to school with their peers. Itard believed, however, that his method of instruction would allow these children to enter normal hearing society, as it would those in the third category. Here are grouped the hearing-handicapped who fail to distinguish among nearly all the consonants but can discriminate among the vowels, which are intrinsically louder. They have difficulty in perceiving and producing intonation. The ordinary means of educating them are useless unless they first receive "physiological training" of hearing and speech. Pupils in the fourth and fifth categories are invariably mute. The former confuse all speech sounds but distinguish them from bursts of noise; the latter are profoundly deaf, and if they detect some intense sounds, it is through the sense of touch and not hearing.

Itard undertook his experiments in 1805 with six children whose hearing loss placed them in the second and third categories. He began by improving their ability to detect sound rapidly and reliably. Then he left off work on absolute sensitivity, and began training differential sensitivity, starting with a broad contrast between loud and soft sounds, which at first the pupils could not reliably distinguish. His third series of exercises engaged his pupils' sense of the timing of sounds as well as of their relative intensities. The fourth series of exercises concerned the perception of rhythm. Edging his way toward speech discrimination, Itard next taught his pupils to distinguish high and low notes on the flute. His pupils reached the point where they perfectly distinguished the *re* and *la* of the musical scale but not the vowels *o* and *a*. To overcome this last difficulty, the teacher placed himself behind the children and pronounced "the five vowels" while writing each in turn on a blackboard. Then the teacher uttered various vowels and the children were to point to the corresponding transcription.

Consonant discriminations proved much more difficult, and Itard (1821) says frankly that he had to use a thousand and one different devices, tailoring his instruction to each individual student. This necessity led him to give an hour's lesson daily to each of the pupils and to reduce the group from six to three. It took Itard about a year to bring his pupils to the point where they could reliably recognize all the vowels and consonants as they occurred in various simple words. And even then, certain confusions persisted.

After a year of physiological training—what would now be called sensory education—Itard's pupils could detect and distinguish the sounds of speech, and the educationally more advanced could understand sentences addressed to them directly and slowly. Since his students had to be taught to speak, Itard proceeded to develop the second half of his program of oral education, speech training, which was described in his second memoir to the Society of Medicine. He developed a careful progression of sounds to be taught, from the highly contrastive to the very similar, from the easily articulated to the more difficult, from the simple to the complex. Moreover, he brought vision and touch into play; he cites Pereire's pioneering work, as well as that of his predecessors, Bonet, Wallis, and Amman.

Itard's progression for teaching speech began with eight simple vowels, then proceeded to the nasal vowels. Next in turn came training in articulating the simple consonants. With sixteen of these and eight vowels to teach, Itard exercised his pupils on the 148 consonant-vowel (CV) syllables that they comprise. Once they had practiced the CV syllables, Itard had them work on the VC syllables (*or, il,* and so on) and then on the CV syllables with a nasalized vowel (as in *ton* and *tin*). Next came CCV (*pre*), then CCV with a nasal vowel (*flan*), then CVC (*par*) and CCVC (*bloc*). Now it came time to tackle the semivowels, which are more constricted than vowels, but less so than consonants (the initial sounds in *oui* and *hier,* like those beginning the

English we and yacht, respectively). In the remaining three series, Itard treated three special problems "as difficult for hearing as for speech"; first, consonant clusters containing s, where there was no vowel to assist in detecting the fricative noise (stade); second, the sound "formed by the junction of g and n" as in peigne; and third, the sole glide that occurs in the middle of words and is usually written ll as in mouiller.

There remained one more crucial class of sounds that Itard's pupils had never learned to distinguish clearly or, therefore, to produce properly; there were the voiced consonants as opposed to their voiceless counterparts: Ba/Pa, Da/Ta, Va/Fa, Za/Sa, Ja/Cha, Ga/Ca. For their mastery, Itard brought sight, touch, and articulatory instructions into play along with hearing.

During the lessons in which Itard's pupils imitated the vowels and consonants of French and their combinations in various kinds of syllables, they also learned to transcribe these syllables and how to read the transcriptions. Soon they were able to write and to read words and simple sentences "more or less intelligibly," but Itard found, to his great disappointment, that they would never speak of their own accord nor could they respond fluently to questions he was sure they understood.

By extensive exercises, with carefully graded materials, Itard was able, nevertheless, to overcome these difficulties of encoding and decoding sentences, at least to a large extent. He believed he would have surmounted them entirely had he been able to separate his pupils from the signing community in which they lived, not just for an hour or two each day, but entirely, so as to oblige them to use speech in expressing their needs and thoughts. Just one year after arriving at the Institution, Itard (1802) wrote:

> [We must] allow no means of communication other than spoken language between the hard-of-hearing child and the people who take care of him; failing this, the first means of training [by speaking loudly and slowly to the child] becomes ineffective; and the child, discouraged by the effort of attention he is obliged to put into speaking or listening, ends up by creating an action language or manual signs, with which he expresses all his needs. Once this modality is discovered and tolerated, the ear loses its sensitivity, the larynx its mobility, and the child remains deaf-mute forever [p. 554].

Among the pupils whom Itard presented to the Faculty of Medicine, the most accomplished speaker was, in fact, the most deaf and the least able to sign. This boy had been given to a governess who worked on training his residual hearing and did not teach him to sign. Itard recognized, however, that the deaf child who is deprived of sign must be taught language in some other mode—for example, the written mode of instruction worked out by Sicard. This education must precede training in spoken language, at least in part, or the pupil will know nothing of the redundancy of language which is the major guide in understanding a sentence. The Society of the Faculty of Medicine warmly acclaimed the performance of Itard's pupils, and the two memoirs that explained his method of oral education. They concluded that:

> Those deaf-mutes who have retained a certain measure of hearing or who have recovered it by sustained treatment, can acquire speech; that in this case, speaking is a prompt and necessary consequence of the functioning of hearing; that once a deaf-mute has been taught to hear, he must be aided and taught to listen to himself; that the development of speech will be the more prompt and more complete the less the subject is able to use manual sign language (Halle & Moreau, 1808 [p. 878]).

American Asylum

1817. Wane. The American Asylum did not teach articulation. "The Principal of the Asylum and his associates [have decided] not to waste their labor and that of their pupils upon this comparatively useless branch of the education of the deaf and dumb. In no case is it the source of any original knowledge to the mind of the pupil. In few cases does it succeed so as to answer any valuable end (Connecticut Asylum, 1819 [p. 7])."

New York Institution

1817. Wax. The Directors of the New York Institution wrote to England for a teacher in the oral tradition. The Braidwood monopoly demanded such an exorbitant fee that they hired instead A. A. Stansbury, who had been an administrator at Hartford. He started a day school with four pupils, and taught articulation and the manual alphabet.

New York Institution

1821. Wane. With 47 pupils, the New York Institution abandoned articulation:

> Mr. Stansbury had not been a teacher at Hartford and his ideas on the method of instruction were rather crude and vague. Consequently, at New York, experience was as yet wanting, and the first teachers, themselves groping in the dark, endeavored by Dr. Watson's work [1809] on deaf-mute instruction, to teach articulation, at least to such of their pupils as retained a remnant of speech or of hearing. The results attained, as might be expected, were so unsatisfactory that the attempt was soon abandoned (Fay, 1893 [Chap. 2, p. 14]).

Itard

1821. Wane. Jean-Marc Itard, the physician who never learned a sign during 40 years among the deaf at the Institution founded by Epée; Itard, who had made no attempt to teach sign language to the mutely gesticulating wild boy from 1801 to 1805; Itard, who founded oral education of the deaf, training six pupils in hearing and speech from 1805 to 1808 without ever employing signs; Itard, who lamented that he could not perfect these pupils' speech because he lacked the authority to isolate them from their peers and thus oblige them to do without sign, "like children whom we wish to teach a foreign language"; Itard surely seems at first look a four-star general in the oralist camp. But in the remaining score of years before his death, Itard came to believe profoundly that sign language was "the natural language of the deaf," whatever their degree of hearing loss. Moreover, he contended that oral education of the partially deaf must be preceded and accompanied by the use of signs. Itard first expounded these views at length in his *Treatise* in 1821. He tried to put them into practice at the Paris Institution, in a program of mixed education in sign and speech, by writing a series of four reports to the administration from 1820 to 1826. This was his argument:

> If, instead of using the covert movements of his larynx and tongue to express his ideas and emotions, man had expressed them by overt movements of his limbs and physiognomy, then vision would have been the most informative sense and the vehicle for intellectual development. It is a mistake to think that the deaf-mute in our speaking society gives an accurate picture of what men would be like were mankind created without the sense of hearing. With the aid of the language of signs, this gestural society would not have advanced less rapidly toward civilization. Written language, which has so greatly aided this progress, would in all likelihood have been invented sooner: for it takes less effort to imagine representing signs than drawing sounds. With this accomplishment, man could have embarked just as rapidly on the vast career that this discovery opened to his intelligence; and, apart from lacking a few ideas concerning sounds, he would have become all that the twofold gift of hearing and speech has made possible. Thus he can do without this gift; far from owing his perfectibility to the perfection of his organs, he can, with senses that function only weakly or incompletely, establish relations with his peers, create signs expressing his thoughts, and convert these fleeting signs into permanent ones. Rising above the limitations of his organs, to realize his full potentialities by dint of his genius alone, man can prove, in accomplishing much with few resources, that he has issued from the intelligence that created everything from nothing (Itard, 1821 [p. 325 of the 1842 ed.]).

Yet if sign language can provide the same intellectual advantages as spoken language, why is the deaf child clearly at a disadvantage?

How can we explain the incomplete intellectual development to which the deaf-mute is condemned by the privation of one of his senses? We can explain it by the resulting isolation which deprives the deaf-mute of the first and the most powerful means of perfecting the human species, the commerce of his equals. Destined by his constitution to understand the speech of the hands, he lives in solitude in the society of speaking and hearing men. If you want to know how much our equal he really can be, make everything equal, let him be born and live among his own kind, and you will presently have the hypothetical society that I have just described (Itard, 1821 [p. 326 of the 1842 ed.]).

In fact, Epée created the nucleus of such a society when he opened the school on the Rue des Moulins, which soon became the National Institution for Deaf-Mutes.

A large and seasoned institution of deaf-mutes, bringing together individuals of diverse ages and degrees of education, represents a genuine society with its own language, a language endowed with its own acquired ideas and traditions, and which is capable, like spoken language, of communicating directly or indirectly all its intended meanings. In fact, the deaf-mute raised in the midst of such a gesturing society sees not only the signs that are made to communicate with him, but also those that are exchanged in conversations among the deaf that are within his view. The impact of this indirect communication explains how these children who have only been taught the names of objects, after several months in a large institution, can conduct sustained animated little conversations with their peers that require a knowledge of how to sign adjectives, verbs, and tenses (Itard, 1827 [p. 192]).

By bringing formerly isolated deaf people together into a signing community, the Paris Institution unwittingly created conditions under which their language could accrete and their society evolve—and with it, the education of those who employed that language and lived in that society.

Comparing our current deaf-mutes with those first pupils trained in the same institution, by the same methods under the same director, we are led to recognize their superiority which can only be due to their having come later, at a more advanced stage of the signing society. There they found two sources of instruction that could not exist in its earliest days: the signed lessons given by the teachers, and their conversations with pupils already educated. Thus it is that instruction is easier and more widely effective than it was twenty years ago. At that time, Massieu was a dazzling phenomenon in the midst of his unfortunate companions, who remained well behind him, still at the first stages of their education; nowadays, he is nothing more than a highly distinguished student. Instruction, powerfully assisted by tradition, has more rapidly developed and civilized his companions; one among them has equalled him, and several have come close and would have surpassed him had they not so promptly left the institution....

Let us contrast Massieu... with Laurent Clerc, this student whom I said was his equal in instruction but who, having come quite recently to the institution, ought to have profited by all the advantages that a more advanced civilization can offer. Massieu, a profound thinker, gifted with a genius for observation and a prodigious memory, favored by the particular attention of his celebrated teacher, benefitting from an extensive education, seems nevertheless to have developed incompletely: His ways, habits, and expressions have a certain strangeness that leaves a considerable gap between him and society. Uninterested in all that motivates that society, inept at conducting its affairs, he lives alone, without desires and ambition. When he writes, we can judge even better what is lacking in his mentality: his style fits him to a tee, it is choppy, unconventional, disorderly, without transition, but swarming with apt thought and flashes of brilliance....

Clerc is entirely a man of the world. He likes social life, and often seeks it out, and he is singled out for his polite manners and his perfect understanding of social custom and interests. He likes to be well-groomed, appreciates luxury and all our contrived needs, and is not insensitive to the goads of ambition. It is ambition that snatched him from the Paris institution, where he had a worthy and comfortable existence as a teacher, and led him across the seas to seek his fortune (Itard, 1821 [p. 327 of the 1842 ed.]).

From all this evidence that sign language was an effective vehicle for the intellectual development of the child, Itard concluded that he had been wrong in opposing it and that indeed it would be foolish to attempt the education of the deaf without its aid. Of the five categories of hearing loss that Itard distinguished, ranging from failure to follow conversation to profound deafness, only pupils in the first category could be educated by purely oral means, he believed. Those in the second category could conceivably manage without sign in those rare cases where a wealthy family could afford a gifted private tutor. But of the largest number of the partially deaf, who could not distinguish among the consonants and thus belonged to the third category, Itard (1824) writes in his unpublished report: "I can affirm even more positively, after numerous attempts, that it is absolutely impossible to educate them exclusively by means of speech [p. 9]."

In his first experiment in oral education, which culminated in 1808, Itard had believed that the use of signs was an impediment to perfecting his students' speech. He realized even then that it was an enormous task to educate them without the aid of signs and that they could not master spoken language without this general education. Nevertheless, were it not impracticable, he would have isolated them from the signing community. In the ensuing decades, Itard became convinced that sign language was the proper vehicle for the general education of the deaf; that it facilitated teaching spoken languages to the partially deaf not only because it brought about their general intellectual development but also because it gave them habits of communication and spontaneous speech and established contact between the teacher and the student. Thus Itard concluded in his unpublished report in 1826:

> What we have said earlier about the advantages that our speaking students would gain from their knowledge and use of sign language in initially developing their ideas and in forming many relationships with children of their own age disposes of the question that came up at the last meeting of the administration concerning the merits and disadvantages of isolating these pupils from the rest of the deaf-mutes. All the advantages I have cited and others would be lost while nothing would be gained, for we cannot delude ourselves that, left on their own with speech as the sole means of communication, they would be able to employ it for their mutual relations.... Rather, they would create their own sign language.... Thus it is not necessary to isolate them, since sign language is as profitable for them as it is indispensable [p. 6].

Itard also believed that sign language was the proper means for the deaf-mute's intellectual growth, and he uses the same words as Sicard to describe oral education, "longue et pénible," in his 1825 report. Speaking of the children to whom he has given physiological training of the ear and voice, he writes in 1821:

> Since they only recover their hearing quite incompletely, it follows that the consonants are only incompletely heard, and spoken signs... create difficulties, blockages, and misunderstandings from which sign language is exempt. It is, I repeat, the natural language of deaf-mutes, and has the great advantage of putting them in communication with each other.... Education that employs hearing and speech as the means of instruction is slower and less complete [p. 391 of 1842 ed.].

Although reading is an important means of education that can stand in for hearing and complement sign, this skill must also be taught to the deaf through sign language: "This powerful auxiliary can be put within his reach either by oral and written instruction, which is very rare and very difficult, or by the method of sign, which is the natural language of the congenitally deaf, whatever his degree of deafness (Itard, 1827 [p. 181])."

Much as Itard was convinced that sign language was the only feasible mode of communication among the deaf, and the proper vehicle for their intellectual development and their learning to read and write, he was equally convinced that they should learn, whenever possible, to understand and produce spoken language. His first reason was that children who have residual hearing and can profit from physiological training can then be returned to speaking society and the full spectrum of communication. His second reason was that sign language is by nature clumsy and imprecise, and that the deaf-mute who supersedes it with spoken language can make his ideas more precise and express them more fluently. In short, Itard came to favor bilingualism for the deaf, and not replacement.

Valade-Gabel

1828. Wane. At Itard's insistence, an articulation class was created with Valade-Gabel as instructor, but only as a supplement; sign was to remain the vehicle of education. "I consider instruction in artificial speech as a complement to the education of the deaf-mute through the vehicle of sign. His intelligence would remain inactive for too long if we were to wait to cultivate it until he mastered the instrument of speech (Valade-Gabel, 1894 [p. 158])." In the United States, articulation was not merely relegated to a minor role, it was abandoned: "The advocates for teaching the Deaf and Dumb to articulate are very few in number; all efforts to accomplish it in the institutions for their instruction are now considered useless; and, even if once made with very sanguine hopes and high professions of success, are wholly abandoned (American Asylum, 1828 [p. 14])."

Ordinaire

1832. Wane. Désiré Ordinaire became convinced during visits to schools for the deaf in Switzerland of the feasibility of oral education. He gave articulation lessons to pupils at the Institution Nationale des Sourds-Muets de Besançon and sent several memoirs on his methods to his Paris counterparts. In 1831 he was appointed director at Paris and undertook to supplant Valade-Gabel's classes in articulation for a few pupils with a generalized oral program throughout the institution. In 1832 he ordered all of the faculty to devote some time each day to teaching speech. Led by distinguished deaf colleagues (Berthier, Lenoir, Forestier), they refused. In 1834, the Board of Directors, which under its late chairman, the distinguished philosopher and oralist Baron Joseph Degérando, had been highly supportive of Ordinaire's efforts, prohibited the use of sign language at the institution and ordered French to be spoken instead. The result is described by a contemporary historian, Esquiros (1847).

> After several trial days, instruction in artificial articulation and lip-reading was abandoned; several instructors, convinced in advance of the sterility of such efforts, did not even deign to try them out on their pupils. Most of the students at the institution found voice exercises repugnant . . . the authorities let themselves in for humiliating defeat since the faculty refused to follow their lead. As a matter of record, the deaf pupils of the institution spoke, but as a matter of fact they did not . . . . This awkward experiment, far from advancing the cause of speech at the Royal Institution, made it regress [pp. 2, 452].

In 1836, Ordinaire obtained a ministerial decree commanding oral instruction but only one professor, formerly no friend of oralism, obeyed. (This was Léon Vaïsse, who had just returned from a 5-year stint at the New York Institution where sign language reigned.) Vanquished finally by 6 years of battling for a lost cause and by failing health, Ordinaire resigned in 1838. A year later the supplementary class in articulation taught by Valade-Gabel from 1828 to 1831 was reinstituted under Puybonnieux and taught intermittently until 1843 when a ministerial decree institutionalized the class and Vaïsse took it in charge. Vaïsse had just returned from visiting schools in Germany, Switzerland and Holland, which were conducted orally. Vaïsse taught this class, one hour each day, for seven years, until J. J. Valade-Gabel (returned to Paris from the Bordeaux school in 1850) took it up again.

Having been a student of Pestalozzi, Valade-Gabel tried—first as director at Bordeaux, then as a teacher in Paris, finally as Inspector-General of all schools for the deaf in France—to introduce Pestalozzi's "mother method" of teaching language. In the case of the deaf, it was necessary to substitute the eye for the ear and writing for speech in order to teach French. In 1857 he published *A Method for Primary Instructors of Teaching the French Language to Deaf-Mutes Without the Intermediary of the Language of Signs.* Although this "intuitive method" as it was called received an award from the Institut and official endorsement by the Ministry it made no major inroads.

Valade-Gabel's son, André, succeeded him as articulation teacher for one year (1851–1852) and was succeeded, in turn, by Volquin (1852–1857). In 1857 André Valade-Gabel resumed the class. Thus, throughout this term of office of Ordinaire's successor, Lanneau (1838–1858), articulation was relegated to a minor role and there was no serious effort at replacing sign language. The dean of the deaf professors, Berthier, wrote:

Thus, articulation, which was to be the exclusive vehicle for the education of the deaf, is relegated nowadays not only to a secondary role but to a special class made up of students whose organs are considered supple enough to receive such lessons and who, for the most part, already spoke in early childhood (cited in Dupont, 1897 [p. 39]).

Likewise, Hartford (cited in Wheeler, 1920), would have none of it and in one report gave these 10 reasons:

1. Too much time is lost in teaching sound, which is to no benefit in mental culture.
2. Under this system a large number of deaf-mutes must be left without instruction.
3. The intonations of the voice and the distortion of the countenance in teaching and practicing articulation are disagreeable.
4. Success in articulation teaching has come principally to pupils who retained their speech after becoming deaf.

5. The ability to converse in general society is not secured by this method of instruction.
6. More teachers are required, resulting in more expense;
7. Religious instruction must be deferred, and religious worship is almost impossible.
8. In teaching articulation, signs are still indispensable.
9. Lip reading must be taught also.
10. The results of instruction by signs are beyond those attained by articulation [p. 372].

Mann

1844. Wax. Horace Mann was the respected and renowned Secretary of the Massachusetts Board of Education. In 1843 he and his colleague, Samuel Howe, Director of the Perkins Institution for the Blind, made a tour of European schools of all kinds, primarily in the United Kingdom and Germany. In his widely publicized Seventh Report to the Board, Mann (1844) stated:

I have seen no institutions for the Blind equal to that under the care of Dr. Howe [but the schools for the Deaf] in Prussia, Saxony and Holland seem to me decidedly superior to any in this country.... With us the deaf and dumb are taught to converse by signs made with the fingers. There, incredible as it may seem, they are taught to *speak* with the lips and tongue... there are hardly any Dumb there... the German teachers of the deaf and dumb prohibit, as far as possible, all intercourse by the artificial language of signs [pp. 74-81].

The report drew an acerbic reply from Hartford in Woodbridge (1844):

We are persuaded that if we should spend a large portion of the period, scanty at best, allowed to each pupil attempting to teach him to articulate and to read on the lips, the cases of partial failure in the far more essential, yet easier, task of teaching the vocabulary and idioms of language would be much more numerous. Articulation has been excluded from the course of instruction after careful and mature deliberation and, in the New York Institution, after actual and patient experiment; not because the object was considered of little account but because the small degree of success usually attainable was judged to be a very inadequate compensation for that expenditure of time and labor which the teaching of articulation exacts—for the many wearisome hours that must be spent in adjusting and readjusting the positions of the vocal organs, in teaching the "seven sounds of the letter *a*," "the hundreds of elementary sounds," as Mr. Mann says, represented by only twenty-six letters, and the thousand capricious irregularities in the pronunciation of the same letters or combinations of letters [p. 333].

The author admonishes teachers of the deaf to remember the disastrous experiment with oralism at the Paris Institution and concludes, "We see no present prospect that the teaching of articulation will be introduced into our institutions at all." Nevertheless, Mann's report did more for replacement than any event before it in the nineteenth century.

Weld

1845. Wane. Lewis Weld, successor to Thomas Gallaudet as principal of the American Asylum, hastened to Europe to see matters first-hand. In his visits to some of the German schools, he was joined by Edward Morel and Léon Vaïsse, professors at the Paris Institution. There he found that—far from Mann's claims—"the communication of actual knowledge to the mind is by manual signs; and, though these may, from the first, be accompanied by speech, the latter is powerless for the great ends of instruction, except as associated with the former (Weld, 1845 [p. 71]." In the British schools, articulatory instruction "is not attempted [in some] and in others but to a very limited extent. In the schools of Cork, Dublin, Manchester and Birmingham, it is not attempted. In those of Liverpool, Doncaster, Edinburgh and Glasgow, it is given to a portion of the pupils. In that of London, it is attempted with all who have good capacity, is part of the regular course for all, and all who cannot succeed in acquiring it to some considerable extent are considered deficient in intellect [p. 37]." Weld (1845) concludes:

Though I cannot recommend the adoption of the German system...still I do recommend as an additional means of usefulness, instruction in articulation and in labial reading to certain classes of pupils in the American Asylum [especially those] who retain in a considerable degree the articulation they acquired before becoming deaf and those who still have some discriminate hearing. These are, on the whole, the classes of persons principally benefitted by articulation in the articulating schools I have visited abroad [p. 121].

In the same year, George Day, representing the New York Institution, made a report that, when published by the New York legislature, ran over 200 pages. Day (1845) visited dozens of schools for the deaf in England, France, Switzerland, and Germany, and concluded:

I can by no means agree with the opinion expressed by a late American writer [Mann] that the schools for the deaf and dumb in Prussia or Saxony are superior to our own, or recommend the introduction of the German mode of instruction. The German method has advantages for the few; the American method for the mass. In attempting to teach all, or nearly all, to employ oral language, the German schools succeed in obtaining solid results with only a select number while the large portion of the scholars are seriously impeded in their progress by the process [p. 182].

As Weld had found, Day also reported that where articulation was taught to all it was taught as an ancillary ability, whereas writing or sign was the vehicle of instruction; where speech was the vehicle of instruction, it was taught to only a few.

A few years later, Harvey Peet, the director of the New York Institution, likewise toured various European schools for the deaf, 27 in all, and concluded as Day had "that instruction in articulation is scarcely ever of decided benefit, except when the faculty of speech has been acquired through the ear (Rae, 1852 [p. 252])."

In 1845, the American Asylum's board voted to give articulation training a trial and in the report for the following year, we find that, of the 182 pupils, 30 with residual speech or hearing were receiving speech instruction through the medium of sign, about 20 minutes a day, collectively. In the New York Institution the figure was 40 out of 192 pupils. Day returned to Europe for a second tour in 1859 and reaffirmed that articulation training was of value only for those pupils deafened after acquiring their oral tongue; these, however, should be taught to speak and lip-read (Day, 1861). Because the teacher who is working with a few hearing students in his class can give no attention during that time to the deaf, the Asylum hired a speech teacher in 1859, the first person so employed in any school in the U.S. She was able to accomplish so little that, in 1863, she was fired and the teaching of speech was dispensed with.

Hubbard

1864. Wane. Despite the Weld, Day, and Peet reports, Howe remained persuaded of the merits of oral education; in this he was joined by Gardner Greene Hubbard, whose daughter Mabel had lost her hearing at the age of four and a half. The Hubbards soon found that the governor of Rhode Island had a daughter much like theirs. Both families had retarded the deterioration of their daughters' speech through oral training at home and both were determined that an oral school should be founded in New England. In 1864, Hubbard applied to the Massachusetts legislature for a charter and appropriation for a new institution for the oral education of those deaf children who could hear a little or had once spoken. Collin Stone, Weld's successor as principal of the American Asylum, vigorously opposed the application on the ground that "the instruction of the Deaf by articulation was a theory of visionary enthusiasts which had been repeatedly tried and abandoned as impracticable (cited in Hubbard, 1898 [p. 24])." The application was refused.

First Oral School

1866. Wax. When Harriet Rogers, a school teacher who had trained a deaf child orally, told Hubbard of her desire to open the first oral school, he took up a subscription. The school opened in Chelmsford, Mass., in 1866, and was limited to seven pupils. Meanwhile, the controversy raged: In 1865, Samuel Howe spoke out again in behalf of oralism in the second report of the Massachusetts Board of Charities (1866). Collin Stone, principal of the American Asylum, responded the following year in the Asylum's 50th Report. Howe next rebutted Stone (1866); in this he was shortly joined by Hubbard (1867), who gave this progress report from Miss Rogers' school:

> No new signs are being acquired by the pupils, and in their recitations and at table, conversation is being carried on by articulation and reading from the lips. When by themselves they sometimes accompany their words with signs, but words are constantly gaining the ascendency... The one great object in educating the deaf-mute is to teach him the English language, and this object is never accomplished by the teachers of the sign language [p. 35].

Clarke School

1867. Wax. Hubbard renewed his request for an appropriation from the Massachusetts legislature; with the governor's support ("I recommend steps to provide for this class of dependents in our own commonwealth") the proposal was referred to a joint special committee (1867), which became the battleground for the pro- and antireplacement forces. Pro: S. G. Howe and F. B. Sanborn, chairman and secretary, respectively, of the Board of State Charities, and G. G. Hubbard and several deaf persons, notably John Carlin, a poet and artist. Anti: Collins Stone and W. W. Turner, principal and professor, respectively, at the American Asylum. A Mr. Clarke from the city of Northampton offered $50,000 (later increased to $250,000) if a Massachusetts School for the Deaf were founded in his city. The committee made a favorable recommendation, the legislature concurred, and the Clarke Institution was opened the same year with Harriet Rogers as principal and G. G. Hubbard as director of the board.

The first report of the school states: "This institution is especially adapted for the education of the semi-deaf and semi-mute pupils, but others may be admitted."

In the same year oral schools were opened in New York City (principal Bernard Engelsmann), Como (Abbé Balestra), and Paris (August Houdin). Edward M. Gallaudet, son of Thomas Hopkins Gallaudet and president of the Columbia Institution for the Deaf in Washington, D.C., was sent abroad by his board to make a thorough examination of schools for the deaf and returned urging the manual method supplemented by articulation training for those who were apt. He recommended a meeting of all American principals at his school to consider this question. This meeting was the first conference of American principals (and the sixth convention of American instructors, which had been postponed since 1861 because of the Civil War).

First Conference of American Principals

1868. Wane.   Fourteen of the 28 schools in existence in the U.S. were represented at the First Conference of American Principals. The new oral schools were not represented. The conference reaffirmed the traditional preference for the manual method "for deaf-mutes *as a class"* (italic theirs). As E. M. Gallaudet and Weld before him, the Conference urged articulation training as a complement "to such pupils as may be able to engage with profit in exercises of this nature; . . . it is not profitable . . . to carry congenital mutes through a course in articulation (1868 [p. 244])."

Bell

1872. Wax.   An event that took place in England during the conference of American principals proved to have profound consequences for the American deaf of the opposite kind. A young school teacher from Edinburgh, Alexander Graham Bell, undertook to teach the deaf at the London School of Susanna Hull, using his father's system of phonetic notation, named "visible speech." Inspired in part by his wife's partial hearing loss, Melville Bell, Alexander's father, had devised a system of symbols indicating the positions of the speech organs, which were combined so as to show the reader how to produce any given vocal sound even if he had never heard it before. On an American speaking tour during 1868, Melville Bell's report of his son's success at the London school caught the attention of Sarah Fuller, who took charge of a new public day school for deaf children in Boston in 1869 (later renamed the Horace Mann School) and organized it along oralist lines.

At about the same time, speech instruction was begun at the Georgia, Illinois, Maryland, Michigan, and Wisconsin schools for the deaf (1868), at St. Joseph's school for the deaf in New York and at the Minnesota School; and the Mystic Oral School for the Deaf was founded in Connecticut (1869).

In 1872, A. G. Bell was invited to the Clarke School (and to the American Asylum) to demonstrate his methods. G. G. Hubbard met Bell at his school on return from a tour of European schools based on replacement. With Hubbard's encouragement, Bell opened his own private oral school in Boston. Hubbard and the father of one of Bell's deaf pupils became his backers and partners in his research on the telephone. In 1873, Bell was appointed professor of vocal physiology at Boston University, which gave him access to electrical and acoustic apparatus in the physics laboratory of the Massachusetts Institute of Technology. That same year, Mabel Hubbard became one of his pupils; 4 years later, she became his wife. In the laboratory, Bell experimented with devices to record sound vibrations so that his deaf pupils would be able to check the sounds they made. This and other experiments led to his invention of the telephone in 1876 (and the audiometer in 1879). About half of the million dollars Bell acquired from his invention he gave in behalf of replacement to the Clarke School, the Horace Mann School, and especially to an association of articulation teachers that he instigated.

The evolution of the American Association to Promote the Teaching of Speech to the Deaf, A. G. Bell, president, is an important part of the history of the replacement movement in the United States. Its roots are in the first convention of articulation teachers in 1874, which was composed of teachers employing "visible speech" in the instruction of the deaf. The second convention met likewise in Massachusetts but was open to speech teachers of the deaf, whatever their method. The third met in New York in 1884 and voted to ask the eleventh Convention of American Instructors of the Deaf to create a special section for the promotion of oralism. No action was taken on the request until the end of the twelfth convention, when it was granted; oral teachers were invited to form an association, which they did, making Bell president and G. G. Hubbard vice-president in 1890. In 1897, the Association established a magazine, now known as the *Volta Review.*

Bell was opposed to the use of sign language at any time or place; it was easier for the deaf to master and more reliable in use, hence it would supplant or preempt speech. It was not only unsuited for integrating the deaf into society, but was a prison intellectually as well as socially, he believed, because it was ideographic rather than phonetic, limited in precision, flexibility, subtlety, and power of abstraction.

"If there is anything that is characteristic of the oral schools," Bell wrote in 1917, "it is their insistence upon the entire disuse of the French sign language of de l'Epée and Sicard, which had been brought to America by Gallaudet and Clerc. They have always insisted on the importance of making speech the usual and ordinary means of communication both in and out of schoolrooms, and claimed that sign language was the usual and ordinary means of communication outside of class in many schools because speech was practically confined to school exercises [p. 26]."

Bell became the outspoken, ardent champion of replacement and E. M. Gallaudet, president of Gallaudet college for the deaf, his chief opponent. Each was an eloquent spokesman and each hoped for many years to convince the other. Toward the end of the century the quarrel became bitter. Bell opposed a congressional appropriation for a teacher-training department at Gallaudet, for he feared that deaf graduates of Gallaudet would eventually be admitted to that department (and, of course, deaf teachers did not advocate replacing their language). Moreover, Bell prepared a statistical paper for the National Academy of Sciences entitled *Memoir upon the Formation of a Deaf Variety of the Human Race* (1883), and advocated eugenic counseling of the deaf.

Those who believe as I do, that the production of a defective race of human beings would be a great calamity to the world, will examine carefully the causes that lead to the intermarriages of the deaf with the object of applying a remedy... The most promising method of lessening the evil appears to lie in the adoption of preventive measures... The immediate cause is undoubtedly the preference that adult deaf-mutes exhibit for the companionship of deaf-mutes rather than that of hearing persons [pp. 41, 45].

Bell advocated four preventive measures to remove this preference: eliminate residential schools, suppress the sign language, prohibit deaf teachers of the deaf, outlaw deaf intermarriage. George Veditz, cited in Mitchell (1971), brought Bell's activities in behalf of this last measure to the attention of the National Association of the Deaf in his presidential address:

The American Stock Breeders Association last autumn [1906] decided to frame a bill for the restriction of matrimony... and to introduce this bill into the legislatures of all the states of the Union. A committee, called the "Committee on Eugenics"... was appointed to draft the bill and to prepare the way for its passage by the dissemination of scientific literature on the subject. The chairman of the committee is our old friend, Dr. Alexander Graham Bell.

Those whose marriage it is proposed to prevent are: (1) Persons mentally, morally, or physically defective, (2) Criminals, (3) Immature children, (4) People of plainly incompatible dispositions, (5) Consumptives, (6) Persons suffering from functional disorders, and (7) The deaf and dumb.

It is evident that the one person upon whom we must cast the odium of having hated the deaf into this category is Dr. Bell, whom his wealth has rendered the most powerful, and his hobby-riding propensity the most subtle, because he comes in the guise of a friend [p. 354].

It would be naive to view these professional activities of A. G. Bell as unrelated to all his others, to his work on the telephone and audiometer, to his promotion of articulation training, to his efforts in behalf of the oral education of the deaf. All were part of a single purpose, to eradicate a deaf minority, to interpret diversity as pathology—to "pathologize" the deaf—and then to treat this pathology with prosthesis, with rehabilitation, with eugenics, and so on. For E. M. Gallaudet, whose mother, uncles, aunts, and many friends and schoolmates were native speakers of ASL, such a course of annihilation for the deaf minority and its language were anathema. Surely it is not irrelevant to Bell's profound commitment to replacement that the deaf near and dear to him, including his mother and his wife, spoke English as a native language and were postlingually deafened. Incidentally, a Hartford professor, E. A. Fay, followed up on Bell's *Memoir* with a thorough study of 5,000 deaf marriages (1898). He found that the large majority of the deaf (73%) married someone who was also deaf. However, this was probably not attributable to residential schools or to the language policy of the schools, because 77% of the day-school deaf, 78% of the oral school deaf, and 62% of the deaf attending no school for the deaf married someone deaf. Undoubtedly, a major factor in these marriages was shared language skills whereas another may have been the shared sensory deficit and social status. In any event, Fay found that only 9% of children from deaf marriages were themselves deaf. A modern estimate gives a comparable global figure (Fraser, 1976).

First International Congress

1878. Wax. The First International Congress, held in Paris under the presidency of Léon Vaïsse, took its origins from the period 1859 to 1872, during which Vaïsse was first chief of studies (*censeur*) and then director of the Paris Institution. To a considerable degree, the struggle between the administration and the faculty under Ordinaire and Lanneau was simply continued under Vaïsse. As *censeur* he was not partisan of oralism, merely of diligent instruction in spoken French for those pupils who profited from it. As director (1866–1872) he tried to go further, replacing sign with French in instruction, but he was opposed by the faculty, by an unfavorable report from the Institut de France, and by a ruling from the Ministry which recommended instruction in articulation only for postlingually deafened children. Vaïsse resigned in disgust, hoping to accomplish outside the Institution what he could not achieve within. This strategy had been tried before. Itard's successors as chief physician of the Institution, P. Ménière and A. Blanchet, were vehemently opposed on the merits of oralism. The debate was brought before the Academy of Medicine (1853) which, however, concluded that the evidence was not in to allow a choice between the French and German methods. Blocked by the hostility of the Paris faculty, Blanchet instigated the establishment of a dozen day schools for the deaf intermixed with hearing children, thus founded on replacement and assimilation. His extraordinary zeal led the Ministry of the Interior to issue a circular in 1858 envisioning the universal integration of the deaf into the public schools. The outcry from oralists abroad who believed no such thing possible caused the Ministry to back down the following year. The integrated schools themselves disintegrated rapidly (perhaps an augur for the prospects of contemporary "mainstreaming"). A commission of the Institut visiting two "Blanchet Schools" in 1861 found integrated along with the deaf and by force of the same arguments, the semi-deaf, the blind, the stammerers, and imbeciles—but no ordinary children. Most of the schools closed on Blanchet's death in 1867. While Vaïsse tried to advance the oralism of the institutions for the deaf in Rodez, Caen, and Alençon that he could not promulgate in Paris, Pereire's grandson and great-grandson opened a private oral school in the capital (1875).

During the French Universal Exhibition of 1878, a meeting of instructors of the deaf was hastily convened. Only 54 people enrolled, 27 of them instructors, and of these 23 were from France. The only American present represented the Horace Mann School. Léon Vaïsse, honorary director of the Paris Institution and long a champion of the oral instruction of the deaf, was elected president of the meeting rather grandiosely called the first International Congress of Instructors of the Deaf and Dumb. The Congress claimed that only oral instruction could fully restore the deaf to society and hence was the educational method of choice, although signing is a useful auxiliary. The Paris Congress appointed a committee of 12 of its own members to make arrangements for a second Congress. Eleven members of the committee were, as it happened, from France and most were advocates of oralism. Milan was selected as the site; in this city were to be found two institutions for the deaf, formerly conducted in sign language, which for the 10 years prior had been predominantly oralist. The head of one of the schools, the Abbé Tarra, was made president of the Second International Congress, and the leading instructor of the other was made secretary.

This was an extraordinary accomplishment! A group of two dozen French oralists constituted themselves, by fiat, as the First International Congress of instructors and by fiat—again without the participation of other French instructors representing the dominant manualist mode of instruction in France, without instructors from other nations, without the deaf themselves —they proclaimed the profession in favor of replacement, appointed a committee of 12 of their own number to organize the Second International Congress, located it in a bastion of oralism, Milan, made oralists its president and secretary, and placed an evaluation of the merits of oralism on the agenda! Such zeal would not go unrewarded.

First French Convention

1879. Wax. The First Convention of French Teachers of Deaf-Mutes, also planned at the Paris Congress, took place in Lyons with Léon Vaïsse elected President. Vaïsse declined, however, "in order to be able to take a more active part in its labors," and his lieutenant, A. Houdin, was elected instead; Houdin ran a private oral school in Paris. By a vote of 14 for and 5 against, the Convention adopted a resolution somewhat more measured than the oralist credo of the Paris Congress:

> While admitting the superiority of articulation to sign language, especially in restoring the deaf-mute more completely to society, yet believing at the same time that it is not possible to accept articulation as the sole basis and essential principle of instruction, [the congress is] of the opinion that a very large part in the instruction of deaf mutes should be left to the sign language, and that consequently the two methods, instead of being regarded as antagonistic, should render mutual aid to each other, and should concur to one and the same end, viz. the instruction and education of the deaf-mute (cited in Fay, 1880 [p. 101]).

Second International Congress

1880. Wax. The Second International Congress was convened in Milan with local oralists as president and vice-president and Vaïsse head of the executive committee. Two days before the opening of the Congress and every afternoon of the convention were devoted to public examinations of the Milan schools, which the delegates were urged to attend. The demonstrations were so impressive, Susanna Hull (1881) wrote to Harriett Rogers, that "the victory for the cause of pure speech was in great measure gained, as many were heard to say afterwards, before the actual work of the congress began[p. 286]." Yet there were reasons to fear that the delegates were taken in. One observer (Denison, 1881) reports that:

> There was evidence of long previous preparation, of severe drilling and personal management to produce the most striking effect. There was an apparently studied absence of definite and all-important special information as each case came up for exhibition.... My neighbors, themselves Italian and articulation teachers informed me that [the best pupils] were not congenitally deaf and had probably mastered speech before entering the institution [p. 45].

Another (Gallaudet, 1881) adds that the deaf pupils' answers:

> were in many instances begun before the examiner had completed his question. That no real examination was made by outside persons; that many pupils were asked very few questions while certain others were examined at great length; that these discriminations were made by the teachers in every instance; that no information was given as to the history of any pupil—that is to say, as to whether deafness was congenital or acquired, and whether speech had been developed before hearing was lost or not. That the impression was thus sought to be conveyed that all the speech possessed by all the pupils had been imparted to them by their teachers, which was certainly not the case [p. 4].

While the exhibitions were going on in the schools, an American delegate (Denison, 1881) was observing the pupils who were waiting their turn outside. They were signing.

> Two or three times a group, noticing the intentness with which I was watching their conversation, abruptly suspended the sign making part of it.... I inquired in signs whether they ever used gestures. The response was a blank mystified look on each face, then a general shaking of heads. But when I reminded them of what I had just observed, they pleaded guilty, with a propitiatory smile, to having partaken of the forbidden fruit of the tree of knowledge [p. 4].

There were various speeches of which the president's, the Abbé Tarra, was considered particularly eloquent. "He spoke of his own original mistake of teaching by signs," Susanna Hull (1881) wrote:

of how his eyes had been opened to see that speech was best.... He acknowledged that it required great courage to do this but signs *must* be abjured.... "It is not the teacher's work to move the arms and legs of the pupil but to open his mouth and train his lips to pronounce the sacred names of father, mother, the holy name of God." Patience, patience, patience, must be the motto of the instructor.... The oral method is possible. The method of signs is in deadly opposition to speech. The combined or mixed system is impossible and illogical.

[The Abbé] pointed out that when God gave a soul to man, He gave him the faculty of speech whereby to express his ideas. Words spring out of the heart; without any visible form, they associate themselves with ideas and become part of them. Signs and gestures appeal to the senses. He had striking proof of this in working in the confessional. When narrating his faults by signs, the penitent revived the passions and sins of which he had been guilty; but it was not so when he *spoke* them out [p. 291].

The representative of the Minister of the Interior in France (Franck, 1880) was equally moved.

I do not need to indicate to you, Sir, the conclusion to which my observations lead: they speak for themselves. We must as soon as possible instruct all the pupils of our two national institutions, and not a select group, with the method of speech. Speech training should be the general rule, the absolute rule, and not the exception [p. 30].

He proposed to the minister that French instructors be sent to Milan to receive training in the oral method, a plan which was carried out the following year. "This kind of instruction should only be introduced little by little and class by class.... It is indispensable for the pupils who receive it to be absolutely separated from those who do not (Franck, 1880 [p. 17])."

This enthusiasm was shared by most of the 164 delegates, all of them hearing, seven-eighths of them from Italy and France, most clerical: "Everywhere the eye fell upon shaven crowns and black cassocks," an American observer (Denison, 1881) wrote.

The Abbé Tarra stated as an undisputed fact the impossibility of conveying by signs any idea of the Divine Being, but ideas gross, material and untrue. But the gesture which he made in illustration was the unmeaning, if not misleading, one of pointing with the index finger to the ceiling. Had he asked Dr. Peet or either of the Gallaudets present [T. H. Gallaudet's sons] to make the appropriate sign, not all his eloquence and enthusiasm would have availed to make his argument on this point a forcible one. On other occasions the gestures he employed to show the inferiority of signs in plainness and precision were only too well calculated to emphasize his remarks. It is possible that he intentionally indulged in travesty or caricature, but it is much more probable that he furnishes in himself an illustration of the fact I have mentioned—that European teachers are very much our inferiors in scientific sign making [p. 42].

The final vote is not surprising. Forty-six of the active members were officers and teachers in the two schools of Milan and three more came from the Pereire school in Paris; 49 votes in all with a constituency of three schools and 200 deaf pupils. The stronghold of signing, the United States, then had 51 schools, 400 teachers, and over 6,000 pupils; it was represented by five votes. All but the Americans voted for a resolution exalting the dominant oral language and disbarring the minority language whatever the nation:

1. The Congress, considering the incontestable superiority of speech over signs, for restoring deaf-mutes to social life and for giving them greater facility of language, declared that the method of articulation should have preference over that of signs in the instruction and education of the deaf and dumb;

2. Considering that the simultaneous use of signs and speech has the disadvantage of injuring speech and lip-reading and precision of ideas, the Congress declares that the pure oral method ought to be preferred. (Franck, 1880 [p. 8]).

In the closing moments of the Congress, the special French representative cried from the podium, "Vive la parole!" This has been the slogan of French instruction of the deaf down to the present time. The final success of replacement in France dates from Milan, 1880. In America, it would come later.

Third International Congress

1883. Wax. The Third International Congress was the largest, with some 250 members (Anon., 1883). A report soon after in the London *Times* (Gordon, 1892) states:

The most remarkable feature of the Congress was that, after the lapse of three years, and in a more widely representative gathering, the decision of the Congress held in Milan in 1880 in favor of the pure oral system was accepted and acquiesced in as final, and thus practically confirmed with perfect unanimity [p. xxxvi].

Fourth International Congress

1900. Wax. A half-dozen meetings of note occurred in the remaining years of the nineteenth century, before the Paris Congress, and all of them were favorable to replacement. The meetings of articulation teachers in the United States were cited earlier. There was a French teachers' convention in 1884, held at the National Institution, where "The teachers present were unanimous in their support of the oral method of instruction." A meeting of the same group also held in Paris in 1885 resolved:

Considering that the pure oral method, after having been admitted in principle at the Milan Congress has been practiced in fact for four years at most of the French institutions, the Congress recommends... a diminution of the numbers of the large schools, the separation of pupils taught by signs from the others, rigorous application of the pure oral method, strict watch of the pupils [to prevent the use of signs], and constant practice in such speech as they already possess (Gordon, 1892 [p. xxxvii]).

In the same year, a Scandinavian convention voted in favor of replacement, 70 to 44. The following year, a Royal Commission conducted a comprehensive inquiry into methods of educating the deaf and the blind (it is important to note the collocation—the deaf were no more viewed as a linguistic minority than were the blind). The Commission found

that every child who is deaf should have full opportunity of being educated on the pure oral system. In all schools which receive government grants, whether conducted on the oral, sign and manual, or combined systems all children should be for the first year at least, instructed on the oral system, and after the first year they should be taught to speak and lip-read on the pure oral system unless they are physically or mentally disqualified, in which case, with the consent of the parents, they should be either removed from the oral department of the school or taught elsewhere on the sign and manual system. (Cited in Gordon, 1892 [p. xlii]).

The presupposition is clearly here that native citizens who do not learn to speak the national language are "physically or mentally disqualified."

In 1888, an International Congress of Deaf-Mutes was held in Paris. Amos Draper, a deaf professor at the National Deaf-Mute College (now Gallaudet College), represented the United States. To gather from his report (1890), little was accomplished. However, his observations on the signing are of interest in signalling an astonishing deterioration of communication in sign in France, originally the citadel of sign language.

On the Continent, signs are much more generally used [than in England]. They are, however, of a halting, broken, indistinct character as if the speaker were obliged at every step not only to search his mind for an idea but also for a means of expressing it. Among the Europeans in two cases only was there a delivery approaching that which can be seen everywhere in America—a delivery in signs that are smooth, clear and cogent; that can win to smiles, affect to tears, provoke to reason, stir to emulation, a delivery, in short, that is lacking in no essential oratory. The possession of such a language seemed at once a cause and a consequence of the high average and comparative development of the Americans [p. 9].

By 1900, a report to the International Congress could state that the pure oral method was the official method of instruction employed in all schools for the Deaf in France (Maudit, 1900). At the National Institution of Deaf Mutes in Paris, entering pupils were first given imitation training, in which they repeated the bodily movements, postures, facial gestures, and finally, articulatory movements of the instructor. After a few days of these exercises, "to interest the pupil, to give him a taste for speech, to facilitate his communication, and to arrest his development of sign language, he is taught to lipread a few easy short words, without decomposing them into their phonetic elements (Institution Nationale, 1896 [p. 42])." Next came the breathing exercises advocated by Itard and then his graded series of phonetic exercises—in which lipreading, however, replaced auditory training with these profoundly deaf children. As the child gained proficiency, writing and reading were introduced.

Thus, by the time of the Paris congress, oralism had become the medium of instruction at Epée's institution. Nevertheless, Edward Gallaudet was on hand, among many others, to contest strongly the merits of the oralist approach. The supporters of oralism are found among the teachers, he declared, whereas the supporters of sign are found among the deaf themselves. The very Congress itself bore witness to his claim: As the hearing professors presented paper after paper in support of oralism, the deaf professors, meeting separately, resolved repeatedly in favor of sign (Gaillard & Jeanvoine, 1900). Gallaudet carried their reiterated demands to meet jointly with the hearing professors to the president and finally to the Congress at large, but each time the request was refused. The pretext was that the official language of the Congress was French, whereas the deaf section communicated in sign. In fact, simultaneous translation would have been possible; many of the deaf had oral skills in any event. Sign might have been a better choice of official language: many of the hearing foreigners frankly admitted that they could not understand the French, and even the French speakers had difficulty with the "barbarisms" perpetrated by the prepared remarks of their guests. That the language problem was indeed a pretext for excluding the deaf, who favored instruction combining sign and speech, was revealed when the president, the third physician to serve the Paris institute after Itard, refused to allow motions passed in the deaf section even to be reported to the hearing section.

Finally, Gallaudet (1900) moved that the Congress resolve in favor of a mixed method of instruction: to tailor the method to the intellectual and physical aptitudes of the individual pupil, to provide initial oral instruction to all, but to continue this mode of instruction only for those who would benefit by it. Although Gallaudet was circumspect enough not even to mention the word sign, the pendulum had swung full arc since his father's visit to Paris in the days of Sicard, and the Congress rejected his motion by more than one hundred to seven. Instead, the meeting passed the following resolution:

> The Congress, considering the incontestable superiority of speech over signs in restoring the deaf-mute to society and giving him a more perfect knowledge of language, declares its adhesion to the decision of the Milan Congress (Fay, 1900 [p. 414]).

At almost the same moment, the deaf professors were voting the opposite (Anon., 1901). Therefore Gallaudet moved that the resolution should read that the hearing section, not the Congress, considers speech incontestably superior to sign. The motion was defeated (Martha & Gaillard, 1901).

Epilogue

Replacement in the United States really gained ground after the Paris Congress of 1900. In 1904, the first year that reliable statistics on oralism were obtained, according to the American Association to Promote the Teaching of Speech to the Deaf, the number of deaf pupils taught wholly by the oral method was 2050 or 18% of the enrollments of schools reporting. This percent grew steadily with each passing year; by 1917 it had reached 30%. The figure corresponds roughly to the number of deaf students enrolled in oral schools, because it is a tenet of oralism that the two languages must not coexist in the same environment. The first decades of this century also witnessed an increase in the number of classes conducted largely in English in institutions where instruction had formerly been given largely in sign. The Association data for these classes (admittedly from a partisan source) show an annual growth comparable to that for classes in exclusively oral schools. Consequently, the percent of deaf pupils in the United States receiving instruction through the vehicle of the majority language, and not merely supplemental training in articulation, rose from virtualy zero in 1867 before the opening of the Clarke School, to a small fraction at the time of the Milan Congress (Clarke was joined by Horace Mann and Mystic), to one third in 1904, to two-thirds in 1917.

Today, in 1978, there are about 175 residential and day schools for the deaf in the United States; all of these use English as the vehicle of instruction. A recent study that attempts to project what the education of the deaf will be like for the next decade gives reason to believe that ASL will not make much headway as the vehicle of instruction, that we will not see much bilingual education of the deaf. Prickett and Hunt (1977) asked 122 experts in the field of education of the deaf who will be in a decision-making role in the next 10 years to rank 48 developments in desirability. "Acceptance of bilingualism— Sign and English" ranked 43; the hiring of deaf elementary teachers ranked 45.

ACKNOWLEDGMENTS

I want to thank the individuals and federal agencies, notably the National Library of Medicine and the National Endowment for the Humanities, who, by maintaining that the deaf have neither a community nor a language but only a handicap and gestures, have redoubled my efforts to trace the social history of the American Sign Language of the Deaf. This article is a precis of a book in progress, and the author would greatly appreciate hearing from individuals who may have suggestions, recollections, or relevant documents.

REFERENCES

American Asylum. See American School for the Deaf.
American School for the Deaf (Connecticut Asylum). *Third Annual Report*. Hartford: Hudson, 1819.
American School for the Deaf (American Asylum). *Twelfth Annual Report*. Hartford: Hudson, 1828.
Anonymous. The Brussels Convention. *American Annals of the Deaf*, 1883, *28*, 254–262.
Anonymous. Resolutions adopted by the deaf section of the Paris Congress of 1900. *American Annals of the Deaf*, 1901, *46*, 108–111.
Barnard, F. A. P. Existing state of the art of instructing the deaf and dumb. *Literary and Theological Review*, 1835, *2*, 367–398.
Barnard, H. *A discourse in commemoration of the life, character, and services of the Reverend Thomas H. Gallaudet*. Hartford: Brockett & Hutchinson, 1852.
Bébian, R. A. A. *Essai sur les sourds-muets et sur le langage naturel*. Paris: Dentu, 1817.
Bébian, R. A. A. *Eloge de Charles Michel de l'Epée*. Paris: Dentu, 1819.
Bébian, R. A. A. *Manuel d'enseignement pratique des sourds-muets*. Paris: Méquignon, 1827.
Bell, A. G. *Memoir upon the formation of a deaf variety of the human race*. New Haven: National Academy of Sciences, 1883.
Bell, A. G. *The growth of the aural method in America*. Northampton: Clarke School, 1917.
Clerc, L. *The diary of Laurent Clerc's voyage from France to America in 1816*. West Hartford, Conn.: American School for the Deaf, 1952.
Conference of Executives of American Schools for the Deaf. Proceedings of the First Conference of American Principals of Schools for the Deaf. *American Annals of the Deaf*, 1868, *13*, 129–146, 242–256.
Connecticut Asylum for the Education of Deaf and Dumb Persons. See American School for the Deaf.
Day, G. E. *Report on the institutions for the deaf and dumb in Central and Western Europe in the year 1844. To the Board of Directors of the New York Institution*. Albany: Carroll & Crook, 1845.
Day, G. E. Report on some schools for the deaf and dumb in Europe. *American Annals of the Deaf*, 1861, *13*, 86–109.
Denison, J. Impressions of the Milan Convention. *American Annals of the Deaf*, 1881, *26*, 41–50.
Desloges, P. *Observations d'un sourd-et-muet*. Paris: Morin, 1779.
Draper, A. G. *Report of Professor Draper on the International Congress of Deaf-Mutes at Paris*. Washington: General Printing Office, 1890.
Dupont, M. *Pages d'Histoire. l'Enseignement de la parole à l'Institution Nationale des Sourds-Muets de Paris*. Paris: Carré, 1897.

Epée, C. M. (Abbé de l'). Institution des sourds-et-muets ou recueil des exercises soutenus par les sourds-et-muets pendant les années *1771, 1772, 1773, 1774.* Paris: Butard, 1774. Reprinted in C. M. Epée, *Institution des sourds-et-muets par la voie des signes méthodiques.* Paris: Nyon, 1776.

Epée, C. M. *Institution des sourds-et-muets par la voie des signes méthodiques.* Paris: Nyon, 1776. Reprinted in C. M. Epée, *La véritable manière d'instruire les sourds-muets confirmée par une longue expérience.* Paris: Nyon, 1784.

Epée, C. M. [*The art of instructing the infant deaf and dumb*] (J. P. Arrowsmith, trans.). London: Taylor and Hessey, 1819. (F. Green, trans.) The true method of educating the deaf and dumb, confirmed by long experience. *American Annals of the Deaf,* 1860, *12,* 1–132.) (Originally published in Paris: Nyon, 1784.)

Esquiros, A. *Paris au XIX siècle.* Paris: Imprimeurs Unis, 1847.

Fay, E. A. The Lyons Convention. *American Annals of the Deaf,* 1880, *25,* 101–102.

Fay, E. A. *Histories of American schools for the deaf, 1817–1893.* Washington, D.C.: Volta Bureau, 1893.

Fay, E. A. *Marriages of the deaf in America.* Washington, D.C.: Volta Bureau, 1898.

Fay, E. A. The Paris Congress of 1900. *American Annals of the Deaf,* 1900, *45,* 404–416.

Franck, A. *Rapport au Ministère de l'Intérieur sur le Congrès International Réuni à Milan du six au douze Septembre [1880].* Paris: Wittersheim, 1880.

Fraser, G. R. *The causes of profound deafness in childhood.* Baltimore: Johns Hopkins University Press, 1976.

Gaillard, H., & Jeanvoine, H. *Congrès International pour l'Etude des Questions d'Assistance et d'Education des Sourds-Muets (Section des Sourds-Muets).* Paris: Imprimerie d'Ouvriers Sourds-Muets, 1900.

Gallaudet, E. M. International convention of instructors of deaf-mutes at Milan. *Education,* 1881, *1,* 279–285.

Gallaudet, E. M. Echoes of the Paris Congress of 1900. *American Annals of the Deaf,* 1900, *45,* 416–426.

Gallaudet, T. H. Letter to the Editor. *Christian Observer,* 1819, *18,* 784–787.

Gordon, J. C. Progress of speech teaching. In J. C. Gordon (Ed.), *Notes and observations upon the education of the deaf.* Washington, D.C.: Volta Bureau, 1892.

Halle, J. N., & Moreau, J. L. (Ecole de Médecine). Rapports sur deux mémoires relatifs aux moyens de rendre l'ouie aux sourds-muets. *Gazette nationale ou le Moniteur Universel,* 1808, *36,*(211), 874–875, 878.

Howe, S. G. *Remarks upon the education of deaf-mutes in defense of the doctrines of the Second Annual Report of the Massachusetts Board of State Charities, and in reply to the charges of Reverend Collin Stone.* Boston: Walker, Fuller, 1866.

Hubbard, G. G. *The education of deaf-mutes: Shall it be by signs or articulation?* Boston: Williams, 1867.

Hubbard, G. G. The story of the rise of the oral method in America as told in the writings of the Hon. Gardiner G. Hubbard. Washington, D.C.: Roberts, 1898.

Hull, S. E. Instruction of deaf-mutes. *Education,* 1881, *1,* 286–293.

Institution Nationale des Sourds-Muets de Paris. *Notice.* Paris: Typographie de l'Institution Nationale, 1896.

Itard, J. M. G. Notes. In A. F. Willich, *Hygiene domestique ou l'art de conserver la santé et de prolonger la vie. II.* Paris: Ducauroy, 1802, (an 10).

Itard, J. M. G. *Traité des maladies de l'oreille et de l'audition.* Paris: Méquignon-Marvis, 1821. (2nd ed., 1842).

Itard, J. M. G. *Deuxième rapport fait en 1824 sur nos sourds-muets incomplets.* Unpublished manuscript. Paris: Institution Nationale des Sourds-Muets, 1824.

Itard, J. M. G. *Troisième Rapport.* Unpublished manuscript. Paris: Institution Nationale des Sourds-Muets, 1826.

Itard, J. M. G. Notes. In J. C. Hoffbauer (Ed.), *Médecine légale relative aux aliénés et aux sourds-muets*. Paris: Baillière, 1827.

Joint Special Committee on the Education of Deaf-Mutes, Commonwealth of Massachusetts. *Report Senate No. 265*. Boston, 1867.

Kloss, H. Bilingualism and nationalism. *Journal of Social Issues*, 1967, *23*, 39–47.

La Rochelle, E. *Jacob-Rodrigues Pereire*. Paris: Dupont, 1882.

Mann, H. Seventh Annual Report of the Secretary of the Board of Education. *Common School Journal*, 1844, *6*, 65–196.

Martha, A. & Gaillard, H. *Congrès International pour l'Etude des Questions d'Education et d'Assistance des Sourds-Muets*. Paris: Imprimerie Nationale, 1901.

Massachusetts Board of State Charities. Second Annual Report, (1865). Boston: Wright & Potter, 1866.

Maudit, N. Les sourds-muets et la méthode orale. In H. Gaillard & H. Jeanvoine (Eds.), *Congrès International pour l'Etude des Questions d'Assistance et d'Education des Sourds-et-Muets (Section des Sourds-Muets)*. Paris: Imprimerie d'Ouvriers Sourds-Muets, 1900.

Mitchell, S. H. The haunting influence of Alexander Graham Bell. *American Annals of the Deaf*, 1971, *116*, 349–356.

New York Institution for the Instruction of the Deaf and Dumb. *Fifteenth Report*. Albany, 1834.

Peet, H. P. Memoire on the history of the art of instructing the deaf and dumb. In *Proceedings of the Fifth Convention of American Instructors of the Deaf and Dumb*. Richmond: Wynne, 1857.

Prickett, H., & Hunt, J. Education of the deaf—the next 10 years. *American Annals of the Deaf*, 1977, *122*, 365–381.

Rae, L. Dr. Peet's European tour. *American Annals of the Deaf*, 1852, *4*, 243–252.

Saboureux de Fontenay, S. Lettre à Mademoiselle XXX. In J. M. Degérando, *De l'Education des sourds-muets de naissance*. Paris: Méquignon, 1827.

Seguin, E. *Idiocy and its treatment by the physiological method*. New York: William Wood, 1866.

Seguin, E. Report on Education. In R. Thurston (Ed.), *Reports of the Commissioners of the United States to the International Exhibition held at Vienna, 1873. Volume 2, Science, Education. Section K*. Washington: U.S. Government Printing Office, 1876.

Sicard, R. A. Art de la parole. In *Séance des écoles normales*. Paris: Reynier, 1795.

Sicard, R. A. *Cours d'instruction d'un sourd-muet de naissance*. Paris: Le Clère, 1801. (2nd ed., 1803).

Sicard, R. A. (Ed.) *l'Art d'enseigner à parler aux sourds-muets de naissance*. Paris: Dentu, 1820.

Société de la Faculté de Médecine de Paris. Procès verbaux. *Bulletin de l'Ecole de Médecine de Paris*, 1808, *15*.

Stone, C. Reply to Dr. Howe. In Connecticut Asylum for the Education of Deaf and Dumb Persons. *Fiftieth Report*. Hartford, Hudson, 1866.

Valade-Gabel, J. J. *Méthode à la portée des instituteurs primaires*. Paris:, 1857.

Valade-Gabel, J. J. *Lettres, notes, rapports*. Grasse: Imbert, 1894.

Watson, J. *Instruction of the deaf and dumb*. London: Durton, & Harvey, 1809.

Weld, L. Report of visits to institutions for the deaf and dumb in Europe. In Connecticut Asylum for the Instruction of Deaf and Dumb Persons. *Twenty-Ninth Report*. Hartford, 1845.

Wheeler, F. R. Growth of American Schools for the Deaf. *American Annals of the Deaf*, 1920, *65*, 367–378.

Woodbridge, W. [Comments on] Seventh Annual Report of the Secretary of the Massachusetts Board of Education. *North American Review*, 1844, *59*, 329–352.

Author Index

Italics denote pages with complete bibliographic information.

Itard, J. M. G., 130, 134, 135, 136, 138, 139, 140, 141, *160, 161*
Itoh, M., 97, *101*

J

Jarvella, R., 48, *58*
Jeanvoine, H., 157, *160*
Johnson, M., 54, *56*
Johnson, N., 53, *57*
Joint Special Committee on the Education of Deaf-Mutes, Commonwealth of Massachusetts, 147, *161*
Jones, M., 64, 70, 71, *78*
Jones, N., 16, *30*
Jones, P., 19, *30*
Jordan, I., 37, 38, 62, *57*

K

Kallman, F., 105, *118*
Kantor, R., 27, *30, 31,* 64, 66, 68, 69, 70, *77*
Kegl, J., 7, 9, 11, 12, 15, 17, 19, 21, 22, 23, 26, 28, *30,* 41, *57,* 69, 70, *77*
Kelly, R. R., 91, 94, *99*
Kimura, D., 81, 82, 86, 89, 97, *98, 99*
Klatt, D., 44, *57*
Klima, E., 4, 5, *6, 6,* 8, 11, 14, 15, *30,* 39, 40, 46, 50, 51, 52, *56, 58,* 64, *76,* 95, *98*
Kloss, H., 119, 129, *161*
Kobayashi, Y., 97, *101*

L

Labov, W., 107, 115, *117*
LaBreche, T. M., 92, 93, 97, *99, 100*
Lacy, R., 7, 21, 22, 25, *30,* 62, 64, 66, *77*
Lane, H., 9, 11, 25, *30,* 39, 40, 41, 42, 45, 46, 47, 48, 53, 54, *56, 57, 58,* 79, 89, 91, 95, 96, 97, *100*
La Rochelle, E., 132, *161*
Leischner, A., 84, 86, 88, *99*
Lentz, E., 26, *30*
Levitsky, W., 80, *99*
Liben, L., 53, *57*
Liberman, A. M., 81, *100*
Liddell, S., 7, 20, 21, 24, *30,* 42, *57, 59*
Long, J., 9, *30*
Lubert, B. J., 86, 89, 91, 97, *99, 100*

M

Mack, J., 86, *100*
Maestas y Moores, J., 62, 68, 69, 73, *78*
Mann, H., 144, *161*

Manning, A. A., 92, 93, 97, *99, 100*
Markman, R., 92, 93, 97, *99, 100*
Markowicz, H., 3, *6,* 8, 11, *29, 31,* 105, 107, *117, 118*
Marslen-Wilson, W., 48, 49, *57*
Martha, A., 158, *161*
Massachusetts Board of State Charities, 147, *161*
Massaro, D., 54, *57*
Maudit, N., 157, *161*
Maxwell, M., 62, *78*
Mayberry, R., 49, *57*
McAdam, D. W., 80, *100*
McCall, E., 41, *57*
McCawley, J., 22, *30*
McIntire, M., 49, *58,* 62, 64, 65, 70, *77, 78*
McKeever, W. F., 92, 97, *100*
Meadow, K., 3, *6,* 61, 62, 63, 67, 75, *78,* 105, 106, *117*
Meckler, R., 86, *100*
Menn, L., 65, 70, *78*
Menyuk, P., 70, *78*
Miller, G., 40, 48; *58*
Milner, B., 80, 81, *100*
Mitchell, S. H., 150, *161*
Mohr, K., 16, *30*
Molfese, D. L., 80, *100*
Moores, D., 61, 66, 68, 69, *77, 78,* 106, *117*
Moreau, J. L., 137, *160*
Morgan, A., 69, *78*
Mori, K., 97, *101*
Murphy, E. H., 80, *100*

N

Nachson, I., 81, 97, *99*
Nebes, R. D., 82, 95, *100*
Nettleton, N. C., 81, *98*
Neville, H., 91, 94, 97, *100*
New England Sign Language Society, 35, *58*
Newkirk, D., 39, 40, 52, *58*
Newport, E., 16, *31*
New York Institution for the Instruction of the Deaf and Dumb, 127, 128, *161*
Nicely, P., 40, 41, *58*
Nowell, R., 53, *57*

O

O'Connor, N., 97, *99*
Ohashi, H., 86, *99*
Oléron, P., 35, *58*
Oliver, S., 109, 112, *118*
O'Malley, P., 69, *78*

Subject Index

A

Acquisition, 3, 35, 61-78
  of action representation, 68
  bilingual, 74
  bimodal, 74
  of classifier usage, 69
  first sign, 64
  iconicity and, 3
  of negation, 66
  of phonology, 65-66
  of semantic relations, 67-68
  of signed English, 74-75
  stages of, 64
  of syntax, 66-67, 70-73
  of verb inflection, 66-67
Agent-Beneficiary Directionality, 108
Agraphia, 87
Agreement point, 17, 21, 22, 23
Ambiguity, 21
American Asylum, 125-126, 128, 137, 145-147
  founded (1817), 125-126, 137
  opposed to oral training, 143-144, 145-147
  reforms (1830), 128
American Sign Language (*see also* Bilingual diglossic continuum)
  effectiveness of communication, 33-38
  historical changes in, 3, 9-10, 103-104, 111-112
  history of, 119-158
  intersign structure, 42
  linguistic description, 7-31
  myths about, 1-6, 82
  origins of, 2
  sociolinguistic aspects of, 2-3, 103-112, 116
  sociolinguistic variation in, 109-112
  vocabulary expansion, 4-5

Ameslan (*see* Bilingual diglossic continuum)
Ameslish (*see* Bilingual diglossic continuum)
Anticipation errors, 40
Aphasia, 80, 83-89
  definition of, 80
  of hearing signers, 86
  of signers, 83-89
Apraxia, 86
Articulation, 43, 44
  rate of, 43, 44
  time, 43
Articulators, 44
Art-sign, 11
ASL (*see* American Sign Language)
Aspect, 16
Assimilation, 11-12
Attitudinal deafness, 105
Autonomous sign language, 83

B

Balanced sentences, 53
Bébian, 126-127
Bell, Alexander Graham, 148-151
Bilingual diglossic continuum, 105-106, 113-114, 116
"Body shift," 17

C

Cerebral Asymmetry, 79-98
  auditory experience and, 92, 96
  in the deaf, 82-98
  electroencephalographic testing of, 94
  to moving signs, 95-96
  in the normally hearing, 79-82
  to static signs, 92-96
  to words plus signs, 92